P9-API-640

SECURITY ARCHITECTURE FOR OPEN DISTRIBUTED SYSTEMS

WILEY SERIES IN COMMUNICATION AND DISTRIBUTED SYSTEMS

Editorial Advisory Board

Professor B. Evans
University of Surrey

Professor G. Pujolle
Université Pierre et Marie Curie

Professor A. Danthine
Université de Liège

Professor O. Spaniol
Technical University of Aachen

Integrated Digital Communications Networks (Volumes 1 and 2)
G. Pujolle, D. Seret, D. Dromard and E. Horlait

Security for Computer Networks, Second Edition
D.W. Davies and W.L. Price

Elements of Digital Communication
J.C. Bic, D. Duponteil and J.C. Imbeaux

Satellite Communications Systems, Second Edition (Systems, Techniques and Technology)
G. Maral and M. Bousquet

Using Formal Description Techniques (An Introduction to ESTELLE, LOTOS and SDL
Edited by Kenneth J. Turner

Future Trends in Telecommunications
R.J. Horrocks and R.W.A. Scarr

Security Architecture for Open Distributed Systems
S. Muftic, A. Patel, P. Sanders, R. Colon, J. Heijnsdijk and U. Pulkkinen

SECURITY ARCHITECTURE FOR OPEN DISTRIBUTED SYSTEMS

Sead Muftic
Stockholm University, Sweden

Ahmed Patel
University College Dublin, Ireland

Peter Sanders
University of Plymouth, UK

Rafael Colon
University of Madrid, Spain

Jan Heijnsdijk
Delft University, The Netherlands

Unto Pulkkinen
Technical Research Centre of Finland

JOHN WILEY & SONS
Chichester · New York · Brisbane · Toronto · Singapore

Copyright © 1993 by John Wiley & Sons Ltd,
Baffins Lane, Chichester,
West Sussex PO19 1UD, England

All rights reserved.

No part of this book may be reproduced by any means,
or transmitted, or translated into a machine language
without the written permission of the publisher.

Other Wiley Editorial Offices

John Wiley & Sons, Inc., 605 Third Avenue,
New York, NY 10158-0012, USA

Jacaranda Wiley Ltd, G.P.O. Box 859, Brisbane,
Queensland 4001, Australia

John Wiley & Sons (Canada) Ltd, 22 Worcester Road,
Rexdale, Ontario M9W 1L1, Canada

John Wiley & Sons (SEA) Pte Ltd, 37 Jalan Pemimpin #05-04,
Block B, Union Industrial Building, Singapore 2057

British Library Cataloguing in Publication Data

A catalogue record for this book is available from the British Library

ISBN 0 471 93472 0

Produced from camera-ready copy supplied by the authors
Printed and bound in Great Britain by Bookcraft (Bath) Ltd

CONTENTS

PREFACE

This book describes various aspects of security in open distributed processing systems: creation and usage of security mechanisms, security services, and security protocols; design of integrated security architectures and secure network applications; and implementation of global secure open systems.

An open distributed processing system is assumed to be the conceptual framework within which computer systems with diverse applications, resources, users, and locations exchange and process various types of data and interact without any previous strict arrangements. Such a computing structure consists of individual, autonomous operational environments (domains) cooperating by dynamic interdomain transactions.

Computer networks constructed within this open distributed framework present a very convenient target for attacks and illegal operations. This means that protection of users, resources and assets in every open computer network is becoming increasingly important.

Computer networks and applications currently exist which have made some attempt to implement various security measures. In many cases, the most effective measures are those which were conceived from the outset to offer security as a prime function, and are typical of networks used by governments, military and financial institutions.

The majority of other computer networks today, however, were not originally conceived with security features in mind. They provide no security, or allow the use only of specific applications which have some security measures built into their facilities on an individual basis. In those cases security services are of limited scope and applicability, and usually incompatible in larger distributed systems.

There are several drawbacks of providing security separately in each application on an individual "ad hoc" basis:

1. The integration and functional completeness of the overall security system in a broader operational environment may not be feasible.

2. It is difficult to analyse and evaluate the overall strength of such a global security system.

3. Implementation, and therefore usage, of individual security algorithms, mechanisms, and services may be duplicated, or interfere with one another.

4. It is not easy to define a formal description of the global security system, suitable for its rigorous analysis.

5. It is very inconvenient to establish a common security architecture and policy for integration and optimization of individual security services.

Therefore, the main aim of this book is to present the design details and principles of usage of a global, integrated security system. The system contains many security features, protocols, services and mechanisms that can be found in existing environments and commercial products and is potentially applicable to a variety of single or distributed computing environments, users or applications. In this book the complete security system is called the *Comprehensive Integrated Security System (CISS)*.

The *Comprehensive Integrated Security System* provides security services for network users, host machines and also for communications functions, such as the transfer of data between user stations or host machines. These services include not only standard *ISO/OSI* security services, but also some new, original services and protocols, designed by the authors. The generality of the *CISS* system means that its concept is applicable to many host systems and to any kind of communication network.

The concept of a *Comprehensive Integrated Security System* can be retrospectively added to existing data processing systems as a security value-added function which may be very attractive to owners, users, and managers of large existing computer networks and network applications. New applications can be written to utilize the available security functions, and existing applications may be modified or updated to use the system, without substantial redesign or reprogramming. The *correctness*, *functionality*, and *integrity* of the *CISS* are demonstrated by application of formal models and methods for verification of security systems.

The basis for security in open systems in this book is the *ISO/OSI Security Architecture* international standard [ISO88]. This document, in the form of a framework, defines security services, security mechanisms, security management functions, and some other relevant aspects of security in open systems, mainly as broad and general recommendations. This book covers many of the aspects of security in open distributed systems and computer networks as *extensions* of the *OSI* security framework.

The main goals and results of this book are therefore the following:

- An overview and analysis of the relevant details of computer network security, including the *ISO/OSI security framework* for *ISO/OSI* environments, and security features in some existing open system applications.

- Extensions of the *ISO/OSI* security framework with *additional* mainframe and data communication security services (since *OSI* is considered primarily as a model for open data communication).

- An overview of some existing *formal security models* and *methodology* for modelling, verification and analysis of distributed security systems, together with design and implementation *security requirements* in open distributed systems.

- A specification of all the *design and implementation details* of the comprehensive global security system for open networks.

- Examples of usage of the comprehensive security system for various applications, operational environments, and global *EDI* systems.

The book has eight chapters. Each describes an autonomous topic, but the chapters are also structured sequentially to give all the relevant details of security in open distributed systems. Therefore, the chapters can be read individually or in groups. The first three chapters are overview chapters, the next three preparatory, and the last two design chapters. All the chapters are self-contained, with short introductory and conclusions sections, as "backward and forward pointers", and chapter summaries.

Chapter 1 is an introductory chapter. It covers the basic concepts of the structure, operations and potential problems in computer networks and distributed systems. It also contains a short overview of security features, services and mechanisms in computer networks and gives all the necessary security terminology needed for subsequent chapters.

Chapter 2 contains an introduction and description of the relevant aspects of the *standard concept of the ISO/OSI Security Architecture*. It describes the general concept of network security in the *OSI* environment, based on sections 5, 6 and 8 of the *ISO/OSI* international standard for security in open systems [ISO88]. Some comments, descriptions and explanations are added to the original text as an introduction to the extensions described in the fourth chapter.

To complete the introductory chapters, *Chapter 3* gives an overview of recommended security services in some existing standardized *OSI* applications and protocols. Security features are described briefly with the intention of matching them against the security concept and the architecture from the second chapter. These features are also the basis (as requirements) for the design of a comprehensive security system for open distributed environments, given in the seventh and eighth chapters.

The basic conclusion derived from Chapters 2 and 3 is that the current concept of the *ISO/OSI* Security Architecture [ISO88] is a good background for security in open systems, but the concept must be thoroughly analysed and extended with some additional security services and mechanisms, both for network host systems and for communication systems. Some suggestions for these extensions are already stated in the original document [ISO88].

An analysis of the standard security architecture for open systems is given in *Chapter 4*. This analysis is the basis for the remaining chapters, which contain the main research results of this book.

The formal approach to the design and verification of secure open distributed systems (formal models and modelling methodology) is described in *Chapter 5*. This chapter introduces readers to the very important aspects of design and use of formal models in secure systems, gives an overview of some of the existing models and their applicability to modelling of security in open distributed systems, and derives security requirements and specifications necessary for the comprehensive integrated security system in open distributed environments. It gives the principles of formal modelling of secure computer networks and distributed systems, describes some existing formal models, analyses their applicability to secure open distributed systems, and suggests some security requirements and specifications. These suggestions are based on the results of the formal modelling and analysis of the standard *ISO/OSI* security architecture and on the principles for designing security systems in open environments.

Chapter 6 covers various aspects of *network security policies.* It begins with a description of the approach to *risk* and *vulnerability analysis,* and gives methods for *rating, verification, selection* and *integration* of individual network security mechanisms. It also contains suggestions for certain *classes of secure systems* in computer networks. This chapter together with Chapter 4 provides the main link to another book by the same authors (*"Security Mechanisms for Computer Networks"* *), since these two chapters contain the results of the analysis of various security mechanisms and services described in that book.

The title of the *Chapter 7* reflects its main contents, the *design* of the comprehensive integrated security system. It includes the following elements:

- The *model* of the comprehensive integrated security system, with all relevant organizational, functional and managerial aspects.

- The *components* of the comprehensive security system: mechanisms, services, agents, protocols, and segments of the security information data base.

- The *security management* functions in a security system, including administration and management activities, event logging, control and recovery procedures, etc.

---

* *"Security Mechanisms for Computer Networks"*, 1989, (reprinted 1991), Ellis Horwood, Ltd., Chichester, England, ISBN 0-13-799180-0

- The *security protocols* for secure communication between individual components of the security system (security agents, security managers and the security data base) and between different security domains.

- Suggestions (guidelines) for the *placement* of new security services and components of the security system within various operational environments.

Chapter 8 is devoted to practical and implementation aspects of *security systems, secure protocols* and *secure applications*. This chapter describes the applicability of the comprehensive security system in various popular operational environments: existing *OSI* systems and applications, *DOS, UNIX, TCP/IP, SNA* and *DECNET* networks. The third part of this chapter contains a description of *prototype implementations* of some of the individual security mechanisms, and also one version of an *integrated security system* applicable to various operational environments. Finally, some possibilities for usage of security in global open electronic systems are also indicated.

The book is based on the second volume of the Project Report which was created as the result of research and cooperation activities in the *CEC COST-11* Ter Project *"Security Mechanisms for Computer Networks"*. The Project was sponsored and financed by the *Commission of the European Communities* for six years (1985 – 1990).

The Project Report is structured in two volumes: the first contains a broad survey of various network security mechanisms and services, and the second (this book) contains the design of a comprehensive integrated security system for various operational environments. The first volume has already been published as *"Security Mechanisms for Computer Networks"*.

The Project Team planned the two volumes should be sequentially related, both methodologically and conceptually. The first book, therefore, contains design, analysis and a broad survey of various *security services* and *mechanisms* for different aspects of networks security: entity authentication and authorization, data communications security, database integrity and security, process control, cryptography, key management, etc., while this book contains an integration of those services and the design of a comprehensive integrated security system applicable to many operational environments.

This book is written to provide guidance to the designers of network security systems: in selection of security mechanisms, services, and protocols; in possible design solutions; and in implementation and use examples of such systems. It is also suitable for users of computer networks, as it gives security solutions for applications and usage of network security systems.

ACKNOWLEDGEMENTS

The authors would like to acknowledge the support and cooperation provided by other people involved in the second stage of the *COST–11 Ter "Security" Project* and also involved in the preparation of this book. The *COST–11 Ter "Security" Project* was sponsored by the Commission of the European Communities (CEC).

Contributions to the Project, other than those by the authors of this book, were provided by the following people: Ciarán Clissmann and Francois Law Min (University College Dublin), Eduardo Perez (Stockholm University), Simon Shepherd and Vijay Varadharajan (University of Plymouth). Other members of the Project Team in the second stage were Dmitri Maroulis (The Greek Computer Society) and Jose L. Morant (University of Madrid). We would like to acknowledge the support and assistance of Herman Weegenaar (the Dutch representative to the COST–11 Ter Concertation Committee) and the financial coordinator of this Project, Jacques Desfosses (the official CEC representative to the COST–11 Ter Project), and Rolf Speth (the Project Director in the third stage of the COST–11 Ter Action).

We would also like to acknowledge the technical assistance of Edina Hatunić, Eduardo Perez and Amra Murtić in the preparation of the book.

We acknowledge the cooperation and support of the Publisher, and our institutions which permitted us to participate in the Project and in the preparation of this book.

A u t h o r s

1

INTRODUCTION TO COMPUTER NETWORK SECURITY

1.1 OVERVIEW OF COMPUTER NETWORKS AND DISTRIBUTED SYSTEMS

1.1.1 Computer Networks and Distributed Systems Infrastructure Technologies

Computer technologies continuously evolve with the development and applications of complex *VLSI* circuits. On that basis the development of microprocessor based computing systems has significantly increased. Trends in the development of computer technology and the emergence of mini and microcomputers make possible the design of computer structures for *distributed* data processing. At present, such structures involve hardware redundancy and thus extra cost, but with future technology advances this disadvantage may soon disappear.

The development of computer technology and user oriented processing has created computing structures with highly distributed computing power. Such structures are based on intelligent, programmable, multifunctional units (user stations), each equipped with its own microprocessor, its own or a shared information base, graphical or multimedia user interfaces, intelligent software applications, etc. These multifunctional user stations are usually connected to a larger computer system, via standard *LAN* or *WAN* arrangements.

The idea of the distributed processing structure largely derives from the concept of transaction-oriented computing functions among its elements, according to the most cost-effective arrangement in a specific data processing environment. Some mini-computers and microprocessors are optimized for message switching, others for input/output functions, and still others for fast, large scale arithmetic calculations. A computing structure may also contain user stations, but these can be considered elements of the structure only if they possess integrated processing power, today usually in the form of personal computers. It is desirable to configure such a computing structure to utilize the capabilities of each component in the most efficient way. Basically, such computing structures are computer networks and distributed processing systems.

The main purpose of computer networks is to permit a wide community of users to share computer resources which are linked through networking infrastructures. Typically, the networking infrastructures are constructed using a variety of technologies, such as circuit switching, packet switching, etc. and they operate over different types of media, such as copper or fibre circuits, satellite channels, etc. These infrastructures are the backbone which support *distributed processing* functions through the use of intelligent machines at different locations, which cooperate by means of communication protocols. Therefore, in this book the terms computer network and distributed system will be used to mean *an interconnected set of autonomous resources or computers*. The categorization of network infrastructures is non-standard. It encompasses all forms of computer networks, regardless of whether they are *LANs* (local area networks), *WANs* (wide area networks), or *VANs* (value-added networks). The important point here is that not only users need security protection, but also the network resources and network management facilities.

Various functions of the intelligent user stations can be implemented as software modules loaded into the memory of the microcomputer. In the distributed computing structure the execution of a program is performed as a sequence of separate functional modules which are topologically distributed up to the lowest level of the computing structure, i.e. user stations. Such a structure may be called a *functionally distributed computing system (FDCS)*. Contrary to the definition of a standard computer network, where computers operate as independent components, in the case of the *FDCS*, computing elements may be mutually dependent. The standard notion of a program (process) executed in some component of a computer network is replaced by the execution of a sequence of functional modules. The execution of several modules in a particular sequence is equivalent to the execution of the whole process.

There are three major advantages of the *FDCS* over some other type of computing structure:

1. *Flexibility.* The *FDCS* is amenable to incremental upward scaling of computer power. The distributed architecture of the system permits that power to be supported by a collection of moderate sized computer systems.

2. *Reliability.* The *FDCS* is more reliable than other computing structures because it is constructed from multiple components at many locations. Some components may be duplicated or may take over the functions of others. Consequently, the *FDCS* is

not even locally susceptible to failure when one component either fails or becomes inaccessible.

3. Efficiency. Since the multifunctional elements of the *FDCS* exist near to where they are most frequently used, the expected effects are: faster access to data, shorter response time, and reduced communication costs.

1.1.2 OSI Reference Model (OSI/RM)

Since *OSI* concepts are used throughout this book, this section gives a global overview of the *OSI* standards. They constitute a framework for defining the communication processes between systems consisting of computers and users.

The basic *OSI Reference Model* (Figure 1.1) has seven layers that define the functions involved in communication between two systems, the services required to perform these functions, and the protocols associated with these services.

The implementation of these functions is achieved by software written to bridge the gap between the application process and the physical medium over which the transmission takes place. The lowest five layers of the *OSI* model provide a reliable connection between source and destination. Level six, the presentation layer, ensures that information is delivered in a form that the receiving system can understand and use. Level seven, the application layer, reflects the behaviour of an application process that is observable in its communication with other application processes obeying the same protocol. Of all the layers, the application layer contains the most user functionality, such as electronic mail, file transfer, virtual terminal, network management, etc.

After selecting the appropriate application layer process, the complete stack of other protocols in the six lower layers is usually selected automatically.

For the purpose of the discussions in this book it is necessary to understand and appreciate that there are two distinct concepts at the application layer:

- the application process; and
- the application entity.

The general purpose application protocols, such as *FTAM, VTP, X.400-MHS, TP, JTM, RDA, X.500-DS,* etc. are network application entities. User applications, such as fault management, performance management, security management, configuration management, name management, and accounting management are termed "application processes". The application processes can access the application entities only via the "user element interface", as shown in Figure 1.2.

It should be noted that the application layer entities may also interface to or support the user application processes. But the user application processes themselves are outside the scope of the *OSI/RM*, because they are user specific and user defined.

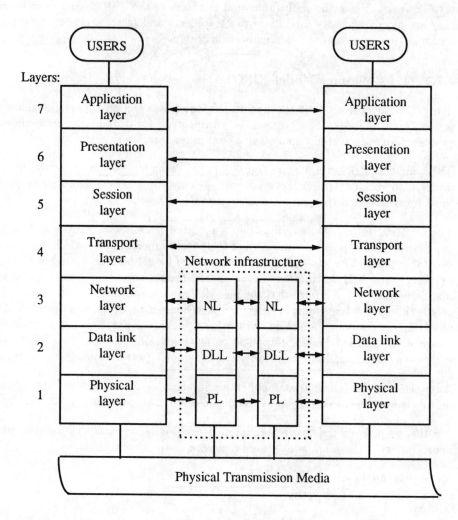

Figure 1.1. Basic OSI/Reference Model

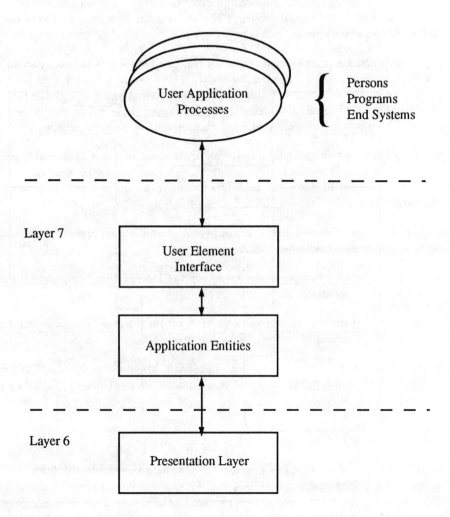

Figure 1.2. General User Application Processes Interface
to Application Entities

The form and function of such user application processes is the responsibility of the system users who access the application layer for a service. It should be further noted that the structure of the application layer is currently being defined by *ISO*. It is expected that a conceptual model of the application layer will be developed to interrelate all the standards at that layer.

An application process is an element within a real open system that takes part in the execution of one or more distributed information processing tasks. For application processes to cooperate, they must share sufficient information to enable them to interact. The shared information is called the "information base". The processes must also have a common understanding of what this shared information means.

In general, application layer standards define conceptual schemes that enable application processes to communicate successfully. Such schemes define the conventions governing the transfer of data, the associated semantics, and abstract syntax to be used in data transfers.

To meet the communication requirements of peer user application processes, the upper layers of *OSI* provide the following services:

- support the negotiation of semantics for the information being exchanged – provided by the application layer service;

- support negotiation of commonly understood representations for the information being exchanged – provided by the presentation layer service;

- enable the application processes to negotiate, maintain and manage the dialogue needed to support their information flow requirements – provided by the session layer service.

Application Layer Model

Within the context of an *OSI* environment, an application process is supported by one or more *Application Entities (AEs)*. An *AE* is accessed through a presentation address. In each *AE*, the user application process has to choose an *Application Service Element (ASE)* to perform its task. A *Service Element (SE)* is a primitive defined at the interface between two adjacent layers. An *ASE* is a set of functionalities that support a typical application program. It represents different kinds of work that the user expects to be performed, such as file transfer or electronic mail, along with all the elements necessary to perform that kind of work.

A group of *ASEs* comprise a particular *ASE* implementation within a computer system (Figure 1.3). For example, *ASE1* could stand for *X.400* based electronic mail and *ASE2* for *X.500* based Directory Service. At any given time, a user application process works with one and only one *ASE* within its environment, controlled by a single association controlling function. For the case of several *OSI* communications, the multiple

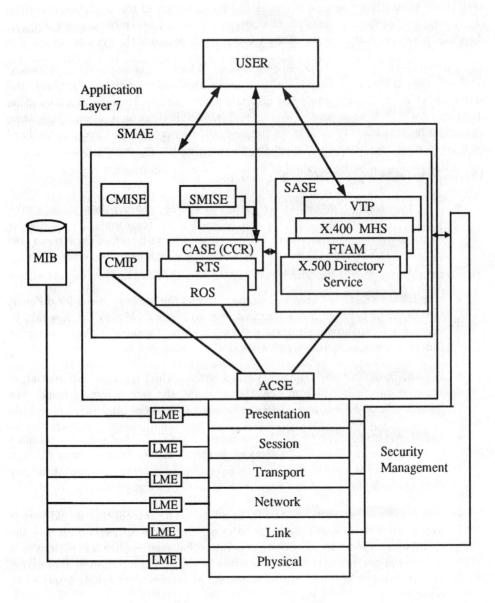

Figure 1.3. Interface of Multiple Applications
to the Security Management through SMAE

association controlling function manages the coordination of the application entities (at the application layer). An *AE* contains one user element interface and a set of *ASEs.* The specific combination of these elements determines the type of *AE.*

The user element interface represents, or acts on behalf of, the application processes. It allows the *ASEs* to communicate with other application entities. In short, the user element interface represents the ultimate source and destination of information transfer. An *ASE* is a coherent set of integrated functions that allow application entities to inter-operate for a specific purpose. *ASEs* may be used independently of each other, or in combination to meet specific information processing goals.

This leads to other types of *ASEs.* For example:

- The *Association Control Service Element (ACSE)* enables other *ASEs* to work together. For instance, *FTAM* can be used alone for simple file transfer or in combination with another *ASE,* such as *Commitment, Concurrency and Recovery (CCR),* for the purpose of achieving a high degree of error recovery. An *ACSE* can also be used to open and close an association.

- *Common ASE (CASE)* represents the common functions required for different jobs or *ASEs* between hosts. For instance, to run *FTAM* or *VTP,* it would be necessary to open communication between hosts. Opening is thus a common function which is applicable to several different protocols.

- Specific *ASE (SASE)* represents the function which permits differentiation between protocols which are capable of doing the same piece of work. For instance, both *FTAM* and *MHS* can be used to transfer files.

- *Reliable Transfer Service (RTS)* was defined by *CCITT* and not *ISO.* Its main function is to interface *X.400 MHS* applications with the session layer through the presentation entity. It does this by grouping several common primitives used by both the *X.400 MHS* and one or more other applications.

- *Remote Operation Service (ROS)* was defined as a protocol that would permit easy interconnection of a workstation or a *PC* with its mail server. It uses the client-server model to represent cooperation between application entities in a distributed environment. It achieves this by splitting a distributed application into modules or agents, some of which act as servers and provide a service to clients.

Application Layer Model for Network Management. The above application layer model is further extended to reflect the network management aspects, such as security management at this layer. Layer management is carried out by *Layer Management Entities (LMEs).* Communication between *LMEs* at a given layer is primarily intended to occur via layer seven application entities, obeying system management protocols. System management is supported by *System Management Application Entities (SMAEs)* resident at the application layer. The *SMAE* is a "tool box" of management services and protocols for management information between open systems. *SMAEs* communicate with each other via a *Common set of Management Information Protocols (CMIP)* and its associated service definition *CMI Service Elements (CMISE)*. In addition, *Specific Management Information–passing Service Elements (SMISEs)* have been defined in terms of the various types of *Management Information Services (MISs)* for which requirements have been identified (e.g. accounting, faults, etc).

In terms of *OSI* network management, *SMAEs* interfacing to user application processes such as fault, accounting, configuration, etc., will utilize the underlying *Application Common Service Elements (ACSE)* for normal access to the presentation and session layers. The *SMAE* in conjunction with *CASE* and *SASE* will provide the operating environment for the user application processes in a standard way. Similarly, *RTS* and *ROS* can also be utilized by the user application processes as stated above.

Summary

This section has presented a broad-brush description of the *OSI/RM*. The emphasis was given to the Application Layer in order to show what interfaces and service elements are available to the user application processes. The implication for security management is that it interfaces with either *CASE, ROS* or *RTS*. This, however, should not preclude one of these *ASEs* being used as an interim measure for a reasonable implementation to be achieved in a given hardware/software environment.

1.2 NETWORK SERVICES AND APPLICATIONS

Figure 1.4 gives three modes of accesses and the structure of the *X.25* network (from [PATE89A]), which are described in the following three subsections.

1.2.1 X.25 Recommendation

The *CCITT X.25 Recommendation* was announced officially in its final version in *1984*, after the debate of a number of previous versions, developed between *1976* and *1980* (an historical overview is given in [MEIJ82] and [FREE88]), with the most recent revision in *1984*. This standard defines the interface between *Data Terminal Equipment (DTE)* and *Data Circuit–terminating Equipment (DCE)* on Packet Switched Data Networks (*PSDN's*). The recommendation includes layers 1, 2 and 3 (packet level) of the *OSI* reference model.

As shown in Figure 1.4 (b), when an asynchronous terminal is connected to the Packet Switched Data Network (*PSDN*), a packet assembler/disassembler (*PAD*) is required. The *PAD* conforms to the *Triple-X (X.3, X.28 and X.29)* standard. Description of functional specifications of layers of the *OSI* reference model can be found in [FREE88] and other textbooks.

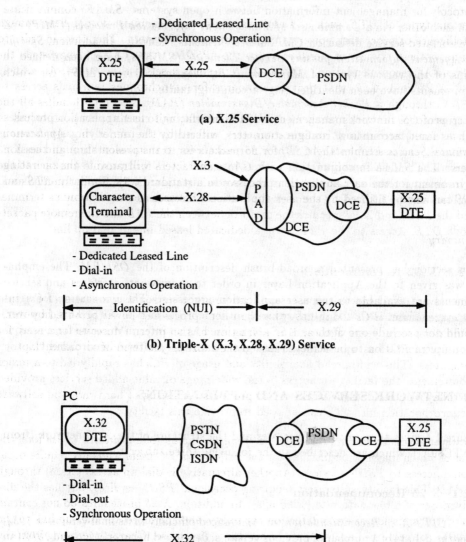

Figure 1.4. Modes of Access to PSDN

1.2.2 Triple-X (X.3, X.28, and X.29)

Certain types of *DTE*, such as simple asynchronous terminals, do not have enough intelligence or processing power to implement an *X.25* system. Therefore, in order to connect these types of terminals to the *PSDNs*, the *CCITT* suggested the *"Triple-X"* recommendation. *"Triple-X"* represents a set of three protocols, namely *X.3*, *X.28*, and *X.29*, that provide standards for asynchronous terminals access to *PSDNs* through a *Packet Assembler/Disassembler (PAD)*. The *PAD* handles all the *X.25* protocol functions (such as call establishment, call clearing, etc.) on behalf of the attached terminals. It accepts characters, entered by the user at the asynchronous terminal, and assembles them into *X.25* packets for transmission through the *X.25* network. The disassembly of *X.25* packets into characters for transmission back to the asynchronous terminal takes place in the reverse direction. *X.3* specifies functions and facilities of the *PAD*, *X.28* specifies the protocol between the asynchronous terminal and the *PAD*, and *X.29* specifies the protocol between the *PAD* and the remote packet-mode *DTE*. Access to the *PAD* is via a dedicated leased line or dial-up line.

1.2.3 X.32 Recommendation

The advent of cheap microprocessors has brought personal computers (*PCs*) into widespread use. *PCs* today have the equivalent processing power provided by mini-computers some years ago, and at a fraction of the price. Moreover the need for mobility of *PCs* has significantly reduced their size in the form of so called "laptop" computers. This widespread availability and usage of *PCs* has rapidly led to a major requirement: the facility for access to the wide range of value-added services provided by today's public data networks. *X.25* products consisting of hardware and software for incorporation into *PCs* can be used to provide this facility.

However access to *PSDNs* through *X.25* requires the use of a *dedicated leased line*, the cost of which may not be justified for the majority of *PC* users who only require occasional access to *PSDN* services. Another alternative is dial-up access (*X.28*) through a *PAD*. This facility suits users requiring occasional *PSDN* services, but has the disadvantage of a low data rate (1200 bps). In addition, *X.28* procedures do not contain any retransmission or error detection capability, and therefore, the dial-up link to the *PAD* is not protected against data errors due to line noise. Character echoing from the *PAD* is often used as a simple form of error correction performed by the user. Some of these problems were overcome in *CCITT* recommendation *X.32*, the final draft version of which was issued in December 1987.

X.32 specifies the functional and procedural aspects of the *DTE/DCE* interface for packet-mode terminals accessing a *PSDN* through a Public Switched Network (*PSN*). In Figure 1.4 (c), the use of a standalone *X.32 DTE* for dial-up access to a remote *X.25* host across a *PSDN* is illustrated. Both dial-in (*DTE* to *PSDN*) and dial-out (*PSDN* to *DTE*) operations over synchronous links are supported. *X.32* embodies the lower three layers of the *OSI* reference model.

X.32 protocol may be viewed as an extension to *X.25* with a number of additional features, such as dial-in, dial-out access and some security issues. The advantages to the user provided by the *X.32* protocol are:

- better error protected transmission than X.28;

- high data rate (2400 to 9600 bps);

- dial-out capability;

- multiple logical channels, compared with X.28, which allows only one logical channel;

- access to OSI end-systems and value-added services for end-to-end communication (message handling systems *(MHS)*, distributed systems, distributed databases).

The *X.32* protocol is suitable for:

- mobile *DTEs (PCs)* for end-to-end mail and *FTAM* applications;

- teletex terminals;

- *DTEs* requiring occasional access to *PSDNs;*

- back-up access to direct *X.25* connections;

- external gateways from Local Area Networks (*LANs*).

1.2.4 X.400 Recommendation

The aim of the X.400 recommendation is to provide an international service for the *exchange of electronic messages* (also named as a generic area of application: *Message Handling Systems* or simply, *MHS*). Two international standardization organizations were involved in the specification of standards for the *MHS: CCITT* and *ISO.* In 1984, the *CCITT* and *ISO* published a set of recommendations known as *X.400 (1984).* Since then, the two organizations have agreed to harmonise their activities, and produce parallel standards with identical text. These later standards are called, respectively, *X.400 (1988)* and *MOTIS (Message Oriented Text Interchange System).* A complete overview of the development of the *MHS* standards can be found in [HENS88].

The basic activity performed by any MHS is the conveyance of electronic messages. As the reader can deduce, the X.400 recommendation belongs to layer 7, the Application Layer of the OSI reference model. A simple model of the MHS is shown in Figure 1.5. This model outlines the basic components involved when a user, the originator, sends a message to another user, the recipient.

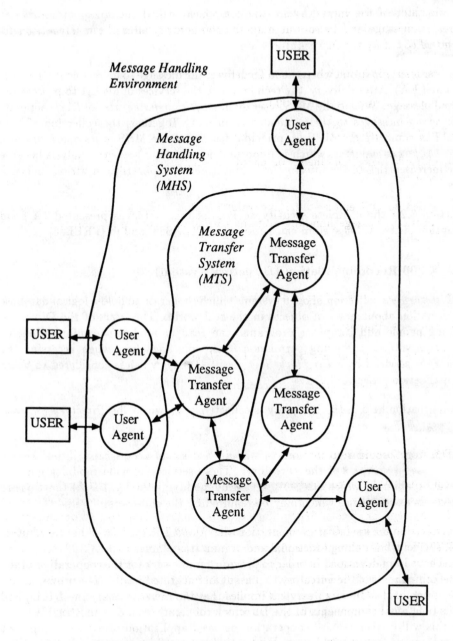

Figure 1.5. The components of the X.400 MHS

The originator of the message uses the component called the *user agent (UA)* to compose a message and to submit it to the component called the *message transfer system (MTS)*.

A UA is similarly involved when the MTS delivers the message to its recipient (the user-associated UA). After delivery, the recipient uses the services of his UA to process the received message. Within the MTS, a set of *message transfer agents (MTAs)* cooperate in conveying messages to their intended recipients. Together, the collection of UAs and MTAs comprise the MHS. A principal feature of the MHS is its operation in a *store-and-forward* manner, which is important for our later security analysis because of the increased risk to the information while stored (temporarily) in various network nodes.

In Section 3.2.4 the complete security analysis of this system is presented. A good description of the *X.400* system can be found in [HENS88] and in [FREE88].

1.2.5 X.500 Recommendation (Directory System)

The Directory is a collection of open systems which cooperate to hold a logical database of information about a set of objects in the real world. The *users* of the Directory, including people and computer programs, can read or modify the information, or parts of it, subject to having permission to do so. Each user when accessing the Directory is serviced by a *Directory User Agent (DUA)*, which is considered to be an *OSI* application process.

The information held in the Directory is collectively known as the *Directory Information Base (DIB)*.

The Directory provides to its users a well-defined set of access capabilities, known as the abstract services of the Directory. These services provide modification and retrieval capabilities, which can be extended by modifying the local *DUA* functions to provide other capabilities which may be required by the end-users.

It is likely that in its full implementation the *X.500* Directory will be distributed, perhaps widely, both along functional and organizational lines. The *X.500* recommendations have been developed in order to provide a framework for the cooperation of the various components of the Directory to present an integrated whole. The provision and consumption of the Directory services implies that the users (actually the *DUAs*) and various functional components of the Directory cooperate with one another. In many cases this will further require cooperation between application processes in different open systems, which in turn requires standardized application protocols to manage this overall cooperation.

The Directory has been designed to support multiple applications, drawn from a wide range of possibilities. The nature of the supported applications will determine which objects will be registered in the Directory, which users will access the information, and which kinds of access they will carry out. Applications may be very specific, such as the provision of distribution lists for electronic mail, or generic, such as the "inter-personal communications directory" application. The Directory also provides the opportunity to exploit commonalities among the applications:

- Single objects in the Directory may be relevant to more than one application.

- Certain patterns of use of the Directory will be common across a range of applications.

To support all Directory functionalities, a number of object classes and attribute types are defined, which should be useful across a range of applications. These definitions are contained in Recommendations X.520 and X.521 (see also Section 3.2.5).

1.2.6 FTAM Recommendation (File Transfer, Access, and Management)

This *OSI* application, also located at the Application layer of the *OSI* reference model, is included in the security analysis of Section 3.2. *FTAM* was defined by *ISO* in a four part document. Part one is a *general introduction* to *FTAM*, part two introduces the concept of a *virtual filestore*, part three the *file service definition* and part four is the *file protocol specification*.

FTAM offers three modes of file manipulation: transfer, access and management. *File transfer* involves the transfer of files between two *OSI* systems and may include transfer of partial or complete files between two filestores on different end-systems. *File access* includes the operations of reading, writing or deleting selected parts of a file residing in a filestore on some end-system, accessed over *OSI* by a user on some remote end-system. *File management* involves remotely reading or altering attributes that define a file within the filestore in which it resides. Figure 1.6 represents the basic concepts of *FTAM*, the virtual filestore and the file access structure. Security aspects of this application are discussed in Section 3.2.6 of this book.

For the interested reader, a detailed description of the *FTAM* application may be found in [HENS88] and in [BLAC89].

1.2.7 Electronic Data Interchange (EDI) Systems

EDI (Electronic Data Interchange) is basically the concept of computer-to-computer exchange of messages (information) relating to various types of activities or business areas, such as banking, trade, software distribution, medicine, publishing, etc. Two basic differences between regular network *MHS* and *EDI* systems are:

- *EDI* information is in the form of special messages, such as banking transactions, orders, invoices, letters, contracts, proprietary materials, etc., exchanged between companies and business partners.

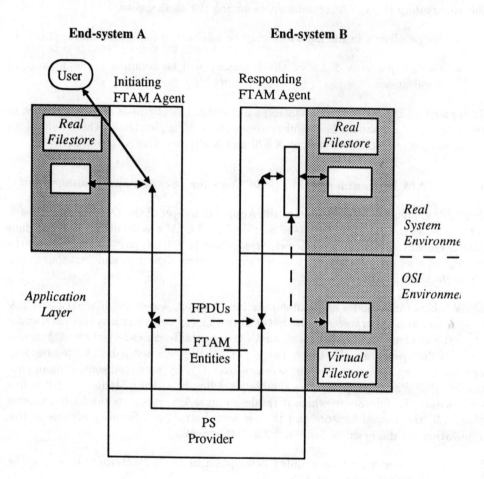

End-system A   **End-system B**

Figure 1.6. FTAM

- Each *EDI* message is transmitted under a special regime or requirements, such as the request for confirmation, the receipt of an "equivalent" message, non-repudiation of content, legal binding, acceptance of special conditions, etc.

It is expected that *EDI* systems will have a tremendous impact on the ways in which companies conduct their business. The use of *EDI* will facilitate networking in banking, trade, publishing, and many other applications in the larger market. Therefore, security, reliability and special functionality will be implicit requirements of *EDI* systems.

There are various ways in which *EDI* systems can be designed and established. *EDI* can be carried out directly between two business partners across a public data communications network or one or more specialized third-party services can be involved.

EDI philosophy and applicability represents an important part of the shift to the electronic ("paperless") society. There are obvious links to *E-mail*, *EFT* (electronic funds transfer) and *POS* (point of sale) systems. While the term "interactive EDI" is sometimes used, *EDI* is currently seen as being distinct from direct client input systems, such as tele-shopping or self-banking. However, the future possibilities of these systems are directed towards global, distributed, homogeneous, multimedia systems, which will cover many aspects of everyday life.

There are many different (functional) aspects to *EDI* systems, but two in particular deserve special consideration, because of their security implications:

- full automation and multimedia facilities, without any special direct human intervention and interpretation;

- the increased possibility for system global distribution and also functional integration.

These two factors together could imply a significant increase in *vulnerability* to failure, error or fraud. Therefore, the information security aspects of this new business environment and this new way of doing business will be very important.

The transition from standard message-exchange systems or E-mail systems to *EDI* systems will result in a significantly increased dependence on internal computer systems operations and network protocols. For those problems there are various strategies which can be adopted and various actions which can be taken. While the problem is common, the solutions adopted can often be tailored to the individual company.

Moreover, with *EDI* a company's dependence on the network, and indeed on the systems of their trading partners, is also increased. General system availability will be important especially when just-in-time techniques, for example, are adopted.

The inter-company aspect of *EDI* brings other special problems. They are "special" in the sense that they imply a need for common solutions. The use of *EDI* means that there has to be agreement on how certain security-related functions are achieved. Any agreement or standard will have widespread ramifications that go beyond the business partners directly involved.

EDI systems will not only be used between direct business partners, but may also be used between a company and other organizations, such as banks, government or administrative organizations, tax authorities, etc. The needs of special groups and professions, such as auditors, have also to be considered.

The *EDI* systems use the capabilities of the *Message Transfer Service (MTS)* of the *X.400* system for receiving and sending messages. This service is provided by the *EDI Messaging System (EDIMS)*, whose functionality is similar to the *IMPS (Interpersonal Messaging System)*, as defined in the Recommendation *X.400*. In some cases the *EDI* service can be used to transmit an *EDI* interchange to a physical reproduction system, such as telex, facsimile or a print.

The *EDIMS* model comprises *EDI User Agents*, *EDI Message Stores* and *Physical Delivery Access Units*, all supported by the *Message Transfer Service (MTS)*. The environment in which EDI messaging takes place can be modelled as a functional object which is referred to as the *EDI Messaging Environment – EDIME*. The *EDIME* consists of lesser objects referred to as the primary objects of EDI Messaging. They include (usually) a single central object to receive, transfer and deliver messages, called the *EDI Messaging System (EDIMS)*, and several "peripheral" objects, called *EDI Messaging System* users.

A user accesses the *EDIMS* through an *Access Unit*, one type of which is the *Physical Delivery Access Unit (PDAU)*. The *PDAU* allows EDI users to send messages to users outside the EDIMS who have no access to MHS. The Message Stores used in EDIMS have specific related functions and can optionally be used by EDI users to take delivery of messages on their behalf, i.e to the Telematic Access Unit.

The *EDI* class of *UAs* create messages containing contents specific to the EDI Messaging Service. The information that is sent from one EDI UA to another is a result of an originator, which is generally an application process, composing and sending a message, called an *EDI Message*. The *EDI Message* carries the EDI Interchange. Only one interchange is present in an EDI Message. The EDI Message is conveyed with an "envelope" when being transferred through the MTS, which contains a header made up of multiple fields. Most of these are mapped directly from equivalent fields in the lead segment of the EDI interchange, with the primary intention of making this information accessible to the message store for retrieval purposes. Additional parts of the message are provided to carry information supplementing that of the EDI interchange, for example, engineering drawings of specifications related to a customer order of complex machine parts. This appears to be a key area in which the flexible, binary structures of X.400 provide advantages over traditional EDI encoding methods.

A new functional component in the EDI Messaging Service, compared with the *X.400* system, is the *EDI Responsibility Notification*. The purpose of introducing the *EDIMS*

Responsibility is primarily to provide a method for confirming the passing of messages amongst *UAs*.

In *EDIMS* a user or user application can request a notification for responsibility of a message by a recipient or recipient application. This notification is requested by an originating *UA* and is generated by the recipient UA taking responsibility for the message. Responsibility implies that the received message is either available to the *EDIMS* user, or that it has been forwarded with certain modifications (message integrity). It is possible to forward a received *EDI* Message unchanged and pass the obligation to respond to the responsibility notification request to the forward recipient or to several intermediate recipients, who must then respond back to the originator of the message.

1.3 BASIC CONCEPTS OF NETWORK SECURITY

In recent years, advances in computing and telecommunication technologies have greatly expanded user requirements, applications, functions and tools available to all users of data processing systems, in almost every field of application. Computer systems are expanding in their capabilities, types and operational characteristics. They may also be connected with communication lines to form very broad, general concepts of *computing networks* and *distributed computing systems.* This development was followed by the emergence of computing structures for *parallel* and *distributed processing* of various application tasks, thus giving users of computer networks and distributed systems great flexibility in the structuring of their systems and in the interactions with other systems.

As a consequence, users and their organizations are becoming more and more dependent on the services provided by their systems and computer networks. Data, computer programs, and information of high confidentiality and value, usually critical to the functioning and survival of the organization, are kept in computer systems and exchanged over telecommunication facilities. This trend raises the need for *dependable systems* and computing structures that process information *securely*, which is a requirement very difficult to achieve with open or distributed systems.

Because of the many different components, operations, resources, and users, computer networks are becoming a very convenient targets for attacks and illegal operations, which means that the *integrity* and *protection of resources* are becoming important operational aspects of each computing structure. More and more computer systems or their components are, first distributed, and then linked together in powerful computing structures which provide a variety of services to their users. Such systems are frequently referred to as *distributed processing systems*, because a single task may require cooperation between processes executing on several end-systems. This structure, in principle, is more complicated than the regular concept of a computer network, and so are the appropriate security measures needed for such systems.

The global functional framework for security in distributed systems is the *Open Sys-*

tems Interconnection (OSI) concept. The objective of OSI is to permit the interconnection of heterogeneous computer systems, so that useful and reliable communication between application processes may be achieved. This, in principle, means *integrity* and *protection* of system resources, plus implementation of additional *security requirements* and *protocols*. Therefore, at various times, security services, controls, and protocols must be used in order to protect resources and information exchanged between the application processes. Such actions should make *the cost* of illegally obtaining or modifying data or programs greater than the potential value of doing so, or make *the time* required to do that so long, that in the meantime the value of data is lost or functions of programs are inadequate.

Generally, security refers to a complex of measures, which may be broadly classified as [ISO88]:

- procedural (e.g. selecting trustworthy personnel, changing passwords regularly, etc.);

- logical (e.g. access controls and cryptography);

- physical (e.g. vaults and door locks, screening against interpretable emissions, etc.);

which are aimed at the

- prevention,

- detection and indication,

- correction

of certain kinds of system misuse, both accidental and deliberate.

Security not only addresses attacks and threats *external* to the system, but *internal* attacks from known user entities. If guarantees of authentication can be provided, it is possible to design a system in which all user entities are subject to strict access control, thus minimizing the internal threat. Of course, it is virtually impossible to stop a user passing information to an attacker directly, so user trust and strong enforcement procedures are also required.

Only authorized users can obtain or provide information which will help to eliminate, as far as possible, misuse of the system, such as eavesdropping on confidential data, abuse of resources, fraudulent activity, forgery of messages, etc. The recommended list of services which a security system should provide is comprehensively addressed in Section 4.2.3 (and synthesized in Table 4.1).

Currently, if a particular application requires security services, these are generally incorporated by hardware/software means *into the application itself* from conception.

In a system where there are several normal (insecure) applications, and only one or two secure services, this approach may be quite satisfactory.

By contrast, in global systems, where there are many possible applications, as with ODP systems, a large number of which may require security facilities, it is clearly wasteful for each application to contain a complete set of internal security services for its own private use, when a majority of the services could be common to most, if not all, applications.

This was the basic approach in designing and implementing the global, integrated security system described in this book: it is structured in a modular way with autonomous functional modules whose various combinations may provide a variety of security mechanisms and services with different levels of strength and efficiency.

Now the definition (concept) of security, as used in this book, will be given. There are many descriptions or definitions as to what is meant by the *secure computer network* or *secure distributed system*. Here, some of them are first stated and then, by comparison, the concept and approach used in this book will be defined. It will be derived as the synthesis of various other definitions, thus, we hope, offering a broader scope of security aspects and functions.

Definition A [ISO88] : *Security* is used in a sense of minimizing the vulnerabilities of assets and resources.

An *asset* is anything of value in a global computing system. A *vulnerability* is any weakness that could be exploited to violate a system or the information it contains. A *threat* is a potential violation of security.

Definition B [ECMA88] : *Security* refers to a complex of procedural, logical and physical measures aimed at prevention, detection and correction of certain kinds of misuse, together with the tools to install, operate and maintain these measures.

From these two definitions, accepted in the international standards concepts, it follows that the following components of a computing structure may require protection:

- *users* of computer networks, including all active components, such as programs, procedures, processes, etc.;

- *data* and *information* (including software, data stored in network data bases, and information produced as results of network usage and operations);

- various network *services* and *functions*, especially communication and data processing services;

- *equipment* and facilities.

Protection must be concerned with various threats and problems, such as:

- *destruction (deletion)* of programs, data, information and/or other network resources;

- *corruption* or *illegal modification* of programs, data and information;

- *theft, removal* or *loss* of programs, data, information and/or other resources;

- illegal, unauthorized *disclosure* of data, information or computer programs;

- *interruption* or *denial* of various network services.

The structured list of threats for OSI environments is given later in Table 1.1.

The concept from Definition A includes three aspects of reliable network operations: *integrity* of network components, *security* of network users and resources, and *privacy* of individuals. These three aspects, as understood throughout this text, are formally defined in the following way:

Definition 1.1 ([DEMO77], [CHAM75]) : *Integrity* of network resources means that:

a. all resources in the network are always *available* to the users, whatever hardware or software malfunctioning or illegal activities may occur (*defence from loss of data*);

- resources of *high quality* are always available, whatever corruption may be attempted to their integrity and consistency (*defence from corruption of data*).

Definition 1.2 [MUFT88A] : *Security* of network resources means that all operations with those resources are always performed in accordance with strictly defined security rules and regulations.

Definition 1.3 [ISO88] : *Privacy* is the right of individuals (network users) to control or influence what information related to them may be collected and stored and by whom and to whom that information may be disclosed.

(*Note:* Because this term relates to the rights of individuals, it cannot be very precise and its use should be avoided except as a motivation for requiring security.)

These three major characteristics of network operations, i.e. *integrity* of network components, *security* of resources and *privacy* of individuals, provide a basis for a reliable network environment. Other aspects are also very important for the regular operation of computing systems: fault avoidance, fault tolerance, formal verification, sensitivity, vulnerability analysis, rating, etc. These aspects, together with integrity, security and privacy, constitute a global concept of *network dependability:*

Definition 1.4 [RUSH86] : *A dependable network* is simply one whose components, resources and operations may be trusted; more precisely, a dependable network is one in which reliance can justifiably be placed on the *quality of services* provided. Quality of services includes *continuity* as well as *correctness* (i.e. conformity with requirements and expectations).

The aspects of network security, given in Definitions 1.1–1.3, are in fact extended in the Definition 1.4. The concept of a dependable computing structure includes not only prevention of *potential problems* and their consequences, but also imposes some additional requirements and operational characteristics. They are all understood under the concept of the *quality of services*, which may be seen as a broader concept than integrity, security and privacy, since it includes all three of them together with some additional characteristics and requirements.

Analysis of recent research papers and reports dealing with various aspects of regular operations of computer networks reveals one additional aspect of modern network usage and applications, namely a number of *special situations, applications and protocols* which are not concerned with any potential problem in the network, but with implementation of special services, additional functions, and applications in an OSI environment. Some of them may be:

- secure *group communications* (teleconferences, multiple signatures, threshold schemes, etc.);

- cooperation of *mutually suspicious users* (coin flipping protocol, mental poker, contract signing schemes, etc.);

- *zero-knowledge* protocols and their applications (user identification and authentication schemes, validation of data and protocols, etc.);

- *special applications* in the open environment (Electronic Document Interchange (EDI) systems, electronic voting schemes, electronic trading, etc.).

So security in OSI and ODP systems is becoming an important area, not only *to prevent undesirable and unauthorized events* (and their consequences), but also *to provide better and broader services and applications* in the open distributed environment.

Therefore, the following definition will be assumed throughout this book:

Definition 1.5 : *Security* is the property of an open system which guarantees at all times :

- correct *status* of all system resources (static characteristics);

- correct *behaviour* of programs, system functions, control modules, and services (dynamic characteristics);

- *availability* of various special security protocols and applications (functional characteristics);

- overall system *dependability* (quality of services).

An open system is *secure* if users in that system may use one or more applications implemented under certain security requirements, which, in that case, may be called *secure applications*. Those requirements are implemented as various *security services* used by secure applications. The security services are the functions of the security system, which, as defined in [ISO88], provide adequate security of individual systems or data transferred between them. Each security service may be implemented in several different ways. Specific implementation of each security service is based on one or more *security mechanisms*. The same security mechanism may be used to implement combinations of various security services.

Which applications need to be secure, what security services will be used within those applications, and how those security services will be implemented, is a matter for each individual system. Those decisions depend on the *security policy*. The security policy is the set of criteria for the provision of security services [ISO88].

In the global computing environment with many interconnected open and distributed systems, one may establish a structural "hierarchy" of security aspects and components:

> *Secure OSI or ODP environment* is a collection of interconnected
> open systems where users may use various . . .

> *secure applications,*   which use one or more . . .

> *security services,*   which are implemented by various . . .

> *security mechanisms.*

Threats to Regular Operations

In order to design and to implement an integrated security system for a computer network, it is necessary, first, to identify *all threats* against which the protection is required. As defined by ISO, *a threat is a potential violation of security.* Identification of threats may be achieved by an *analysis* which consists of three global stages:

1. *vulnerability analysis* (identifying potential weak elements of the network);

2. *threat assessment* (evaluation of which problems may appear due to weak elements of the network);

3. *risk analysis* (analysis of potential consequences which these problems may cause).

The results of this stage are called *security requirements.* Threats may be classified in three different ways: by their *type* (accidental or intentional, passive or active), by their *consequences,* or by *sources* and *objects* of threats [ISO88].

As a checklist for potential users, and also as a reference list for further topics and solutions in this book, a "standard" list of threats will be given, compiled from various international standard documents and research papers ([ISO88], [VOYD83], [DENN79], [GRAH72]). Threats in the list are grouped in four types of network resources: users, communication messages, data base objects, or programs (processes), being sources or objects of threats. Users and programs may only be *sources* of threats, while all four categories of network resources may be *objects* of threats.

Elimination of some or all of these threats is the ultimate goal of the design and usage of every security system.

Table 1.1.   The List of Threats for OSI Environments

1. *Masquerade (Source: users or programs):* occurs when some legal entity (user or program) successfully pretends to be a different entity. This threat may take the following forms: *(a)* impersonation and misuse of the credentials (security parameters) of another legal entity, *(b)* incorrectly executed sign-on procedure, *(c)* false claim of the origin (source) of entity parameters, *(d)* impersonation of the supervisory entity to a legal entity (user), *(e)* impersonation of one user to another network user.

2. *Illegal associations (Source: users or programs):* the threat may occur if the intruder (illegal entity) conforms to the rules of the authentication and access control services, but violates the authentication or authorization policies, altering the identification information or providing illegal identity. This threat may cause establishment of illegal logical relations (associations) between network entities and resources.

3. *Non-authorized access (Source: users or programs, Objects: various network resources):* the intruder (who may be a legal user) succeeds in total violation of the access control service, for example, by modifying the content of the control file. This threat may be caused by an illegal user or by some legal network user, performing actions outside of his security profile (legal operational capabilities).

4. *Denial of service (Source: users or programs):* occurs when a legal network user is prevented from performing his functions, or prevents other users from performing their functions. Denial of service may take the form of denial of access, denial of message transfer (communication), deliberate suppression of messages sent to a particular recipient, or a generation of extra traffic.

5. *Repudiation (Source: users or programs):* this threat occurs when some network user falsely denies submitting or receiving a message, or, in general, denies participation in an action or association. Repudiation threats take the form of denial of origin, denial of delivery, denial of submission, and denial of a specific action.

6. *Leakage of information (Release of contents) (Source: users or programs, Objects: messages in a communication system or data in databases):* this problem may take the following forms: *(a)* loss of confidentiality occurs when an entity gains unauthorized access to information transferred by some message or stored in some segment of a data base, *(b)* loss of anonymity (because anonymity is sometimes a security requirement in an ODP environment), *(c)* misappropriation of messages or data records happens when some network user, other than the intended recipient, receives a message or accesses a database by some unauthorized means, such as masquerade, misuse of legal user credentials, or causing some network component to function incorrectly.

7. *Traffic analysis (Source: users or programs, Objects: messages in a communication system):* in this case the intruder may observe protocol control information or the lengths, frequency, sources and destinations of transmitting messages. This may cause a violation of a communication process, even if data are not intelligible to the intruder.

8. *Invalid message sequencing (Message stream modification) (Source: users or programs, Objects: messages in a communication system):* this threat may be achieved by illegal modification, deletion, re-ordering or replay (playback) of the valid sequence of communication messages.

9. *Data modification or destruction (Source: users or programs, Objects: messages in a communication system or data in databases):* involves intentional (illegal) or unintentional modification or deletion of communication messages, data or programs in databases. This may occur as

selective changing or deletion of sensitive fields in the message (e.g. its labels, attributes, recipient address, originator identity, etc.) or as a random modification of some portions of valid messages, data or programs.

10. *Deduction of information (Source: users or programs, Objects: data (information) stored in data bases):* this threat is based on the distribution of publicly available summaries (statistical data) derived from individual data items in a database. Since summaries inherently contain vestiges of the original information, an illegal user may reconstruct individual values of the original information by processing enough summaries. This deduction may be performed in two ways: *statistically,* using methods of information theory (*deduction by inference*) or *analytically,* using exact mathematical methods and formulas (so called *trackers*).

11. *Illegal modification of programs (Source: users or programs, Objects: programs stored in libraries):* this threat is known in three different forms, as viruses, Trojan horses, and worms. It may destroy modules of the host operating systems, communications software, or user application software.

Security Policy

The next stage in designing and implementing a comprehensive security system for an ODP environment is to define the *security policy*. It is basically the decision:

- which *threats* should be eliminated and to what extent;

- which network *resources* to protect and to what degree;

- by what *means* security should be implemented;

- what should be the overall *price* for network security in terms of implementation expenses, operational expenses, and potential damages.

When the security policy is defined, the next step is *the selection of the security services*. Security services are the individual functions which enhance the security of the open system. Each of the security services may be implemented by various *security mechanisms,* and in order to use them efficiently, additional activities are needed to support their operations, called *security management* functions.

Security management [ISO88] in the network is the control and distribution of information to various open systems for:

- use in providing security services and mechanisms;

- reporting on security services and mechanisms;

- reporting on security relevant events that have occurred.

From this short introductory discussion on security policy, it follows that an integrated network security system may be specified in the form of *a list of security services.* The broader this list, the better the possible protection in the network. Such a list may be a conceptual framework for more formal definitions of a secure computer network.

The framework for this book is the OSI Security Architecture. This international standard in its current form is just a recommendation for development, implementation and usage of security services and mechanisms. In order to become the security architecture, this concept must be further analysed, designed and specified, and possibly extended with some additional aspects, security services, protocols and applications. This is the content of the second, third, and fourth chapters of this book. They are the results of original research, while the third and fourth chapters include also some recent results from ISO [ISO91].

2

OSI
SECURITY ARCHITECTURE

2.1 GENERAL DESCRIPTION OF SECURITY SERVICES AND MECHANISMS

2.1.1 Overview

This section describes the security services and security mechanisms specified in the *ISO/OSI Security Architecture* international standard [ISO88]. The security services described below will in practice be invoked at different OSI layers and in appropriate combinations to satisfy the security policy and/or user requirements. Practical realizations of security systems may use combinations (sequences) of security mechanisms and services.

2.1.2 Security Services

Security services recommended within the framework of the *ISO/OSI Basic Reference Model* are treated as generic groups of services, since each service may be applied in different variations, to different entities, situations and resources.

Most of the services require some control information stored locally, some data (parameters) to be transmitted to or received from a remote location, and some control information stored remotely for completion of the service. The organisation of those control data structures and rules for their manipulations will be described in detail in Chapter 7.

Since communications within the ISO/OSI reference model are performed between adjacent layers on the stack and also between corresponding layers on two sides of the association, *ISO/OSI* security services may be applied between two neighbouring layers on the same stack and between corresponding layers on communicating stacks.

2.1.2.1 Entity Authentication Security Services

This group of services provides the authentication of a peer entity (*peer-entity authentication*), authentication of the source of messages (*data origin authentication*) and mutual partners authentication (*peer-to-peer authentication*), as described below.

Peer Entity Authentication

This service, when provided to some layer of the OSI model, provides assurance to the layer entity that the peer entity on the higher layer is the claimed entity.

This service is provided for use at the establishment of, or at times during, the data transfer phase of a connection to verify the identities of one or more other entities. This service provides confidence, at the time of usage only, that an entity is not attempting a masquerade or an unauthorized replay of a previous connection. Mechanisms based on one-way and mutual peer-entity authentication schemes, with or without a liveness check, are possible for the implementation of this service and can provide varying degrees of security.

Data Origin Authentication

This service, when provided at some layer, provides the assurance to an entity on that layer that the source of the received messages is the claimed peer entity on the same layer of the stack at the other side of the connection. This service provides confirmation of the identity of the source of a transmitted message. Simple implementation of this service may not provide protection against duplication or modification of control data units.

Peer-to-Peer Authentication

This service is equivalent to the peer entity authentication. When provided by some layer, it gives a possibility for both parties to authenticate each other, i.e. it provides assurance to both layer entities that the partner entity is the claimed entity.

This service may also be provided at the establishment of, or during, the data transfer phase of a connection. It confirms the identities of two or more other entities. This service provides confidence, at the time of usage only, that both of the entities involved in an association are not attempting a masquerade or an unauthorized replay of a previous connection. The same mechanisms as for the peer entity authentication are applicable to this service.

2.1.2.2 Access Control Security Service

This service provides protection against unauthorized use of resources accessible on OSI systems. These may be *OSI* or non-*OSI* resources accessed via *OSI* or non-*OSI* protocols. This security service may be applied to various individual types of access to a resource (e.g. the use of a communications resource; the reading, the writing, or the deletion of an information resource; the execution of a processing resource, etc.).

Mechanisms available for this security service may be simple *access control lists* based on access control attributes, *multi-level* access control procedures based on security labels, user categories and resource classifications, or may be *extended access control mechanisms*, taking into account various relevant processing parameters and conditions, like processing history, conditional access schemes, etc.

2.1.2.3 Data Confidentiality Security Services

This group of services provides protection of data from unauthorized disclosure or protection of traffic in a communication subsystem, as described below.

Message Confidentiality

This service may be applied to messages in a communication system or to data instances in network data bases. For messages in transfer, protection may be applied to connection oriented transmission, when the connection is established first, or to connectionless transmission, when messages are transmitted before connection has been previously established.

Connection confidentiality. This service provides confidentiality of all messages in a connection-based association.

Note: Depending on use and layer, it may not be appropriate to protect all data, e.g. expedited data or data in a connection request.

Connectionless confidentiality. This service provides confidentiality of all messages in a single connectionless association.

Selective Field Confidentiality

This service provides confidentiality of selected fields within each message in a connection-based or in a connectionless association.

Traffic Flow Confidentiality

This service provides protection of the information which might be illegally derived from observation of traffic flows. This information may be source and destination addresses, time of transfer, frequency of transmission, special routing policies, etc.

2.1.2.4 Data Integrity Security Services

These services counter active threats against illegal modification of messages, files or traffic and may take one of the following forms: *message integrity with or without recovery, selective fields integrity, file (records) integrity, and traffic (session) integrity.*

Note: The use of peer entity authentication during the establishment of a connection and the use of data integrity service during the life of the connection can jointly provide for the corroboration of the source of all messages transferred on the connection and the integrity of those messages. They may additionally provide for the detection of duplication of messages (traffic integrity) by the use of sequence numbers or time stamps.

Connection Integrity With or Without Recovery

This service provides integrity of all messages on an association and detects any modification, insertion, deletion or replay of any data within an entire message. This service may be implemented with recovery or without it.

Selective Field Connection Integrity

This service provides integrity of selected fields within the message of an entire sequence of messages transferred over a connection. It may be based on determining whether the selected fields have been modified, inserted, deleted or replayed.

Connectionless Integrity

This service provides for the integrity of a single connectionless message and may be based on a determination of whether a received message has been modified. Additionally, a limited form of detection of illegal replay may be provided.

Selective Field Connectionless Integrity

This service provides the integrity of selected fields within a single connectionless association and determines whether the selected fields in the message have been illegally modified.

2.1.2.5 Non-repudiation Security Service

This service may basically take the following three forms in any combination:

Non-repudiation with proof of origin. With this service the receiver of data is provided with proof of the origin of the message. This will protect against any attempt by the sender to falsely deny sending the message or its contents.

Non-repudiation with proof of delivery. In this case the sender of data is provided with the proof of delivery of data. This will protect against any subsequent attempt by the recipient to falsely deny receiving the data or its contents.

Notary service. In the case where either or both parties are suspicious users, some special arrangement must be used. This may be a third party, acting as an unbiased arbitrator, called a *notary.* When used, it confirms or denies the claims of sending or receiving the data or its original contents. The other solution may be special message transmission protocols to provide both users with the required level of confidence in the transmission.

2.1.3 Specific Security Mechanisms

The following mechanisms may be used in order to provide some of the services described in Section 2.1.2.

2.1.3.1 Cryptography

Cryptography can provide confidentiality of either data or traffic flow information. It can be used alone or in combination with a number of other security mechanisms, as described in the following sections of this chapter.

Cryptographic algorithms must be reversible and there are two general classifications of reversible encryption algorithms:

- *symmetric* (i.e. secret key) cryptographic algorithms, in which knowledge of the encryption key implies knowledge of the decryption key and vice-versa; and

- *asymmetric* (e.g. public key) encryption, in which knowledge of the encryption key does not imply knowledge of the decryption key or vice-versa. The two keys of such a system are sometimes referred to as the *"public key"* and the *"private key"*.

The existence and usage of cryptographic mechanisms imply the use of some *key management scheme*. Some guidelines on key management methodologies are given in Section 2.3.4.1.

2.1.3.2 Digital Signature Mechanisms

These mechanisms consist of two procedures :

a. *signing* a message; and

b. *verifying* a signed message.

The first process uses information (cryptographic key) which is private (i.e. unique and confidential) to the signer. The second process uses procedures and information which are publicly available, but from which the signer's private information cannot be deduced.

The signing process involves either an encryption of the entire data unit or the production of a checkvalue of the message and then signing it, using the signer's private information (private key).

The verification process involves using the public procedures and information to determine whether the signature was produced with the signer's private information.

The essential characteristic of the digital signature mechanism is that the signature can only be produced using the signer's private information. Thus when the signature is verified, it can subsequently be proven to a third party (e.g. a notary) at any time that only the unique holder of the private information could have produced the digital signature.

2.1.3.3 Access Control Mechanisms

These mechanisms may use the *identity* of an entity or information about the entity (such as membership in a known set of groups) or *capabilities* of the entity, in order to determine and enforce the access rights of the entity. If the entity attempts to use an unauthorized resource, or an authorized resource with an improper type of access, then the access control function will reject the attempt. It may additionally report the incident for the purpose of generating an alarm and/or recording it as part of a security audit trail. Any notification to the sender of a denial of access for a connectionless data transmission can be provided only as a result of access controls imposed at the origin.

Access control mechanisms may, for example, be based on the use of one or more of the following (usually a combination of these are used):

a. *Access control information bases,* where the access rights of users are maintained. This information may be maintained by authorization centres or by the entity being accessed. It may be in the form of an access control list or a matrix of a hierarchical or distributed structure. This presupposes that peer entity authentication has been assured.

b. *Authentication information,* such as passwords; the possession and subsequent presentation of which is evidence of the accessing entity's authorization.

c. *Capabilities,* the possession and subsequent presentation of which is evidence of the right to access the entity or resource defined by the capability.

d. *Security labels,* which when associated with a user or resource may be used to grant or deny access, usually according to a security policy.

e. Some other *predetermined conditions,* such as the time of attempted access, the route of attempted access, the duration of access, user's processing history, user's processing capabilities, etc.

Note: All access control parameters which are used to determine access rights must be unforgeable and should be conveyed in a trusted manner.

Access control mechanisms may be applied at either end of a communications association and/or at any intermediate point. Access controls involved at the origin or any intermediate point are used to determine whether the sender is authorized to communicate with the recipient and/or to use the required communications resources.

The requirements of the peer-level access control mechanisms at the destination end of a connectionless data transmission must be known a priori at the origin, and must be recorded in the corresponding segment of the *Security Management Information Base (SMIB)* (for details, see Sections 2.3.1 and 7.3.2).

2.1.3.4 Data Integrity Mechanisms

Two aspects of data integrity are the integrity of a single message or a field and the integrity of a stream of messages or fields (traffic integrity). In general, different mechanisms are used to provide these two types of integrity service, although provision of the second without the first is not practical.

Determining the integrity of a single message involves two processes: one at the sending side and one at the receiving side. The sending side appends to a message a quantity which is a function of the data itself. This quantity may be supplementary information, such as a *block check code* or a *cryptographic checkvalue*. For effectiveness of this mechanism, this control quantity must be cryptographically protected, otherwise anybody could, after modification of a message, modify that control quantity too.

The receiving entity generates a corresponding quantity using the original message and compares it with the received quantity to determine whether the message has been modified in transit. This mechanism alone will not protect against the replay of a single message. In appropriate layers of the *OSI* architecture, detection of manipulation may lead to a recovery action (for example, via retransmission or error correction) at the same or at a higher layer.

For connection-mode data transfer, protecting the integrity of a sequence of messages (i.e. protecting against misordering, losing, replaying and inserting or modifying data) requires some additional form of explicit ordering, such as *sequence numbering, time stamping,* or *cryptographic chaining*.

For connectionless data transmission, *time stamping* may be used to provide a limited form of protection against replay of individual messages, but time synchronisation of the two ends is necessary, which is not such a simple task as it may seem.

2.1.3.5 Authentication Exchange Mechanisms

Some of the techniques which may be applied to the authentication exchange mechanisms in order to implement a peer-to-peer authentication security service are:

- the use of authentication information, such as passwords – supplied by a sending entity and checked by the receiving entity;

- cryptographic techniques;

- the use of characteristics (biometrics) and/or various possessions of the entity (in case of human entities).

The mechanisms may be incorporated into any *OSI* layer to provide peer entity authentication. If the mechanism does not succeed in authenticating the entity, this will result in rejection or termination of the connection and may also cause an entry in the security audit trail and/or a report to a security management centre.

When cryptographic techniques are used to implement this mechanism, they may be combined with "handshaking" protocols to protect against replay (i.e. to ensure the "liveness" of the communication).

The choice of authentication exchange techniques will depend upon the circumstances in which they are to be used. In many circumstances they will need to be used with:

- time stamping and synchronised clocks;

- two- and three-way handshakes (for unilateral and mutual authentication respectively);

- non-repudiation services achieved by digital signature and/or notarization mechanisms.

2.1.3.6 Traffic Padding Mechanisms

Traffic padding mechanisms can be used to provide various levels of protection against traffic analysis. These mechanisms can be effective only if the redundant traffic padding information is protected by a data confidentiality service.

2.1.3.7 Routing Control Mechanisms

Routes in a network can be chosen either dynamically or by prearrangement, so as to use only physically secure sub-networks, relays or links. End-systems may, on detection of possible manipulation attacks, wish to instruct the network service provider to establish a connection via a different route. Messages carrying certain security labels may be forbidden by the security policy to pass through certain sub-networks, relays or links. Also the initiator of a connection (or the sender of a connectionless message) may specify routing requirements which request that specific network components be avoided.

2.1.3.8 Notarization Mechanisms

Information concerning the messages, communicated between two or more entities, such as their integrity, origin, time, and destination, can be protected by the provision of some non-repudiation mechanisms. The potential conflicts about these issues may be resolved by a third party, the *notary*, which must be trusted by both communicating entities. In order to perform its function, the notary must hold the necessary information to provide the required assurance in a testifiable manner.

Each instance of communication may use a digital signature, cryptography, or integrity mechanisms as appropriate to the service being provided by the notary. When such a notarization mechanism is invoked, the messages are communicated between the entities using this protection form and possibly via the notary. The notarisation mechanisms may be used "in real time", during the lifetime of an association or "in a delayed form", after an association has been closed.

2.1.4 Pervasive Security Mechanisms

This section describes a number of mechanisms which are not specific to any particular service. Therefore, in Section 2.2 they are not explicitly described as being in any particular layer. Some of these pervasive security mechanisms can be regarded as aspects of security management (treated also in Chapter 7, Section 7.3.6). The importance of these mechanisms is, in general, directly related to the level of security required. The level of security (security classes) will be precisely and formally defined in Chapter 6.

2.1.4.1 Trusted Functionality

Trusted functionality must be used to extend the scope of, or to establish the effectiveness of, other security mechanisms. Any functionality which directly provides, or provides access to, security mechanisms, should be trustworthy. These functionalities are designed in the form of *security management centres*, which may be implemented as combinations of hardware and software tools, as will be described later in Section 7.2.3. The procedures used to ensure that trust may be placed in such components are outside the scope of the *ISO/OSI* security standard and, in any case, vary with the level of perceived threat and the value of information to be protected.

The procedures to implement trusted functionality are in general costly and complex. The problems can be minimized by choosing an architecture which permits implementation of security functions in modules which can be made separate from, and provided from, non-security-related functions. Such an approach is followed in Chapter 7.

Any protection of associations above the layer at which the protection is applied, and in extreme cases above the OSI layered model, must be provided by other means, e.g. by appropriate trusted functionalities.

2.1.4.2 Security Labels

All network resources extended to the granularity of individual data items, may have *security labels* associated with them to indicate a *sensitivity* or *protection level*, for example. It is often necessary to transfer the appropriate security label with messages in transit. A security label may be implicit, e.g. implied by the use of a specific key to encrypt data, or implied by the context of the data, such as the source or route. Explicit security labels must be clearly identifiable in order that they can be appropriately checked. In addition they must be securely bound to the data with which they are associated.

2.1.4.3 Event Detection

Security-relevant event detection not only includes the detection of apparent violations of security, but may also include detection of "normal" events, such as a successful access (or logon). The specification of what constitutes a security-relevant event is maintained by the Event Handling Management (see Section 2.3.3.1). Detection of various security-relevant events may, for example, cause one or more of the following actions:

    a. local reporting of the event;

    b. remote reporting of the event;

    c. logging the event;

    d. recovery action (see Section 2.3.3.3).

Examples of such security-relevant events are:

- a specific security violation;

- a specific selected event;

- an overflow on a count of a number of occurrences.

Standardization in this field will take into consideration the transmission of relevant information for event reporting and event logging, and the syntactic and semantic definition to be used for the transmission of these operations.

2.1.4.4 Security Audit Trail

Security audit trails provide a valuable security mechanism, as they can permit detection and investigation of breaches of security by security audit. A security audit is an independent review and examination of system records and activities in order to test for adequacy of system controls, to ensure compliance with established policy and operational procedures, to aid in damage assessment, and to recommend any indicated changes in controls, policy and procedures. A security audit requires the *recording* of security-relevant information in a security audit trail, and the *analysis* and *reporting* of information from the security audit trail. The logging or recording is considered to be a security mechanism and is described in this section. The analysis and report generation is considered a security management function (see Section 2.3.3.2).

Collection of security audit trail information may be adapted to various requirements by specifying the kind(s) of security-relevant events to be recorded (e.g. apparent security violations or completion of successful operations).

The known existence of a security audit trail may serve as a deterrent to some potential sources of security attacks.

OSI security audit trail considerations take into account what information will optionally be logged, under what conditions that information will be logged, and the syntactic and semantic definitions to be used for the interchange of the security audit trail information.

2.1.4.5 Security Recovery

Security recovery deals with problems of establishing consistent security states after security failures by taking various recovery actions, organised as the result of certain verification criteria and testing rules. These recovery actions may be of three kinds:

- immediate;

- temporary;

- long term.

For example:

Immediate actions may cause an abort of operations, like immediate disconnection. Temporary actions may produce temporary invalidation of an entity. Long term actions may be the introduction of an entity into a "black list" or the changing of a cryptographic key.

Topics for further standardization within *ISO/OSI* model include specifications of protocols and supporting data sets for recovery actions and for security recovery management (see also Section 2.3.3.3).

2.1.5 Illustration of Relationship of Security Services and Security Mechanisms

Table 2.1 below, illustrates which mechanisms, alone or in combination with others, are appropriate for the provision of each security service. This table presents an overview of these relationships and is not definitive. The services and mechanisms referred to in this table are described in Sections 2.1.2 and 2.1.3. The relationships are more fully described in Section 2.3.

Table 2.1 Relationship between Security Mechanisms and Services

MECHANISM SERVICE	Enci-pher-ment	Digit. Signa-ture	Access Cntrl	Data Integ-rity	Auth. Exch-ange	Traff. Padd-ing	Rout. Cntrl	Nota-riza-tion
Peer Entity Authentication	Y	Y	•	•	Y	•	•	•
Data Origin Authentication	Y	Y	•	•	•	•	•	•
Access Control Service	•	•	Y	•	•	•	•	•
Connection Confidentiality	Y	•	•	•	•	•	Y	•
Connectionless Confidentiality	Y	•	•	•	•	•	Y	•
Selective Field Confidentiality	Y	•	•	•	•	•	•	•
Traffic Flow Confidentiality	Y	•	•	•	•	Y	Y	•
Connection Integrity with Rec.	Y	•	•	Y	•	•	•	•
Connection Integrity without Recovery	Y	•	•	Y	•	•	•	•
Selective Field Connection Integrity	Y	•	•	Y	•	•	•	•
Connectionless Integrity	Y	Y	•	Y	•	•	•	•
Selective Field Connectionless Integrity	Y	Y	•	Y	•	•	•	•
Non-repudiation, Origin	•	Y	•	Y	•	•	•	Y
Non-repudiation, Delivery	•	Y	•	Y	•	•	•	Y

Legend :

• The mechanism is considered not to be appropriate.

Y *Yes:* the mechanism is considered to be appropriate, either on its own or in combination with other mechanisms. **Note:** In some instances, the mechanism provides more than is necessary for the relevant service, but could nevertheless be used.

2.2 THE RELATIONSHIP OF SECURITY SERVICES, MECHANISMS, AND LAYERS

2.2.1 Security Layering Principles

In Chapter 1 the layers of the *OSI* reference model were explained. In principle, the transfer of messages in an *OSI* system is organised as a number of logical processes, all in a hierarchical order, constituting the layers of the *OSI* model. Each of these processes may need some security services. Therefore, the use of the security system in an *OSI* environment may be organised by calls to those services by different *OSI* layers, as appropriate. This is called *layering* of security services in *OSI* systems.

The main problem in allocating security services to layers is to determine some principles (criteria) for allocation. The following principles were used by the *ISO* in order to determine the *allocation* of security services to layers and the consequent *placement* of security mechanisms in the layers:

a. that the number of alternative ways of achieving a service should be *minimized;*

b. that it is acceptable to build secure systems by providing security services in more than one layer;

c. that additional functionality required for security should not unnecessarily duplicate the existing *OSI* functions;

d. that violation of layer independence should be avoided;

e. that the amount of trusted functionality should be minimized;

f. that, wherever an entity is dependent on a security mechanism provided by an entity in a lower layer, any intermediate layers should be constructed in such a way that security violation is impracticable;

g. that, wherever possible, the additional security functions of a layer should be defined in such a way that implementation as a self-contained module(s) is not precluded;

h. that the *ISO/OSI* standard is assumed to apply to open systems consisting of end systems containing all seven layers and to relay systems.

Definitions and implementations of standard *OSI* communication services at each layer must be slightly modified to provide an interface for security requests. Some suggestions for this interface at the Application layer are given in Section 8.2.1.

2.2.2 Model of Invocation, Management, and Use of Security Services

This section is closely related to Section 2.3 and Chapter 7 which contain a discussion on security management issues. It is intended that security services and mechanisms can be activated by the appropriate entity through the programming interface and/or service invocation modules. Those are, in fact, special security protocols, and they are also described in Chapter 7.

2.2.2.1 Determination of Security Services for an Instance of Communication

This part describes the invocation of security services for connection-oriented and connectionless instances of communication. The security services may be requested or granted at connection establishment time and also later during the lifetime of the association. This applies both to connection and connectionless associations.

In order to simplify the following description, the term "service request" will be used to mean either a connection establishment or a connectionless request. The invocation of security for selected data can be achieved by requesting selective field protection. For example, this can be done by establishing several connections, each with a different type or level of security.

ISO/OSI security architecture accommodates a variety of *security policies*, including those which are *rule-based*, those which are *identity-based* and those which are a *mixture* of both. (For discussion of security policies see Chapter 6, Section 6.2). The security architecture also accommodates protection which is administratively imposed (therefore established at user registration time), dynamically selected (at the moment of logging on or establishing associations) and a mixture of both.

Security Service Requests

For each communication service request, the entity may also request some security services. The request must identify the desired security services together with all necessary parameters and any additional relevant information (such as sensitivity information and/or security labels).

Prior to each instance of communication, the initiating module has to access the *Security Management Information Base (SMIB)* (see also Chapter 7, Section 7.3.2). The *SMIB* contains information on the administratively-imposed security requirements associated with the receiving entity. It must reside at some trusted system, which is a convenient way to enforce various security requirements. (In this book the trusted functionality will be called a *Security Management Centre.*)

Provision of the security services during a communication session may require *negotiation* of the security services that are required or negotiations of their specific versions. The protocol required for negotiating mechanisms and parameters can be carried out either as a separate procedure or as an integral part of the regular connection establishment procedure.

When the negotiation is carried out as a separate procedure, the results of the agreement (i.e. on the type of security services and mechanisms and the security parameters that are necessary to provide such security services) may be permanently entered in the *SMIB* for subsequent use. When the negotiation is carried out as an integral part of the normal connection establishment procedure, the results of the negotiation may be temporarily stored in the *SMIB* to last for the lifetime of an association only. Prior to the negotiation stage, each communicating entity may access the *SMIB* to get information required for the negotiation.

Some lower *OSI* layer may reject the service request coming from the upper layer, if it violates administratively-imposed requirements for the upper layer entity registered in the *SMIB*. The lower layer may also add to the requested security services any security services which are defined in the *SMIB* as mandatory to obtain the target security scheme.

If the upper layer entity does not specify a desired security scheme, the lower layer will follow a security policy in accordance with specifications in the *SMIB*. This could be to proceed with communication using a default security specification within the range defined for the upper layer entity in the *SMIB*.

2.2.2.2 Provision of Security Services

After the combination of administratively-imposed and dynamically selected security requirements has been determined, as described in 2.2.2.1, the service providing layer will attempt to achieve, as a minimum, the target security scheme. This may be achieved by either, or both, of the following methods:

a. invoking security mechanisms directly within that layer; and/or

b. requesting security services from the lower layer. In this case, the scope of protection must be extended to the corresponding communications service by a combination of trusted functionality and/or specific security mechanisms in the particular layer.

Note: This does not necessarily imply that all the modules in that layer have to be trusted.

Thus, the particular layer determines if it is able to achieve the requested security scheme. If it is not able to achieve this, no instance of a (secure) communication occurs.

Establishment of a Secure Connection Between Two Layers

The following discussion addresses the provision of security services within the particular layer (as opposed to relying on security services at the lower layer). In certain protocols, to achieve satisfactory security, the sequence of operations is crucial.

1. Outgoing access control. The layer may impose outgoing access controls, i.e. it may determine locally (from the *SMIB*) whether the secure connection establishment may be attempted or is forbidden.

2. Peer-entity authentication. If the required security scheme includes peer-entity authentication, or if it is known (from the *SMIB*) that the destination entity will require peer-entity authentication, then an authentication exchange must take place. This may employ two- or three-way handshakes between corresponding layers to provide unilateral or mutual authentication, as required.

Sometimes, the authentication exchange may be integrated into the usual connection establishment procedures. Under other circumstances, the authentication exchange may be accomplished separately from the normal connection establishment procedures.

3. Access control service. The destination entity or intermediate entities may impose access control restrictions to incoming requests. If specific information is required by a remote access control service, then the initiating entity supplies this information within the outgoing message or via communication management channels.

4. Data confidentiality. If a total or selective data confidentiality service has been selected, a secure connection must be established. This must include the establishment of the proper working key(s) and negotiation of cryptographic parameters for the connection. This may have been done by prearrangement, in the authentication exchange stage or by a separate protocol.

5. Data integrity. If integrity of all messages, with or without recovery, or integrity of selective fields has been selected, a secure connection must be established. This may be the same connection as that established to provide the data confidentiality service and may also provide entity authentication. The same considerations apply as for the data confidentiality service for a secure connection.

6. Non-repudiation services. If non-repudiation with proof of origin has been selected, the proper cryptographic parameters must be established, or a protected connection with a notarization entity must be established. If non-repudiation with proof of delivery has been selected, the proper parameters (which are different from those required for non-repudiation with proof of origin) must be established, or a protected connection with a notarization entity must be set up.

Note: Establishment of the secure connection may fail owing to the lack of agreement on cryptographic parameters (possibly including nonpossession of the proper keys) or through rejection by an access control mechanism.

2.2.2.3 Operation (Usage) of a Secure Connection

During the data transfer phase over a secure connection the following effects (actions) will be visible at the "boundary" of the communication service:

a. peer-entity authentication (at various time intervals);

b. protection of selective fields;

c. reporting of active attacks (for example, when manipulation of data has occurred and the service being provided is "connection integrity without recovery").

In addition, the following may be needed:

a. security audit trail recording;

b. event detection and handling.

Those services which are amenable to selective applications are:

a. data confidentiality;

b. data integrity (possibly with authentication);

c. non-repudiation (by receiver or by sender).

Notes:

1. Two techniques are suggested for marking by the user those data items selected for the use of a security service. The first involves using *strong typing.* It is anticipated that the presentation layer will recognise certain types of messages as those which require certain security services to be applied. The second involves some form of *flagging* of the individual data items within a message to which specified security services should be applied.

2. One scenario for providing the selective application of non-repudiation service may be the following: Some form of negotiating dialogue occurs over an association prior to both entities agreeing that a final version of a data item or a particular message is mutually acceptable. At that point, the intended recipient may ask the sender to apply a non-repudiation service (of both origin and delivery) to the final agreed version of the data item. The sender asks for and obtains this service, transmits the data item, and subsequently receives notice that the data item has been received and acknowledged by the recipient. The non-repudiation service assures both the originator and recipient of the data item that it has been successfully transmitted.

3. Both the non-repudiation services (i.e. of origin and of delivery) are invoked by the originator.

2.2.2.4 Provision of Protected Connectionless Data Transmission

Not all the security services available in connection-oriented protocols are available in connectionless protocols. Specifically, protection against deletion, insertion and replay attacks, if required, must be provided at connection-oriented higher layers. Limited protection against replay attacks can be provided by a time-stamp mechanism. In addition, a number of other security services are unable to provide the same degree of security enforcement that can be achieved by connection-oriented protocols.

The security services which may be appropriate to connectionless data transmission are the following:

1. peer-entity authentication (Section 2.1.2.1);

2. data origin authentication (Section 2.1.2.1);

3. access control (Section 2.1.2.2);

4. connectionless confidentiality (Section 2.1.2.3);

5. selective field confidentiality (Section 2.1.2.3);

6. connectionless integrity (Section 2.1.2.4);

7. selective field connectionless integrity (Section 2.1.2.4);

8. non-repudiation, origin (Section 2.1.2.5).

These services may be provided by cryptography, signature mechanisms, access control mechanisms, routing mechanisms, data integrity mechanisms and/or notarization mechanisms (see also Section 2.1.3).

The originator of a connectionless data transmission will have to ensure that each of his messages contains all the information (parameters) required to make it acceptable at the destination.

2.3 SECURITY MANAGEMENT

2.3.1 General

OSI security management is concerned with security aspects which are outside normal instances of communications, but which are needed to *support* and *control* the security of those communications.

There can be many security policies imposed by the administration(s) of distributed open systems and *OSI* security management standards should support most or all such policies. Entities that are subject to a single security policy, administered by a single authority, are sometimes collected into what has been called a *"security domain"*. Security domains and their interactions are an important area for future extensions of the *ISO/OSI Security Architecture* and many relevant aspects are already described in this book.

OSI security management is concerned with the management of *OSI* security services and mechanisms. Such management requires the distribution of management information to these services and mechanisms, as well as the collection of information concerning the operation of these services and mechanisms. Examples are the distribution of cryptographic keys, the setting of administratively-imposed security selection parameters, the reporting of both normal and abnormal security events (audit trails), and service activation and deactivation. Security management does not address the passing of security-relevant information in protocols which call up specific security services (e.g. parameters in connection requests).

Most of the information needed for security management will be stored in the *Security Management Information Base (SMIB)*. The *SMIB* is the conceptual repository for all security-relevant information needed by open systems. This concept does not suggest any contents or form for the storage of the information, its implementation or usage. However, each end-system must contain the necessary local information to enable it to enforce an appropriate security policy. The *SMIB* may be implemented as a *distributed* information base to the extent that it is necessary to enforce a consistent security policy in a (logical or physical) grouping of end-systems (security domain). In practice, parts of the *SMIB* may or may not be integrated with the *Management Information Base (MIB)* of the open system.

Note: There can be many realizations of the *SMIB*, e.g.:

- a table of data;

- a single file or a (distributed) set of data base segments;

- data or rules embedded within the software or hardware of the real system.

Rules for inserting, maintaining, deleting and using information in the *SMIB* constitute security management protocols. Management protocols, especially security management protocols, and the communication channels carrying the management information, are potentially vulnerable. Particular care must therefore be taken to ensure that the management protocols and information are protected, so that the security provided for usual instances of communications is not weakened.

Security management may require the exchange of security-relevant information between various system administrations, in order that the *SMIB* can be established or extended. In some cases, the security-relevant information will be passed through non-*OSI* communication paths, and the local systems administrators will update the *SMIB* through methods not standardized by *OSI*. In other cases, it may be desirable to exchange such information over an *OSI* communication path, in which case the information will be passed between two security management applications running in the real open systems. The security management applications will use the communicated information to update the *SMIB*. Such updating of the *SMIB* requires the prior authorization of the appropriate security administrator or access control of other authorized entities.

Special application protocols (interfaces) must be defined for the exchange of security relevant information over *OSI* communications channels. Some of them will be described in Chapters 7 and 8.

2.3.2 Categories of OSI Security Management

There are three global categories of *OSI* security management activities:

    a. system security management;

    b. security services management;

    c. security mechanisms management.

In addition to providing security to normal instances of communications, security of *OSI* management functions and control data must also be considered (see Section 2.3.2.4).

The key functions performed by the three categories of security management are summarized below.

2.3.2.1 Security System Management

Security system management is concerned with the management of security aspects of the overall *OSI* environment. The following list is typical of the activities which fall into this category of security management:

    a. overall security policy management, including updates and maintenance of consistency;

    b. interaction with other *OSI* management functions;

    c. interaction with security services management and security mechanisms management functions;

    d. event handling management;

    e. security audit management;

    f. security recovery management.

2.3.2.2 Security Services Management

Security services management is concerned with the management of individual security services. The following list is typical of the activities which may be performed in managing a particular security service:

    a. determination and assignment of the target security scheme for the service;

    b. assignment and maintenance of rules for the selection (where alternatives exist) of the specific security mechanism to be employed to provide the requested security service;

    c. negotiation (locally and remotely) of available security mechanisms which require prior management agreement;

    d. invocation of specific security mechanisms via the appropriate security mechanism management function, e.g. for the provision of administratively-imposed security services;

    e. interaction with other security service management functions and security mechanisms management functions.

2.3.2.3 Security Mechanism Management

Security mechanism management is concerned with the management of particular security mechanisms. The following list of security mechanism management functions is typical, but not exhaustive:

    a. key management;

    b. encryption/decryption management;

    c. digital signature management;

    d. access control management;

    e. data integrity management;

    f. authentication management;

    g. traffic padding management;

h. routing control management;

i. notarization management.

Each of the listed security mechanism management functions is discussed in more detail in section 2.3.4.

2.3.2.4 Security of OSI Management

Security of all *OSI* management functions, control data structures and of the transmission of *OSI* management information are important aspects of *OSI* security. This category of security management will invoke appropriate choices of the listed *OSI* security services and mechanisms in order to ensure that *OSI* management protocols and information are adequately protected. For example, communications between management entities involving the Management Information Base will generally require some form of protection.

2.3.3 Specific Security System Management Activities

2.3.3.1 Event Handling Management

The management aspects of event handling visible in *OSI* are the *remote reporting* of apparent attempts to violate system security and the *modification of thresholds* used to trigger event reporting.

2.3.3.2 Security Audit Management

Security audit management may include:

a. the selection of events to be logged and/or remotely collected;

b. the enabling and disabling of audit trail logging of selected events;

c. the remote collection of selected audit records; and

d. the preparation of security audit reports.

2.3.3.3 Security Recovery Management

Security recovery management may include:

a. maintenance of the rules used to react to real or suspected security violations;

b. the remote reporting of apparent violations of system security;

c. security administrator interactions.

2.3.4 Security Mechanism Management Functions

2.3.4.1 Key Management

Key management may involve:

a. generating suitable keys at intervals commensurate with the level of security required;

b. determining, in accordance with access control requirements, which entities should receive a copy of each key;

c. making available or distributing the keys in a secure manner to entity instances in real open systems.

Some key management functions may be performed outside of the *OSI* communication environment. These include the physical distribution of keys by trusted means.

Exchange of working keys for use during an association is a normal layer protocol function. Selection of working keys may also be accomplished by access to a key distribution centre or by pre-distribution via management protocols.

2.3.4.2 Cryptography Management

Cryptography management may involve:

a. interaction with key management;

b. establishment of cryptographic parameters;

c. cryptographic synchronization.

The existence of a cryptography mechanism implies the use of key management and of common ways to reference the cryptographic algorithms.

The degree of granularity of protection provided by cryptography, i.e. which entities within the *OSI* environment are independently keyed, is determined by the security architecture and specifically by the key management scheme.

A common reference to specific cryptographic algorithms can be obtained by using a register of cryptographic algorithms, by prior agreements between entities, or by a negotiation process in the connection establishment stage.

2.3.4.3 Digital Signature Management

Digital signature management may involve:

    a. interaction with key management;

    b. establishment of cryptographic parameters and algorithms;

    c. use of a protocol between communicating entities and possibly a third party.

Note: Generally, there exist many similarities between digital signature management and cryptographic management.

2.3.4.4 Access Control Management

Access control management may involve distribution of security attributes (including passwords) or updates to access control lists or capabilities lists. It may also involve the use of a protocol between communicating entities and other entities providing access control services.

2.3.4.5 Data Integrity Management

Data integrity management may involve:

    a. interactions with key management;

    b. establishment of cryptographic parameters and algorithms;

    c. use of a protocol between communicating entities.

Note: When using cryptographic techniques for data integrity, there are many similarities between data integrity management and cryptographic management.

2.3.4.6 Authentication Management

Authentication management may involve distribution of descriptive information, passwords or keys (using key management), to entities required to perform authentication. It may also involve use of a protocol between communicating entities and other entities providing authentication services.

2.3.4.7 Traffic Padding Management

Traffic padding management may include maintenance of the rules to be used for traffic padding. For example these rules may be:

    a. pre-specified data rates;

    b. specifying random data rates;

    c. specifying message characteristics such as length; and

    d. variation of the specifications, possibly in accordance with the date and time.

2.3.4.8 Routing Control Management

Routing control management may involve definition of the links or sub-networks which are considered to be either secured or trusted with respect to particular criteria.

2.3.4.9 Notarization Management

Notarization management may include:

    a. the distribution of information about notaries;

    b. the use of a protocol between a notary and the communicating entities;

    c. interaction with notaries.

2.4 CONCLUSIONS

As stated in the Preface, the *ISO/OSI Security Architecture* [ISO88] international standard has been taken in this book as the basis for security in open systems. This document has been briefly reviewed and quoted in this chapter. It is obvious that, in the form of a framework, it defines security services, security mechanisms, security management functions, and some other relevant aspects of security in open systems, but only as a conceptual, broad and general set of recommendations.

This book covers many aspects of security in open distributed systems and computer networks as *extensions* of the *ISO/OSI* security framework. Therefore, the basic principles of computer networks, networks security, and *ISO/OSI* security architecture have been reviewed in the first two chapters to provide the necessary background for the topics that follow.

3

OVERVIEW
OF SECURITY FEATURES
IN STANDARDIZED
OSI PROTOCOLS
AND APPLICATIONS

3.1 INTRODUCTION

This chapter has three main goals: *(a)* to describe security features in existing *OSI* applications and protocols, *(b)* to analyse security concepts in existing *OSI* applications and protocols against the security architecture from the previous chapter, and *(c)* to indicate possible approaches to practical implementation, design, integration, or extensions of security functions in the *OSI* or *ODP* environments.

The chapter is structured in two sections: the first one is introductory, while the second, the main section of this chapter, contains detailed descriptions of security services in existing standard *OSI* applications and protocols, together with a short overview of some current standardization activities and results. This section is based on many available *ISO* documents, official standards, research papers, and specifications.

A number of applications have been developed based on the specifications of the *OSI* basic reference model, but security was not the primary goal of their design. The following standardized *OSI* applications and protocols, with certain security services and mechanisms, will be discussed in this chapter: *X.25*, *Triple-X*, *X.32*, *X.400*, *X.500*, and *FTAM*.

The analysis of security features, and more important security requirements, of each of the standardized *OSI* applications assumes all potential problems and attacks in the open environment. A standard list of threats (Table 1.1) is assumed for each *OSI* application. These threats will be analysed in the context of the basic security services suggested by *ISO* [ISO88], (described in detail in Chapter 2). In addition, possibilities for *extending* existing *OSI* applications with some new security services or *integrating* those applications in some secure architecture will be briefly discussed in the next chapter.

In terms of their functionalities, three *OSI* protocols (*X.25*, *X.32*, and *Triple-X*) are concerned mainly with data transmission. Security for them means primarily the application of *communication security services*. At the seventh layer the very useful and popular *X.400* (Electronic Mail System), *X.500* (Directory Services), and *FTAM* (File Transfer, Access and Management) *OSI* applications have some security specifications and features. They will all be briefly described in this chapter.

3.2 OVERVIEW OF SECURITY FEATURES
IN STANDARDIZED OSI PROTOCOLS AND APPLICATIONS

Security in existing *OSI* protocols and applications is treated in this section with respect to three relevant aspects:

- description of the *standard security services*, as specified in the *ISO/OSI 7498/2 Security Architecture* for each *OSI* protocol and application;

- analysis of the efficiency and applicability of security services and mechanisms in the existing standardized applications;

- some segments of the *security architecture*, which exist in the *OSI* protocols and applications and are used in the design of the complete security architecture found in later chapters.

3.2.1 Security of the X.25 System and the Transport Layer

The *X.25* system provides the following *standard OSI security services: entity authentication, data integrity,* and *access control. Access control* may be implemented with certain optional *X.25* facilities. *Data confidentiality* and *non-repudiation* are not included in *X.25* specifications.

Considering the threats previously defined in Section 1.1 for users, host computers and communication lines (Table 1.1), the following standard *OSI* security services may be required for *X.25* network users:

1. Entity authentication. This security service is essential, since network components which are accessible through the *X.25* lines must be certain about the positive identification of their users.

The *X.25* protocol provides facilities for entity authentication in the association establishment stage. Various techniques can be used to obtain an authenticator of the caller's *PAD* network address and include it in the call establishment packets (call request and incoming calls). The *X.25* networks provide *the identity of the caller* to the called user by means of an *address identifier* included in the packet. Based on this address the called user must accept or deny the incoming call.

2. Data integrity. Messages transmitted over communication lines must be protected against illegal or accidental modifications during the transmission. This is usually achieved by some kind of a *checksum.* The *X.224* standard recommends a 16-bit *checksum algorithm* for implementation of the data integrity security service. This feature in fact is not a part of the *X.25* recommendation; it belongs to the *OSI Transport layer.* Since that layer is on top of the *X.25* protocol, the checksum mechanism provides reliable message transfer over the *X.25* network.

The following symbols are used in the specification of the checksum message integrity algorithm:

- C_0, C_1 : variables used in the algorithm;

- i: the number (i.e. position) of an octet within the message;

- n: the number (i.e. position) of the first octet of the checksum parameter;

- L: the length of the complete message;

- X: the value of the first octet of the calculated checksum;

- Y: the value of the second octet of the calculated checksum.

Addition in the algorithm may be performed in one of the two following modes:

a. modulo *255* arithmetic;

b. *one's complement* arithmetic in which if any of the variables has the value minus zero (i.e. *255*) it shall be regarded as though it was plus zero (i.e. *0*).

The algorithm for data integrity consists of two parts: the algorithm for *generating* the checksum and the algorithm for *verifying* the checksum.

The algorithm for generating the checksum:

Step 1. Set up the complete message with the value of the checksum field set to *zero.*

Step 2. Initialize variables C_0 and C_1 to *zero.*

Step 3. Process each octet in the message sequentially from $i=1$ to L by

    a. adding the value of the octet to C_0; then

    b. adding the value of C_0 to C_1.

Step 4. Calculate the values X and Y such that

$$X = -C_1 + (L - n) * C_0,$$

$$Y = C_1 - (L - n + 1) * C_0.$$

Place the values X and Y in octets n and $(n+1)$ respectively.

Note: This algorithm calculates:

$$C_1 = \sum_{i=1}^{L} (L - i + 1)\, a_i$$

which should be equal to zero, since:

$$\sum_{i=1}^{L} (L - i + 1)\, a_i = (L + 1) \sum_{i=1}^{L} a_i - \sum_{i=1}^{L} i\, a_i = 0$$

The algorithm for verifying the checksum:

Step 1. Initialize variables C_0 and C_1 to *zero.*

Step 2. Process each octet of the message sequentially from $i=1$ to L by

    a. adding the value of the octet to C_0; then

    b. adding the value of C_0 to C_1.

Step 3. If, when all the octets have been processed, either or both of C_0 and C_1 does not have the value *zero*, the checksum formulas have been satisfied, and the message contents may be accepted as valid.

Note: The nature of the algorithm is such that it is not necessary to compare explicitly the stored checksum bytes.

3. The *access control* security service in *X.25* may be implemented by a number of *X.25* optional facilities which can enhance communication security. These are the following *X.25* features:

- *Incoming calls barred*, in order to prevent all remotely originated calls from being passed to the local user.

- *One-way logical channels*, outgoing/incoming, which may be used to restrict the assignment of logical channel numbers to outgoing or incoming calls only.

- *Closed user groups*, may be used to provide a level of control associated with specific user groups.

- *Bi-lateral closed user groups*, which is a variation of the closed user group that can be implemented to restrict calls between two parties.

- Network *user identification*, usually implemented for billing purposes.

- *Local charging prevention*, also concerned with billing, prevents reverse charging of incoming calls.

As *additional security services*, the *X.25* protocol provides various mechanisms to guarantee the *integrity of the overall communication process*. Users must be protected against packet alteration, suppression and also against the insertion of packets copied from previous associations. There are mechanisms to verify that all the packets in a particular association will be received in the same *order* as they were sent and *without duplicates*. Also for *time authentication* a procedure can be used to associate the actual time with the time when the call was established. Cryptographic mechanisms, as additional means, may be used to implement *origin authentication* or *data confidentiality*.

X.25 does not rely on any *security architecture*. All standard security services are available through parameters exchanged *directly* between communicating entities, by including them in the association messages. However, some researchers propose certain extensions of the *X.25* specifications to include additional security services or some alternative implementations of available services. In those cases some elements of the security architecture are also needed.

3.2.2 Security of the Triple–X (X.3, X.28, X.29) System

Triple-X (X.3, X.28, X.29) is the protocol for connecting an asynchronous terminal to the *X.25 PAD* via dial-up access.

Prior to establishing an *X.28* connection between an asynchronous terminal and a *PAD,* the user at the terminal has *to identify himself* to the *PAD* using his *Network User Identification (NUI) number.* This number is composed of the *account number* and the *password.* The *NUI* is assigned to the user when subscribing to the service and the *PTT* authority providing the network service. Identification of the user is required for dial-up access and ensures collection of charges for use of the *PSDN* services. The *NUI* is not based on any cryptographic transformation and is sent as cleartext (therefore it is vulnerable to line tapping). Thus, the use of a *NUI* does not protect against masquerade, if a dishonest person has obtained the *NUI* of an authorized *PAD* user.

It is common today for business people and other mobile users to gain access to *PSDN* services in different countries using *portable mobile terminals.* This means that the user has to be registered with each of the network administrations, and must also be assigned different *NUIs* by each of the network administrations in the different countries. This may pose problems if network administrations are not allowed to send bills to addresses outside their own country.

The use of the *X.32* protocol, which supports services for the identification and authentication of the user, can provide the solution to *PSDN* access from different countries. The *X.32* user is only required to register with his home administration and information about the user profile is provided by the home administration to any other network administration, on request. Thus, in this case, the cooperating environment of interconnected open systems, whereby different network administrations cooperate in the provision of a comprehensive *X.32* service, has to be established first.

3.2.3 Security of the X.32 System

The *X.32* protocol specifies the functional and procedural aspects of the *DTE/DCE* interface for packet-mode terminals accessing a *PSDN* through a Public Switched Network (PSN).

Before a user at an X.32 workstation (DTE) can gain access to services provided by a packet switched data network, it has to establish a dial-in connection and then initiate procedures for the *identification/authentication* of the workstation to the network. Thus, there is a requirement for an *X.32 DTE* to identify/authenticate itself to the *PSDN* during a dial-in operation in order to obtain a particular service type. On the other hand there may also be a requirement for the *PSDN* to identify/authenticate itself to the *DTE* during a dial-out operation, so that the *DTE* can select certain parameters pertaining to that particular network.

The two parties involved in the identification protocol are referred to in the *X.32* recommendation as the *identifying party* and the *challenged party*. For example, in a dial-in operation the challenged party is the *DTE* and the identifying party is the *DCE*.

The type of service provided by the *PSDN* to an *X.32 DTE* during a dial-in operation depends on the *level of identification* achieved by the *DTE*. The higher the level of identification, the greater the range of *PSDN* facilities made available to the *DTE*. Three types of service are identified in the *X.32* recommendation. They are, in ascending order of level of identification:

1. *Non-identified service:* No identification is required for this type of service and the *DTE* will only be allowed use of free services provided by the network.

2. *Identified service:* To avail of this service type requires a simple identification procedure, e.g. conveying an *identity element* and a *password*. The *DTE* may then have access to paid network services.

3. *Customized service:* Provision of this service requires an *authentication procedure*. In this case the *DTE* is offered a range of network services, not available in the previous service types.

All three service types are characterized (implemented) by the appropriate set of attributes. These attributes are:

• *DTE Identity:* This attribute defines the identity element of the *DTE*. The exact format of such an identity element has not been clearly specified in the *X.32* recommendation at the time of writing this text.

• *DTE Identification Method:* This attribute defines the *DTE's* identification method for establishing the *DTE's* identity/authenticity. *DTE* identification can be carried out using Link layer or Network layer protocol procedures. These procedures are governed by an identification protocol which is described later.

• *DTE Address:* This attribute defines the address for use in the calling *DTE* address field of the network layer packets. The exact format for the address was not clearly defined in the *X.32* recommendation at the time of writing this text as it is still under study. The *DTE* address can be an *X.121* number from the *PSDN* or *PSN* numbering plan. An *X.121 PSDN* number consists of the *Data Network Identification Code (DNIC)*, followed by the *Network Terminal Number (NTN)*. On the other hand, an *X.121 PSTN* number consists of the *DNIC* assigned to the *PSTN*, plus the *National Number (NN)* or *0 + Telephone Country Code (TCC) + National Number (NN)*.

• *Registered Address:* This attribute defines the address for use in the called *DTE* address field of *Call Request* packets. Its provision or non-provision by the calling *DTE* causes different actions to be taken by the *DCE*. If provided, the *DCE* checks first whether a switched access connection to the called *DTE* already exists. If so, then the *DCE* uses the existing switched access connection, otherwise the *DCE* performs a dial-out operation to the *DTE*. If not provided, the *DCE* performs a dial-out operation regardless of whether a switched connection already exists or not. This results in a busy signal if a switched access connection already exists and causes the incoming virtual call to be cleared. The exact format for a registered address is not yet defined in the Recommendation.

- *Registered PSN Number:* This attribute defines the *X.121 PSN* number used by the *DCE* for dialling out to the *DTE*.

- *X.25 Subscription Set:* This attribute defines the set of parameters and their values for the *X.25* link and network layer optional user facilities.

- *Logical Channel Assignment:* This attribute defines the number of logical channels of each type (dial-in, dial-out) assigned to a particular *DTE*. The direction of the virtual call placement that is allowed on the logical channel(s) is governed by the direction of the dial operation as shown in Figure 1.4 (c).

- *Availability of PSDN Dial-out:* This attribute specifies whether or not dial-out operation by the *PSDN* is supported.

- *Dial-out Access Type:* This attribute allows the DTE to choose modem characteristics that are to be used for PSTN switched access operation. Different characteristics pertaining to *CSDN* and *ISDN* may also be selected or required.

- *X.32 Optional User Facilities:* This attribute specifies the availability of *X.32* temporary location and secure dial-back facilities (these are described later).

- *DCE Identity Presentation:* This attribute specifies the identification method used by the *PSDN* for identification to the *DTE* during a dial-out operation. This may be required so that the *DTE* can select certain parameters pertaining to that particular network.

- *Link Layer Address Assignment:* This attribute defines the method used for Link layer address assignment. Link layer addresses may be assigned depending on the direction of the switched access connection or depending on the role of the system as a *DTE/DCE*.

The provision or non-provision of attributes by the PSDN depends on the *DTE* service type. When the attributes are provided, they are either set to a default value specified by the network, or are set to values selected by the user from a range of values provided by the network (user selectable).

X.32 provides two levels of security:

Security Level 1. This level provides a simple exchange of messages between the two communicating parties. The challenged party sends its *identity (Id),* and optionally its *signature (SIG)*, to the identifying party. *SIG* can be a password assigned by the identifying party, or the challenged party's *Id* signed using its secret key *KSc* (i.e. $SIG = D_{KSc}$ *(Id)* using the RSA cryptosystem). The identifying party then checks that both *Id* and *SIG* are correct, and the challenged party is validated. Otherwise, the access path is disconnected. In both cases, the identifying party sends back the appropriate *diagnostic message (DIAG)* to the challenged party.

Security Level 1 does not provide any protection against *replay of messages*. For example, an intruder can tap the communication line and record both *Id* and *SIG*. The intruder can later use them to establish a connection, masquerading as the real *DTE*. This has certain advantages for the intruder, since the real *DTE* will get billed for use of network resources by the intruder. Security level 2 solves this problem by the use of a *challenge–response* mechanism based on *digital signatures.*

Security level 2. This level incorporates both security level 1 and an additional authentication exchange based on a challenge–response mechanism. Thus, the challenged party sends its *Id* and *SIG* to the identifying party, and if they are valid, the identifying party generates a *random number (r)* and sends it to the challenged party. To authenticate itself, the challenged party signs number *r* using its secret key, *KSc*, and sends back the result (i.e. $D_{KSc}(r)$) to the identifying party. If enciphering of the $D_{KSc}(r)$, using the challenged party's public key *KPc*, results in the random number *r*, the appropriate diagnostic message *(DIAG)* is sent to the challenged party and the authentication process is successfully completed. Otherwise, an error diagnostic message is returned and the access path is disconnected. A simple protocol for security level 2 is illustrated in Figure 3.1.

The use of a random number in the handshake guarantees the "freshness" of the challenged party's response, and thus prevents any replay from a previous connection by an intruder. The use of digital signatures guarantees the authenticity of the challenged party, provided the challenged party's key has not been compromised.

X.32 Security Procedures

Identification and authentication of the *DTE/PSDN* can be carried out either at the Link layer or at the Network layer of the *OSI* reference model. After establishing the physical *PSTN* connection during a dial-in operation, the user can then initiate a *network* or *link layer* security procedure to obtain a required service. Link layer identification can only take place when the logical link has not yet been set up. On the other hand, Network layer identification takes place when the logical link has been set up but prior to any virtual circuit *(VC)* establishment; i.e. all *VCs* must be in the idle state.

At the *link layer*, the identification and authentication procedures involve exchanges of security related information in *eXchange IDentification (XID)* frames while the link is in its disconnected state.

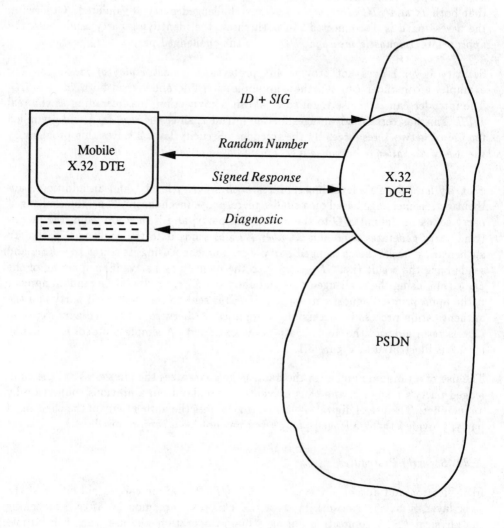

Figure 3.1. X.32 Level-2 Security: Challenge--Response Mechanism

Authentication must be carried out at the link layer if negotiation of link layer parameters is required. At the link layer, *exchange identification (XID)* frames are used for the exchange of security information based on the *X.32* security protocol. *XID* response frames are used for acknowledging receipt of *XID* command frames.

When transmitting an *XID* command frame, the *DTE/DCE* starts a *timer T1*. The timer is stopped on receipt of an *XID* response frame. If *T1* expires before an *XID* response is received, the *DTE/DCE* retransmits the *XID* command frame.

The maximum number of attempts made by the *DTE/DCE* to complete a successful transmission of the *XID* command frame is defined by a link level parameter.

At the *network layer*, the identification and authentication procedures involve exchanges of *Registration Request* (from *DTE*) and *Registration Confirmation* from *DCE* packets. (The *DCE* is the remote or *PSDN DCE* and not the local modem which is also regarded as a *DCE*.) Network layer identification takes place prior to virtual circuit establishment.

At the network layer of the *X.32* protocol, *registration packets* are used for exchanges of security information between the *DTE* and *DCE*. The *DTE* will send identification information in the registration field of the *registration request* packets, while the *DCE* will respond by sending the appropriate response in the *registration confirmation* packets.

The exchanges of link layer *XID* frames and network layer registration packets are governed by the *identification protocol*. Two levels of security are defined in the protocol, as described earlier. Security level *1* involves a simple identification of the *DTE/DCE*, whereas security level *2* incorporates procedures for authentication of the *DTE/DCE*. The security mechanism for authentication is based on digital signatures using the *RSA* public-key cryptosystems.

Because of the *X.32 DTE* mobility and the inherent security features, the provision of an *X.32* service by national *PTTs* will require *additional management overheads* (compared with say an *X.25* service). In addition to the billing functions, the national *PTTs* will have to provide for extra administrative functions and security management functions to support the *X.32* identification and authentication procedures. Moreover, inter-working between different national *PTTs* is required.

3.2.4 Security of the X.400 System

3.2.4.1 Introduction

The main function of the *X.400 Message Handling System* recommendation has been to carry out the interconnection of electronic mail systems. Security facilities were not taken into account in the first version of the *X.400* recommendations, so these systems, in most cases, have been used to perform the exchange of messages (letters) without any serious security requirements.

The new *X.400* set of recommendations (1988) defines a number of security services and procedures capable of directly supporting a wide range of security policies. These services constitute optional extensions to the standard *MHS* and can be used to minimize the risks of attacks and threats. Nevertheless, extensions to the existing *X.400* protocols by themselves, with the inclusion of some security attributes, are not enough to get a true secure Message Handling System. They have been outlined assuming the availability of a broader secure environment.

The security capabilities in the *X.400* system have been achieved by means of different mechanisms, for example: the inclusion of new elements in the exchanged messages by user cooperation during the association establishment stage; or by adding information in the *MHS* envelope. It should be emphasized that security capabilities included in the *MHS* system define only how to transfer and use relevant security parameters. Rules about generation and interpretation of these parameters are not in the *X.400 MHS* recommendations. Its aim is to provide security independent of the communication services supplied by other entities of higher or lower levels.

3.2.4.2 Security Services Available in the X.400 System

Standard *OSI* security services are provided by the *X.400 system* in the following way:

- *Entity Authentication.* The following services facilitate *peer entity authentication* and *data source authentication:*

  1. *Message Origin Authentication,* enables the recipient to authenticate the identity of the originator of a message (i.e. signature).

  2. *Probe Origin Authentication,* provides the recipient with unforgeable proof of the origin of a probe.

  3. *Report Origin Authentication,* allows the originator to authenticate the origin of a delivery/non-delivery report.

  4. *Proof of Submission,* provides the originator with unforgeable proof that he submitted the message for delivery to the originally specified recipient.

  5. *Proof of Delivery,* provides the originator with unforgeable proof that the message was delivered to the recipient.

In a *MHS* with capabilities for storing or forwarding messages, a direct communication between the originator and the recipient of messages does not exist. For this reason, there is no possibility of using some kind of handshake (i.e. a backwards reply) to confirm accuracy of connection before sending the message.

However, there is a useful service provided by a *MHS*, even if it is not trusted by the users. This service is the transmission of a positive proof of delivery to a particular recipient. It can be provided by sending back to the originator some *token* generated only when the recipient has received the message. If used in an appropriate way, this kind of proof could be strong enough to ensure that once issued, the recipient cannot repudiate it.

In an electronic mail system, this proof can be requested from a recipient, but it is not required. It must be generated by the recipient, so that it is possible to provide a proof of non-repudiation of delivery only after the recipient has accepted the contents of a message, and not before.

This is a useful security service, but it is not perfect, because the generation of the proof is a discretionary action for the recipient.

• *Access Control.* This service is concerned with protecting the resources against unauthorized usage, mainly the *MTAs*. Access control is based on mutual authentication between *MTAs and MTA* users. It establishes the credentials of the subjects in interaction.

• *Data Confidentiality.* This service is used in order to protect data against unauthorized disclosure.

Content Confidentiality: Prevents unauthorized disclosure of a message to a party other than the intended recipient.

• *Data Integrity.* This service is provided to counteract active threats against the Message Handling System.

Content Integrity: Enables the recipient to verify that the original content of a message has not been modified.

Message Sequence Integrity: Allows the originator to provide to a recipient proof that the sequence of messages has been preserved.

• *Non-repudiation.* This security service provides a guarantee to a third party (an arbitrator, not involved in the communication) that some particular message has been sent, deposited or delivered. This security service may have the following variations:

1. *Origin non-repudiation* security service provides the recipient(s) of the message with unforgeable proof of the origin and the content of the message and the associated message security labels.

2. *Deposit non-repudiation* security service provides the originator of the message with unforgeable proof that the message has been deposited in the Message Transfer System for delivery to the intended recipient.

3. *Delivery non-repudiation* security service provides the originator of the message with unforgeable proof that the message has been delivered to the intended recipient.

3.2.4.3 Management of Security Services in Message Handling Systems

Security of the *X.400* Message Handling System also requires certain management functions and support. Only the authorized entities may change user credentials or security labels.

Most of the techniques (mechanisms) used to implement the described security services are based on *cryptography*. Security services of the Message Handling System allow the selection of alternative algorithms. Nevertheless, in some cases, asymmetric cryptographic algorithms are the only methods that are suggested in these recommendations. Alternative mechanisms using symmetric cryptographic algorithms have been planned for future versions.

The service elements needed to implement security in the *X.400* system must be supported by the *Directory Authentication* environment, defined in the *X.500* recommendations (see Section 3.2.5). The Directory System stores certificated copies of the user public keys of the Message Handling System that can be used to provide authentication and facilitate the exchange of user credentials. Thus, mechanisms to secure data confidentiality and integrity are provided.

Despite the availability of security services in Message Handling Systems, certain attacks still may occur against communications between users and the Message Handling System or between users themselves. To avoid the consequences of these attacks, the intention is to extend current security services and models in the near future.

Although the *X.400* security recommendations provide the means for secure messages, there are a number of limitations when using them:

1. If a "combined" security service for full protection of messages is used, the security services should be applied in the following order: *integrity, authentication* and *confidentiality*, which does not necessarily mean a new service called "authorship" by [MITC89].

The *X.400* recommendations use a token with encrypted data, where the "authorship" security service is not provided; a way to solve this deficiency could be the definition of the token, where the signature would be calculated before performing encryptions, although it may increase the time and resources needed for the security processes.

2. Proof of non-delivery is not recommended by the *X.400* recommendations, but the proof of delivery is, except when the end point of the delivery service is a message store and the message is encrypted. The message store is not able to decrypt the message and perform any proof of delivery check.

3. Proof of transfer is not provided by the *X.400* system when the submitting *MTA* is in a private domain and the message is sent to a *MTA* in a public domain, owing to certain protocol limitations.

4. *X.400* recommendations do not provide security against attacks based on *traffic flow analysis.*

In addition to all these restrictions, there may be some incompatibilities between the security services and some other *MHS* services, owing to the use of encrypted messages by the former.

3.2.5 Security of the X.500 (Directory) System

Two security services are suggested in the *X.500* recommendation to be used when accessing the information in the *OSI* Directory: entity authentication, i.e. a special key exchange protocol between parties involved in the communication, and some rudimentary aspects of access control.

3.2.5.1. X.509 Directory: Authentication Framework

The *X.509* recommendation defines a framework for the provision of an entity authentication security service by the Directory to its users. These users include the Directory itself, as well as other applications and services. The Directory can usefully be involved in meeting their needs for authentication and other security services, because it is a natural place from which communicating parties can obtain authentication information about each other. The Directory also holds other information which is required for communication and which can be obtained prior to communication taking place. Obtaining the authentication information of a potential communication partner from the Directory is, with this approach, similar to obtaining an address. Owing to the wide reach of the Directory for communications purposes, it is expected that this authentication framework will be widely used by a range of applications.

The *X.509* recommendation:

- specifies the form of authentication information held by the Directory;

- describes how authentication information may be obtained from the Directory;

- states the assumptions made about how this authentication information is created and placed in the Directory;

- defines three ways in which applications may use this authentication information to perform authentication and describes how other security services may be supported by authentication.

The *X.509* recommendation describes two levels of authentication: *simple authentication*, using a password as a verification of claimed identity, and *strong authentication*, involving credentials formed using cryptographic techniques. While simple authentication offers some limited protection against unauthorized access, only strong authentication should be used as the basis for providing secure services. In the *X.509* recommendation it was not intended to establish this rule as a general framework for authentication, but it can be of general use for applications which consider these techniques adequate.

Authentication (and other security services) can only be provided within the context of a defined *security policy*. It is a matter for users of an application to define their own security policy which may be constrained by the services provided by a standard.

It is a matter for *OSI* network applications which use the authentication framework to specify the *protocol exchanges* which need to be performed in order to achieve authentication based upon the authentication information, obtained from the Directory. The protocol used by applications to obtain credentials from the Directory is the *Directory Access Protocol (DAP)*, specified in recommendation *X.519*.

The strong authentication method specified in the *X.509* recommendation is based on public-key cryptosystems. It is a major advantage of such systems that user certificates may be held within the Directory as attributes, and may be freely communicated within the Directory System and obtained by users of the Directory in the same manner as other Directory information. The user certificates are assumed to be formed by "off-line" means, and placed in the Directory by their creator. The generation of user certificates is performed by some off-line *Certification Authority* which is completely separate from the *DSAs* in the Directory. In particular, no special requirements are placed upon Directory providers to store or communicate user certificates in a secure manner.

In general, the authentication framework is not dependent on the use of a particular cryptographic algorithm. Potentially a number of different algorithms may be used. However, two users wishing to authenticate themselves must use the same cryptographic algorithm for authentication to be performed correctly. Thus, within the context of a set of related applications, the choice of a single algorithm will serve to maximize the community of users able to authenticate and communicate securely.

Similarly, two users wishing to authenticate each other, must support the same *hash function* needed in forming credentials and authentication tokens. Again, in principle, a number of alternative hash functions could be used, at the cost of narrowing the communities of users able to authenticate.

3.2.5.2 X.509 Directory: Access Control Framework

Directory users are granted access to the information in the *Directory Information Base (DIB)* on the basis of their *access control rights,* in accordance with the access control policy applied for protection of that information.

Access control security service is left in the *X.500* recommendation as a local matter in each security domain. However, it is recognized that implementations of this security service will need to introduce some means of controlling access and that future versions of the *X.500* recommendations are likely to define a standardized means of creating, maintaining and applying access control information.

The two principles that may guide the establishment of procedures for managing access control are:

1. There must be some means of protecting information in the Directory from unauthorized detection, examination, and modification, including protecting the *Directory Information Tree (DIT)* from unauthorized modification.

2. The information required to determine user's rights to perform a given operation must be available to the *Directory Services Agents (DSAs)* involved in performing the operation in order to avoid further remote operations solely to determine these rights.

The following levels of security are presently identified in the *X.500* recommendations:

- protection of an entire subtree of the *DIT;*

- protection of an individual entry;

- protection of an entire attribute within an entry;

- protection of selected instances of attribute values.

A need for at least six *categories* of access is envisaged in the *X.500* recommendation. If access is not granted to a protected item in any category, then the Directory, in so far as is possible, responds as though the protected item did not exist at all.

The categories of access are: *detect, compare, read, modify, add/delete,* and *naming.*

One scheme for managing access control associates with every protected item, either explicitly or implicitly, a list of access rights. Each item in such a list pairs a set of users with a set of access categories.

Determining if a user is in one (or more) of the noted sets must be possible from the information supplied with the request – either from the authenticated identity and credentials of the user as supplied in the **bind** macro (a specially defined *X.500* function), or from information carried in the operation argument.

There are at least two possibilities:

1. The sets are described in terms of the distinguishing names of the users they identify – either the distinguishing name of the user or distinguishing name of a superior with a flag specifying that the entire subtree is included.

2. The sets give only a capability, and implicitly include all users having that capability. This scheme requires that such users' capability be available locally or else carried in the **bind** macro, or as the operation argument. The latter may require some extensions to the protocols currently defined in the *X.500* recommendation.

3.2.6 Security of the FTAM System

The purpose of the *File Transfer, Access, and Management (FTAM)* international standard is to facilitate the transfer and management of files, local and remote, by the open system user. The *FTAM* recommendations are organized in three parts:

1. *Virtual file definition.* A generic file virtual format is offered by means of a presentation protocol. Each user will realize locally the conversion between this format and the original file format. The definition is made in terms of:

   - *Structure. FTAM* implements a hierarchical model; each node of the tree defines a sub-tree called *File Access Data Unit (FADU),* which can be individually accessed.

   - *Attributes.* File related properties.

   - Allowed *actions* over the whole file or the individual *FADUs.*

2. *File services definition.* A set of primitives and parameters allowing the creation of a working environment in which the user can access files in a secure and reliable way.

3. Specification of the *file protocol* that the *FTAM* service offers. It must be responsible for the use of the representation services needed for the conversion of files, from virtual to local. It is also used for the establishment of the session links and the necessary check points for the access to remote files.

The starting point of the definition of any security architecture must always be the determination of an *authorization security policy* which for *FTAM* can be defined as a set of rules (specifications) of user access restrictions to files or their parts.

Given that the security offered by a service or an application will rely on the good definition of this policy, its demonstrability will often be required. In such cases a formal security model is needed; i.e. a precise and manageable description of the system behaviour, which permits the use of formal tools for security validation.

The security service that guarantees the authorization requirement, supported or not by a formal model, is called *Access Control* and must be supplied directly by the *FTAM*. It must also ensure that users cannot evade this security service, by using other appropriate security services and mechanisms that, in general, will be obtained from the operating system of the host machine or from lower levels of the *OSI* reference model.

In order to simplify the overall approach to security in the *FTAM* system, and disregarding those potential threats to the *FTAM* system with low probability, two main categories of attacks are distinguished:

a. *Identity falsification.* This is the case when an intruder complies with the access control services, but evades the authorization policy, altering the information on which the access authorization relies. For example, falsifying its identity or privilege level.

b. *Non-authorized access.* This case is related to the total violation of the access control mechanism. For example, altering the file contents during its transmission.

3.2.6.1 *Access Control Service of the FTAM*

Regardless of the security policy, two types of access control services can be distinguished:

1. *Rule based* (Mandatory Access Control). Security levels are defined for the information, and for user privilege levels; authorization restrictions are defined based on these levels. For example, a user cannot read a file with a security level higher than his privilege level.

2. *Identity based* (Discretionary Access Control). The authorization relies directly on the user identity and the type of information requested. For example, user X has the access right to read file F.

In both cases, an essential aspect of the security service on which the application of these restrictions depends is its granularity; in other words, the precision with which access attributes are distinguished with respect to:

- *Access subjects.* Different users should have different authorizations.

- *Requested operations.* Each *FTAM* operation must be authorized independently, either for complete files (create file, change attributes, erase file, etc), or just for its elements, i.e. File Access Data Units (*FADU*) (allocate new *FADU*, read existing *FADU*, insert new *FADU*, replace, add and erase).

- *The accessed objects.* In the simplest case, the access authorization refers to complete files, in general, even though the file structure will be more complex. Distinction between access to different file elements (each one with its own identity and security levels) will be needed.

In *FTAM,* the granularity of the access control service corresponds to the structure of the virtual file, hierarchically structured. Each *FADU* (individually accessed file component) will have associated security attributes on which the access control service relies.

- *Rule Based Access Control Attributes.* A security level is related to each *FADU* (or to a complete file). When an *FTAM* user requests access to a specific *FADU,* the protocol is responsible for accomplishing the security policy, allowing only the authorized activities described by its security level and privilege level (obtained by *FTAM* via the Request primitive).

The most serious problems in a distributed environment may be the linkage (cooperation) of file systems when different security policies are used for them. However, regardless of the correct implementations of these policies, their interaction can produce deficiencies that sometimes are difficult to detect. *FTAM* must consider these interactions to allow access only when it will not affect security.

- *Identity Based Access Control Attributes.* The information that permits establishment of a logical relation between the user identity and the authorization for access to a *FADU* for a specific operation, can be associated with:

  - *User:* each user provides the identity information, which is received by *FTAM* in the Service Request primitive.

  - *FADU:* incorporated in it, as an additional security attribute, may be the list of users authorized for the specific operation.

As before, the protocol must take care of the possible interactions for the case of different solutions implemented in a heterogeneous environment.

3.2.6.2 Identity Authentication Service

Assuming that the different security policies in use in a distributed environment are correct, and that the interaction problems between them are solved, some users may try (using potential deficiencies of the access control security service) to falsify their privilege levels or identity, in order to achieve non-authorized effects. To avoid this, the *FTAM* should use security services that guarantee the security of the operation being performed. In a simple way, these services depend on:

1. *Operating System.* It must guarantee to the *FTAM* that the user will not be able to modify its access control attributes:

   - *security level;*

   - *user identity;*

   - *discretionary access information,* when available.

2. *Communications services.* The lower *OSI* layers must guarantee secure services, based on the assumption that any intruder can interfere with the communications through the network, causing the delivery of false access control attributes to the remote *FTAM.* The communication protection services for elimination of these problems are:

   - message integrity protection by even/odd parity or message authentication codes;

   - message origin authentication.

Given that the access control service is established in terms of the user identity, then the presentation layer delivers this service to the *FTAM* and lower layers will not be able to provide the appropriate granularity.

3.2.6.3 File Contents Security Service: Confidentiality and Integrity

Some users may illegally try to elude completely the access control mechanisms using the security weaknesses on:

- *The operating system.* The possibility of non-authorized access realized via a variety of techniques (Trojan horses, hidden channels, etc.), must be considered.

- *The communications path.* The nature of the communications service allows access to the contents while files pass over the network.

In response to these threats, the *FTAM* relies on the security services directly concerned with the individual *FADU's,* such as file confidentiality and content authentication (integrity) during the storage or transmission periods.

3.2.7 Security of EDI Systems

3.2.7.1 Introduction

Security in *EDI* systems relates most specifically to the transmission and receipt of *EDI* messages. The person who sends an *EDI* message must first be authorized to do so. *EDI* messages must arrive at the correct destination without modification. In addition, the person who sends the message should not be able to deny having sent the message and the person who receives the message should not be able to deny having received it (*non-repudiation*). This applies to the *receipt* as well as to the *contents* of the messages.

The basic *EDI* security services are therefore :

1. *Authentication:* there must be some form of unforgeable proof that the message originated from an identifiable, authorized person.

2. *Confidentiality:* the content of the message must be protected during transmission.

3. *Integrity:* there must be some form of proof that the message has not been modified either accidentally or deliberately.

4. *Non-repudiation:* procedures must be available to avoid the denial of the sending or receipt of a specific message.

A global approach has to be taken to the basic *EDI* message security services identified. A number of questions related to these services should be addressed:

a. How can these security services be implemented within the message itself, and how much can be done at the message handling level?

b. Do users have to modify their internal procedures and network applications, and if so, in what way and to what extent?

c. What can value-added or third-party services do in this area?

d. What are the ready-made products and tools available today in the market?

e. What kind of infrastructure (network facilities) is required?

f. How to determine a balance between the risks and the costs?

The means of ensuring user authentication, message confidentiality, message integrity and non-repudiation of transmission or receipt have to be legally credible across international borders. In these circumstances electronic archiving and notarization services on, or associated with, public networks may also be necessary.

There are already some international standards for *EDI* messages (*EDIFACT*) and for message handling systems (*X.400*). In addition, there is a set of *"Uniform rules of conduct for interchange of trade data by tele-transmission"*. These rules, the *UNCID* rules, have been published by the *ICC (International Chamber of Commerce)*.

The acceptance of formal, contractual responsibility by third parties may be as important a factor as the actual technology available. The legal credibility of the solutions adopted has also to be ensured.

3.2.7.2 EDI Specific Security Requirements

The *EDI* security requirements which are not fully recognized within the current *X.400* documents are concerned with the concept of *responsibility* for messages at each stage of the message path through the *MHS* environment. In an *EDI* context, the increased possibility of a number of service providers offering commercial services may require the transfer of responsibility to be clearly identified and assured to provide further protection, not only to the end users, but also to the service providers. In the *EDIMS* security model an important issue concerned with security is the *responsibility domain*. Identified responsibility domains are:

- *EDIMS* user environment plus *EDIMS UA;*

- *MTS* Management Domain;

- *IMS* Message Store.

EDIMS user environment and EDIMS UA. In the *EDIMS* user environment with the *EDIMS UA*, an additional security requirement, not defined in the existing *X.400* documents, is the *proof of receipt.* This security service is necessary because the existing *proof of submission* and *proof of delivery* services do not operate end-to-end, and in particular do not take into account the *EDIMS* scenario where the recipient *EDIMS UA* and Message Store are not co-located. Such receipt notification needs to be associated with the subject of the message.

3.2.7.3 MTS: Specific Services

Audit Trail. Loss of individual messages in the Message Store, whether malicious or accidental, will require the provision of a secure *Audit Trail facility* to enable detection of such a loss. Such a service has to be provided to the *EDIMS* user and to the *MS* management. Secure *MS Audit Trail* could be realized as a pervasive mechanism.

Repudiation. The existing *MHS* services only cover some areas of transfer between responsibility domains, which could be of significance in an *EDIMS* environment, i.e. between *MTS* Management Domains, between a Message Store and a receiving *EDIMS* user. The existing services in *MHS* (Non-repudiation/Proof of delivery) do not provide protection in the case of delivery to a Message Store which is not a part of the receiving *EDIMS* users' environment. Therefore new Non-repudiation/Proof of Retrieval and Non-repudiation/Proof of Transfer services covering transfer of responsibility to the recipient *EDIMS UA* are necessary. Proof of Retrieval may be realized by a secure *MS Audit Trail* to record *EDIMS* user actions on the Message Store. Another service which seems to be necessary is Non-repudiation/Proof of Receipt by the *EDIMS UA* in order to provide protection for the originating *EDIMS* user. Such services are relevant in the case of autoforwarding, redirection etc. and have to be defined as additional services to the EDIMS originator. The vulnerability to manipulation of information by the EDIMS user may be countered with another service, i.e. Non-repudiation/Proof of Content.

In the course of development of the *EDI* conceptual model, special attention has been devoted to the vulnerability of the *EDI* services. This vulnerability, as well as the specific mechanisms and services required to counter the threats to *EDIMS*, are complementary to the existing security services as defined in recommendation *X.400*. Therefore, additional security services for *EDIMS* proposed recently may be summarized as follows:

- Non-repudiation/Proof of Receipt;

- Non-repudiation/Proof of Retrieval;

- Non-repudiation/Proof of Transfer;

- Non-repudiation/Proof of Content;

- Secure MS Audit Trail;

- Secure MT Audit Trail.

These specific security services for *EDIMS* are concerned with the concept of *responsibility* for messages at each stage of the message path through the communication network. In an *EDI* context, with the increased possibilities of many service providers offering commercial products and services, security issues have to be clearly identified and assured, to provide protection not only to the end-users, but also to the service providers.

4

ANALYSIS
OF SECURITY REQUIREMENTS
FOR OPEN
DISTRIBUTED SYSTEMS

4.1 ANALYSIS OF THE ISO/OSI SECURITY ARCHITECTURE

This section contains comments and suggestions concerning the concept and framework for security within the *OSI* environment, as defined in [ISO88] and described in the previous chapter. Most of these comments are derived from suggestions and remarks given in the original *ISO* document, which itself indicates possible variations and future extensions of the concept of *ISO/OSI Security Architecture*.

The analysis of the *ISO/OSI Security Architecture* in this chapter is given in the form of open problems, possibilities for future activities, and extensions to the basic *OSI* security framework. These comments may be considered as the basis for all the research results described in this book with specific extensions, described in detail in subsequent chapters.

Most of these extensions are based on three characteristics of the *ISO/OSI* security architecture:

1. The architecture is just *a framework* (recommendation) for security in open systems, therefore it needs further design and implementation details.

2. *OSI* is only a *communication environment,* so security services needed in vari-

ous applications are likely to be located mainly in the Application Layer. This suggests that security in Open Distributed Processing (ODP) systems should be considered as extensions of the standard *OSI* security architecture.

3. There are other operating environments, different from *OSI*, which may use security systems derived from the *OSI* security architecture concept.

The objective of security in *OSI* systems is to permit the interconnection of heterogeneous computer systems, so that useful and secure communication between application processes may be achieved. Therefore, at various times, security services must be applied and security controls must be established in order to protect the information exchanged between the application processes. Such services and controls should make the cost of obtaining or modifying data greater than the potential value of doing so, or make the time required to obtain the data so great that the value of the data is lost.

The emphasis for security measures in any computing structure must be on users and application processes. Data communication functions are just supporting functions for cooperation of application processes in distributed environments. *OSI* security functions are concerned only with those visible aspects of a communication path which permit end-systems to achieve the secure transfer of information between them. *OSI* security is not concerned with security measures needed in end-systems, installations, and organizations, except where these have implications for the choice and position of security services visible in *OSI*. These latter aspects of security may be standardized, but not within the scope of *OSI* standards. This approach is derived from the basic principles of *OSI* systems, while security must be concerned with total systems operations, and not just communication functions [ISO88]. Therefore, security in an *OSI* environment is just one aspect of data processing/data communications security.

If they are to be effective, the protective measures used in an *OSI* environment require supporting measures which lie outside *OSI*. They must be located either in the application layer or in application processes. For example, information flowing between systems may be encrypted, but if no physical security restrictions are placed on access to the systems themselves, encipherment may be in vain. Also, *OSI* is concerned only with the interconnection of systems. For *OSI* security measures to be effective, they must be used in conjunction with measures that fall outside the scope of *OSI*. Many of them are described in the subsequent chapters of this book.

Creating a secure open environment assumes that the communications can be protected from several types of threats, including: interception or alteration of traffic, insertion of bogus traffic, illegally obtaining the identities of the communicating partners, interruption of legitimate activities, etc. (see Table 1.1). To protect the communications from all of these problems, security functions must be distributed among many computers and in several different layers of the *OSI* reference model. A problem is that in an internetworking and interworking environment the large number of subnetworks and computers involved can make security solutions difficult to implement or manage.

For example, at the internetworking level, consideration must be given to the existence of subnetworks with different security services that are used in the routing of messages. Internetworking gateways must also be secured, so that their behaviour cannot be altered by unauthorized parties. Information concerning the security capabilities of all attached subnetworks must be distributed to the gateways, so that they can incorporate security in routing decisions. Also, traffic presented to a gateway must specify the level of security it requires, as it is moved across different subnetworks.

This example can be generalized to the cooperation of different security domains, which may exist even within the same subnetwork in an open system. This implies that special consideration must be given to secure interdomain communications, which may be conceptually structured as a separate component of security management.

The interworking environment must also protect individual computers from attack by remote processes. Individual operating systems must be constructed to supply the necessary security mechanisms and then be integrated into the interworking environment. Protocols and services must be defined so that computers can interact and exchange the necessary information among themselves as well as with special security-management computers.

This aspect is somewhat different from previous considerations. The basis for secure *OSI* operations and applications is security in individual host systems. Security in the *OSI* system may be built by adding communication security services onto security services in host computers. Since *OSI* is a concept for interconnection of heterogeneous computer systems, this applies also to security within those systems. Security measures in individual hosts may be heterogeneous, and cooperation of such systems in a secure way is also an extension of the *OSI* security architecture.

Special emphasis in design, implementation and use of security services must be given to the protection of the control security data, such as passwords, encryption keys, and access codes, and the means for altering or distributing that information. If security features are not addressed in a timely manner, many network administrators may adopt solutions that will be incompatible with future *OSI* standards. This problem may be stated as requirements for secure, reliable and trustworthy operations of security management functions, combined with protection and integrity of data in the security management databases.

As indicated in this section so far, extensions of the *OSI* security architecture may be organized in two directions:

1. The design and precise specification of all necessary components of the *ISO* security standards (security management databases, security protocols, verification of a secure system design, etc.), that would make the current framework

a real security architecture.

2. Extensions of the security concepts and services to the open distributed processing environment.

Security in *ODP* systems is a very broad area, with many problems still open. Some of them will be indicated in the remaining subsections as possible extensions of the standard *ISO/OSI* security architecture.

Some additional security services for communication environments are suggested in Section 4.2.1. Security services in end-systems are discussed in Section 4.2.2 and security management services in Section 4.2.3. Applications of formal models for secure systems are suggested in Section 4.2.4, and the integration of individual security services towards the design of integrated security systems is treated in Section 4.2.5. The last two subsections are concerned with rating, selection, and classification of security mechanisms and the assessment of global security in *ODP* systems.

4.2 EXTENSIONS OF THE ISO/OSI SECURITY ARCHITECTURE

4.2.1 Additional Security Services in the OSI Environment

OSI is a model for a data communication environment and therefore its security services are primarily data communications security services, as described in the *ISO/OSI* Security Architecture international standard [ISO88]. *ISO* has suggested the use of five types of security services: *authentication, access control, data confidentiality, data integrity,* and *non-repudiation.* Based on a thorough analysis of these security services and functionalities of the *OSI* reference model, the following could be suggested as additional communication security services for *OSI* systems, or perhaps extensions and modifications of the standard security services:

a. *Subliminal channel.* This is a special form of secure communications which may be called "double" data confidentiality. This kind of communication has two levels of security: the secret message can be recovered from the protected message using some regular mechanism, but an additional mechanism is needed to obtain the subliminal message. This allows two entities to communicate secretly while an illegal eavesdropper is fooled into thinking that he can read their communications. This kind of network security service is called a *subliminal channel* or "prisoners' problem" ([SIMM84]).

b. *Prevention of denial of message delivery* [VOYD83]. This security service prevents attacks in which the intruder either *discards* all messages passing on an association or, in less drastic action, *delays* all messages going in one or both directions. An illegal user may do this by generating so much bogus or dummy traffic that regular messages may not pass on the communication line. The subtle difference between message stream modification attack and denial of message service attack is a function both of the degree of the attack and of the state of an association. For example, security mechanisms protecting against message stream modification can detect temporary denial-of-service attacks, but, if an association is quiescent (i.e. no messages are outstanding in either direction), a protocol entity at one end of the association may have no way of determining when the next message should arrive from its correspondent peer entity. In this state, it would thus be unable to detect a denial-of-service attack that completely cut off the flow of incoming messages. To handle attacks of this sort, security mechanisms additional to the *OSI* security services are necessary.

c. *Secure group communications.* This is the case when a group is involved in a communication as a logical entity. This type of communication may have three different forms: *secure broadcasting* (distribution one-to-many), *multi--origin delivery* (distribution many-to-one), and the combination of the first two cases, *secure group-to-group communication.* It seems that in this case, simple *OSI* security services, designed for secure peer-to-peer (one-to-one) communications, may not be simply "multiplied", because of special security requirements: *multisignatures* ([BOYD86], [TATS88]), *threshold schemes* [SHAM79A], or *secure teleconferences* [INGE82].

d. *Anonymous communications.* A stronger requirement for secure exchange of messages, compared with the *ISO traffic flow confidentiality* security service, occurs when the real identities of the communicating entities (registered in the network and used for secure entity identification) should be hidden not only from passive attacks by illegal users, but also from the partner(s) in the association. This case may be called anonymous communications. With this security service a user may employ a different identity for each of his associations, thus hiding his real identity, not only from intruders, but also from his peer entities as well. One mechanism suggested in the literature for this security service is digital pseudonyms [CHAU81].

4.2.2 Security Services in End-Systems

In order to provide security in *ODP* systems, security services in end-systems are essential. They are concerned with various user functions and requirements, data processing and data storage operations performed in end-systems. Most of the standard *OSI* security services may also be applied (implemented) in end-systems, for instance: *entity authentication, access control, data confidentiality* and *data integrity.*

One of the interesting possibilities for additional forms of secure user cooperation in *ODP* systems is *cooperation of mutually suspicious users.* For most of the *OSI* security services and their corresponding mechanisms it has been implicitly assumed that two *mutually confident* entities communicate in the untrustworthy open environment. This means that the sources of threats to an association are logically located *outside* of that association. A more serious requirement would be to provide secure exchange of information between two *mutually suspicious* entities; the case when neither trusts the other. In this arrangement no private (secret) information should be exchanged without reciprocity, i.e. without receiving the same or equivalent secret information. This type of security service for two participants is called *contract signing* ([BLUM83], [RABI83], [MUFT90B]) and may be extended to simultaneous cooperation of several entities (*multilateral associations*) ([BAUE83], [DENN83]). The first case is known as *bilateral contract signing* and the second *multilateral contract signing*.

For mutually suspicious entities, some other security services have also been suggested in the literature. Electronic *coin flipping* allows two mutually distrustful entities to flip a coin in the network environment, so that the resulting coin toss is random, unbiased, and neither entity can influence its outcome ([BLUM81], [EVEN85]). This basic security service may be used to implement some other network functions and protocols in a secure way (mental poker, disclosure protocol, secure distributed computing, computing with encrypted data, zero-knowledge interactive protocol, etc.) [BRAS87].

Secure registered mail is the service provided when the sender of the signed letter is willing to deliver the letter to the intended receiver only under condition that in return he/she receives a proof of the delivery and of the correct letter content.

Another example of cooperation of mutually suspicious entities is the case when n users constitute a closed communication group, and are willing to establish secure communication only if at least k of them are active at the same time. This security service is called a *(k, n)-threshold scheme*, and may also be used to establish access categories (levels) of participating entities [SHAM79A].

Finally, two important security services also dealing with the cooperation of mutually suspicious users are the *secure copyright* and *secure licensing* schemes. The first provides the possibility of distributing authorized (copyright) materials and the second of licensing network resources with certain conditions (limited number of copies, predetermined distribution, etc.). These two security services may be particularly important when distributing software and other proprietary materials by electronic means.

The *OSI* security services *access control, data confidentiality* and *data integrity* may also be applied (implemented) to database and process protection in end-systems, in which case "data" means data in the databases or instructions in computer programs. Additional services may be suggested, concerned with *dynamic* database and process protection schemes; for example:

- *Security-consistent flow of data.* This must be applied when classified data in the database is copied from one group (segment) to another group (segment). In that case, this security service regulates the dissemination of values among the data sets in such a way that the security mechanisms, related to the original data, will also be applied to new elements of the database [DENN79].

- *Prevention of inference (generation).* This security service prevents confidential values, derived from individual data, stored in regular or statistical databases, from being collected and correlated, so that sensitive data cannot be inferred by illegal users [DENN79].

- *Consistency control of database use.* This is the security service which provides protection and integrity of individual database items, based on their values (so-called "value-dependent" restrictions). Successful implementation of this service in the network means that data in the database is always logically consistent and that sensitive data values are disseminated only under special authorization [CONW72].

- *Context protection.* This is the security service, based on dynamic database protection schemes, that must also be included in the database protection system. With this security service, protection of an individual database object at a particular instant of time depends on the overall security environment and previous operations executed with the same object ("history-dependent" restrictions) [HART76].

- *Prevention of unauthorized information generation.* This is the service that prevents an entity from inferring information classified above his security level, without direct access to that information in the database or without collecting and correlating statistics (as with the inference threat), but based on certain logical relations between data values [MUFT77].

These additional security services in end-systems, as well as most of the *OSI* services, may be applied to the protection of *ODP* processes when treated as system resources. Other interesting questions concerning processes in *ODP* systems are implementation of *memoryless processes* and *secure distributed computing:*

- *Implementation of memoryless subsystems.* By treating a process in an *ODP* system as a finite state machine, a "memory" of that machine can be a source for illegal, unauthorized penetration into confidential system resources, information, activities or subsystems. This memory may be realized by accumulating various individual values, by generated information, or by a special sequence of states of the process. In order to eliminate this threat, implementation of *memoryless subsystems* must be one of the *ODP* system security services. Application of this service means that no process may derive protected information either by keeping (accumulating) data and information or by executing any specific sequence of states (operations).

- *Secure distributed computing.* This service is the case when a process must derive some value $f(x_1, x_2, \ldots, x_n)$ out of n arguments, when these n arguments *(a)* are not individually or publicly available [YAO82], or *(b)* are in encrypted form [FEIG86].

4.2.3 Security Management Services

Besides operational security services, security management services are very important. These services are concerned with the correct management of various parameters and security protocols, needed for correct operation of the security system. In addition, all security relevant parameters and events must be properly recorded for monitoring and auditing purposes. In the case of security violations, there must be services to allow recovery from undesired situations.

One of the most important security management services is *key generation*. It applies to symmetric and asymmetric cryptographic systems and guarantees that the keys are generated according to predetermined (mathematical) requirements and properly used and managed. With symmetric cryptographic systems the generated keys must be verified not to be:

    a. one of possibly weak or semi-weak keys;

    b. generated by a random repetitive process, so that a newly generated key has not been used (recently) by the same user.

With asymmetric cryptographic systems, this service must provide key pairs, with certain desired properties. The key pair will be secure if it fulfills the following conditions:

1. The generated keys are not trivial, predictable keys of small size.

2. There exists no duplicate (identical) key pairs in the same security domain.

3. The corresponding algebraic field is secure (for the RSA system this means that the modulo number is the product of two large prime numbers p and q and they are both chosen safely according to the corresponding mathematical rules, while for El'Gamal's system the modulo is a truly prime number).

4. The keys are mathematically correct (i.e. for the RSA system the keys are multiplicative inverses in the modulo number of the generated field, while for El'Gamal system they fulfil the required conditions about their size).

5. There is no possibility of the requested key pair being compromised when generating, transferring, or using it in the network.

The key generation service must provide a protocol for the organizations used in defining the common security domain, for establishing the same modulo field, and for easily defining key pairs for new users registered in that domain, as needed.

Two other very important security management services are *logging* of security relevant events and *security recovery*, which must be organized with special precautions, since their malfunctioning may cause serious damage to the whole security system.

For later reference and as design goals, the security services to be provided by the comprehensive integrated security system are given in the following table.

Table 4.1. Security Services in the *ODP* Environment

A.   Communication Security Services

   A.1. Standard (ISO/OSI) Security Services

      1. Entity Authentication
      2. Data Confidentiality
      3. Data Integrity
      4. Access Control
      5. Non-repudiation

   A.2. Additional Communication Security Services

      6. Subliminal Channel
      7. Prevention of Denial of Message Service
      8. Secure Group Communications
      9. Anonymous Communications

B.   Security Services in End-Systems

   B.1. Security Services for Cooperation of Suspicious Users

      10. Contract Signing Protocol
      11. Decision Making Protocol
      12. Secure Electronic Mail
      13. Threshold Schemes
      14. Secure Copyright Schemes
      15. Secure Licensing Schemes

   B.2. Database Security Services

      16. Secure Flow of Data
      17. Prevention of Data Inference
      18. Context-Oriented (Dynamic) Protection Schemes
      19. Prevention of Information Generation

   B.3. Security Services for Software and Processes

      20. Software Authenticity and Integrity (Viruses)
      21. Security of Operating Systems
      22. Implementation of Memoryless Subsystems

C.   Security Management Services

      23. Generation, Storage, and Distribution of Cryptographic Keys
      24. Logging and Auditing Security Relevant Events
      25. Security Recovery
      26. Notary Service

4.2.4 Application of Formal Models

The design of a security system involves the *building of a formal representation* of the system which will eventually be implemented. This representation may be further analysed to derive some important *system characteristics* and to detect potential *design errors* prior to the implementation.

From the point of view of *ODP* security, the formal representation essentially provides a basis for determining *whether or not a system is secure,* according to the prespecified criteria. If insecure, the model helps to identify and to detect the design flaws and insufficiencies. The formal representation must be mathematically rigorous enough to be able to verify the security of the system in order to determine whether it meets the security constraints and requirements.

Most of the formal models of secure systems are based on the concept of the *finite state machine.* Operations of the system and security parameters are used to define the states of the machine. Various requirements and constraints are imposed on the security system in order to meet the definition of security. The model is used to verify formally whether the secure system meets the specified requirements.

As stated in Section 2.1.2, *ISO* has suggested the use of five types of security services: *entity authentication, access control, data confidentiality, data integrity,* and *non-repudiation.* Most of the existing formal models, although modelling secure systems through global system states and verifying overall system behaviour, are primarily concerned with one particular security service. For instance, the Bell–LaPadula model [BELL73] is primarily concerned with access control, while with Sidhu [SIDH86] it is authentication, and with Goguen and Meseguer [GOGU82] it is noninterference, which may be applied to authentication and data integrity, etc.

The most important property of formal models based on a finite-state machine concept is that they are models for *sequential computation.* In *ODP* systems, there are many concurrently active processes, and therefore finite-state machine models, in general, are not adequate (without appropriate modification) for modelling security systems based on the *OSI* or *ODP* security architecture.

This inadequacy may be overcome in two different ways. Existing models may be used to verify partial properties of the security systems, and their results may be methodologically "linked" together in order to derive security characteristics and properties of the complete security system. The other approach would be the development of new, original models, which would inherently include *concurrent computations,* and therefore would be more suitable for modelling of secure *OSI* and *ODP* systems.

In Chapter 5 a survey and short analysis of the applicability of existing formal models to the *OSI* security architecture is given. A new, original model is presented and applied to the analysis of secure *ODP* systems.

4.2.5 Integration of ODP Security Services (ODP Security Architecture)

Integration of the *ODP* security services may be achieved through the concept of a common security management consisting of:

a. segments of the *Security Management Information Base (SMIB)*;

b. *security management modules* which perform security related functions in the *ODP* system.

Both of these components constitute a concept of *ODP security management,* concerned with the management of security services and mechanisms. Such management requires the *distribution of management information* to security services and mechanisms as well as the collection of information concerning the operation of the integrated security system.

The Security Management Information Base (*SMIB*) is the conceptual repository for all security-relevant information needed by open systems. In order to be efficient, the *SMIB* will be a distributed information base. Segments of the *SMIB* must be *structured* in such a way as to support implementation of all security services and mechanisms in the *ODP* environment, and be *distributed* in such a way as to enable the most efficient access to the security relevant information.

Collection, distribution and use of the information from the (distributed) *SMIB* require special procedures and protocols, which may be called *security management protocols.* They define the exchange of security-relevant information between logical components of the security management system. The components of that system (called *Agents*) are:

1. User Agent;

2. Security Services Agent;

3. Security Mechanisms Agent;

4. *SMIB* Agent;

5. Security Administrator Agent;

6. Agent for interactions with the operational environment;

7. Monitoring Agent (regular monitoring, event handling, auditing, etc.);

8. Recovery Agent;

9. Associations Agent;

10. Interdomain Communications Agent.

These suggested agents, their individual functions, their mutual cooperation (security protocols), and their integration (in a form of a global security system) are discussed in Chapter 7, while some problems in this area are still open for further study.

4.2.6 Rating, Classification, and Selection of Security Mechanisms

Rating is the process of verifying that the specific mechanism or mechanisms used to implement the security services provide security and operational efficiency in conformance with the pre-specified criteria. For this purpose a number of methods may be considered: the *analytical formula* developed by Eloff [ELOF83], the authors' concept of rating based on *security capabilities* [MUFT88B], some *mathematical tests*, the elements of *information theory* (unicity distance, work factor, etc.). The prototype implementation of the comprehensive integrated security system described in Section 8.3 has been organized with empirically recognized acceptable security mechanisms (*DES, RSA, MAC, MD2, MD4*, etc.). Verification methods and models, as very important problems, are areas for further research studies.

4.2.7 Assessment of Security in ODP Systems

Selection of security services and mechanisms to achieve certain objectives for a particular security system depends on a number of factors, such as the perceived security threats, the required level of security, and the cost-effectiveness of achieving this level. These factors are part of the overall *security policy* for the particular *ODP* system. Essentially, security policy is the high level specification that dictates the security requirements without any concern for how these requirements are to be achieved. In that sense, different systems will have different security policies because of their different threats, resources, and security requirements.

The first stage in the *selection* of security services and mechanisms for a particular system is to *identify the specific threats* against which the protection is required. This is known as *threat assessment* and involves [ISO88]:

- Identification of potential threats (listed in Table 1.1).

- Identification of the vulnerabilities of the system (*vulnerability analysis*).

- Analysis of the risks of threats aimed at exploiting these vulnerabilities (*risk analysis*).

- Assessment of the *consequences* of each threat being successfully carried out.

- Assessment of the *cost* of each realized threat to the system.

- Assessment of the *cost* of potential countermeasures.

The next stage, after the assessment of threats, is to identify all possible security services and mechanisms that may counter the identified threats. The security mechanisms and algorithms should then be rated according to certain established criteria (one important criterion is the strength of the security mechanisms and algorithms; however, this may be offset by some limiting factors such as the cost and the speed of implementation). Finally, the optimal security services and mechanisms, based on their ratings, should be selected to achieve the required security level.

The basic approach to selecting network security mechanisms is to consider which security services are really needed and what cost can be justified in introducing them in the network. The most relevant factors in determining the need for security are the vulnerabilities in the company's or organization's business operations. Loss of goodwill and public confidence due to breach of personal integrity or disclosure of commercially sensitive information may in turn lead to loss of income. Various national laws and statutory requirements may demand the use of security services, e.g. Data Protection Acts and international security standards in banking.

Assessing the vulnerabilities in an open system should be done as part of an overall risk analysis. In short, this consists of identifying the potential threats and evaluating them with respect to expected probabilities or possible frequency of occurrence. If a specific threat, successfully carried out, leads to unacceptable consequences in the opinion of top management, then a security service to eliminate this threat is required.

As already indicated, the security objectives and requirements must be set by top management. There are several reasons for this. Security measures necessitate investments, but are commonly believed to decrease productivity or service levels and they seldom show a directly evident profit.

So security needs sensitive and careful decisions which must be made by top management in order to win undisputed acceptance. The need for security measures should be expressed in formal statements and these constitute the company's *security policy.*

The security requirements expressed in the security policy must be accompanied by financial, organizational, and other means for implementing the services, which is usually the responsibility of senior management.

An overall security policy will of course cover many aspects outside the network and may lead to security measures like administrative routines, vetting of personnel, physical access control systems, protection against sabotage and fire, and so on.

The concepts of security policy and the methodology for conducting risk analyses have been extensively treated in the literature. A good overview may be also found in annex A in the document [ISO88].

The important points to remember are:

- The security policy is the steering document set by top management.

- The security policy should express the general goals for the level of security.

- The required security services will be decided upon from the results of a risk analysis conducted within the system. Evaluation of potential threats and their possible consequences for the operation is then undertaken.

- Network security is a part of the overall security required to fulfil the goals of the security policy.

- Vulnerability of an information system may change with time, depending on the growth of the volume and level of protected information, change of data sensitivity, new business position, evolution of the network, newly discovered attack possibilities, etc. For this reason the process of establishing a security policy, conducting risk analyses and implementing security services may have to be repeated at intervals.

A brief overview and a methodology for assessment of security are given in Chapter 6. This should be a guidance to managers, users, and system personnel in establishing a secure environment based on ideas and results from this book.

4.3 CONCEPTUAL APPROACH TO SECURITY
IN OPEN DISTRIBUTED SYSTEMS

A conceptual approach to the analysis and design of security systems will now be described. It will be used as methodological guidance (framework) in subsequent chapters.

4.3.1 Operational Environment and Security Policies

Security systems are always implemented in some operational environment. In the most general case this will be an *ODP* environment, which will be assumed to be a collection of data processing (distributed) end-systems, interconnected with one or more general *OSI* systems. The interpretation of such a global environment varies from a single *PC* up to the most general intercontinental networks.

The main topic of this book is the design of a comprehensive security system for any kind of operational environment, conforming to a broad list of formal specifications and user requirements. The basic purpose of such a security system is to provide, through its functions, procedures and protocols, security for users and resources of the underlying operational environment. The design of a security system means the establishment of a system with the desired requirements, while its implementation and operation means that the system meets the design specifications.

Each security system depends on the appropriate security policy, which in turn depends on the security requirements and specifications of the particular operational *ODP* environment. General security requirements and specifications for secure *ODP* systems were given in Section 4.2, and they should be interpreted and followed when designing and implementing each specific security system.

An operational environment consists, basically, of three main components relevant for security: *(a)* hardware components included in the *ODP* system and their topological structure, *(b)* software components, consisting of host operating systems, network communication software, and user applications, *(c)* security policy constraints and requirements.

These components will be structured into groups (of users and resources) under the same security policy. As given in Definition 5.1 in Chapter 5, the *security policy* can also be considered as a set of criteria for the provision of security services. The security domain is therefore a logical structure of various components of the *ODP* system that operate under the regulations of the same security policy.

Each security policy is enforced and managed by a *security administrator*. The security administrator is a logical component of the security system in charge of implementing and controlling the operations of the system. The set of tools used by the security administrator will be called the *security manager*. All parameters, access control rules and security attributes needed for operations in a security system will be recorded in the *Security Management Information Base (SMIB)* (see Definitions 5.12 to 5.14 in Chapter 5). The complete security structure and organization in a security domain, i.e. Security Administrator, Security Manager, and Security Management Information Base (SMIB), will constitute one *Security Management Centre (SMC)*.

A secure *ODP* system will be treated as a collection of secure domains interconnected (dynamically) by a number of mutual relations, called *secure associations*. Associations may be established within and between domains, depending on the required connections. Security of the global *ODP* system may be achieved in two autonomous steps: first, security in each domain must be established, verified, and guaranteed, and then establishment and use of secure associations between domains must be considered. This model may therefore be called an *association security model* of a secure *ODP* system. In other words, security in such a model may be achieved in practice by establishing *SMCs*, providing secure communication of users and applications with their local *SMCs* and providing secure cooperation between *SMCs*.

For the purpose of design and implementation of a comprehensive integrated security system, all the resources of the operational environment will be functionally structured into three operational areas: *user area, data processing area,* and *communications area.* This structure may be superimposed on the logical organization of the system resources and formed into security domains. This approach has certain advantages in designing and implementing components of the comprehensive integrated security system. The details of this functional structure will be given in Section 7.2.2.

4.3.2 Security Domains and their Administration

The security domain is a managerial/control concept that defines the scope of a particular security policy [ISO88]. Where the number of security subjects and objects is large, they may be formed into subgroups for ease of management. Such a subgroup is referred to as a *sub-domain*. Normally, the policy of the overall domain will apply to all sub-domains. Thus, a domain covers all or part of a given distributed system.

One authority will dictate the policy for one domain, and another authority will dictate policy for another domain. A successful *secure association* between two or more entities, belonging to different domains, should only be possible if the security policies, services and mechanisms of both end-systems are compatible. Although there should be no logical difference between local activities and remote activities, a local activity may be assured of compatibility within a security policy local to the domain, whereas a remote activity may require interdomain negotiations to ensure effectiveness of an overall security policy. This may be necessary in the case of security incompatibilities between domains. The incompatibilities may be arbitrated and resolved either by negotiation in an association establishment stage or by reference to a higher authority. This situation will be modelled in Chapter 5 as activities within a single domain and activities organized between two or more security domains. In the latter case, some negotiation is necessary in order to establish common sets and levels of security parameters.

Higher level authorities may take the form of *regional* and then *national* committees, that must meet given codes of practice, contractual specifications, or the *ISO* standards (see Figure 4.1). Any authority dictating policy, but not conforming to these standards will by default exclude itself from connectivity within the complete open security framework. A good example of cooperation of entities in an open environment with coordination of higher level authorities is the *X.509* authentication protocol.

Within each domain, the Security Administrator is responsible for the implementation of the domain policy and for assuring its continuing effectiveness. This responsibility includes the *installation* of trusted hardware and software components of the security system; *insertions, modifications,* and *deletions* of various security parameters; *monitoring* day–to–day operations; and *recovery* in case of breach of security or fault conditions.

Within this framework, any user entity or application entity that is allowed by the security policy to use security services, can obtain/provide information securely to other authorized users within the *ODP* environment. A user entity may request access to an object or service in a normal (insecure) mode (either accidentally or intentionally), but if this object or entity is itself subject to the security policy, then that policy will force the security services to be invoked for this activity, or access will not be possible at all. This approach to security policy will account for both human error and attempts at criminal misuse of the system.

The basic conclusion in this section, and therefore in this chapter, is that a compre-hensive security system, to be described later in this book, will be based on potential extensions of the *ISO/OSI* security architecture and will be organized as cooperating security domains.

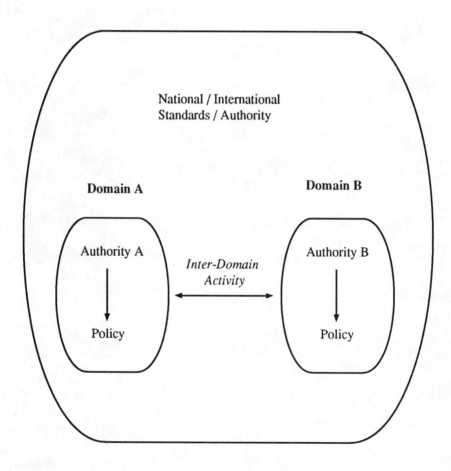

Figure 4.1.   Security Authority and Policy Concept

5

MODELLING SECURITY IN OSI AND ODP SYSTEMS

This chapter deals with the specification of security requirements for open systems, especially for an extended OSI security architecture. The approach is based on formal analysis and the application of formal models. The first section gives the principles of formal modelling and verification of security systems. The second section gives an overview of some of the formal models frequently quoted in the literature, together with an analysis of their adequacy for verification of *OSI* and *ODP* security architectures. Since most of the existing models were developed for analysis of specific security services and mechanisms (usually in closed, dedicated systems), in the third section a new set of security specifications and requirements has been defined and used in Chapter 7 for the design of secure open distributed systems. It is based on the relevant characteristics of the existing formal models, but compared with them it is designed especially for the *OSI* security architecture concept, security services and mechanisms in a distributed environment. The results of the formal analysis of the *OSI* and *ODP* security architectures in this chapter are:

- indications of possible *extensions* of the standard *OSI* security architecture;

- specifications of *requirements* and *properties* of the comprehensive integrated security system for the *OSI* or *ODP* environments;

- *design* and *verification principles* and *criteria* for practical implementations.

These results have been used as guidelines for the design and later verification of the extended *OSI* security architecture of Chapter 3.

5.1 PRINCIPLES OF FORMAL MODELLING, ANALYSIS, AND VERIFICATION OF SECURITY SYSTEMS

Each security system, and therefore its formal model, depends on the corresponding security policy. This means that in order to be secure (by the definition) the security system must conform to the prespecified criteria stated in the security policy.

Definition 5.1 *[ISO88] : Security policy is the set of criteria for provision of security services. It may be rule-based or identity-based.*

A rule-based security policy is based on global rules for all users, which rely on comparison of the sensitivity of the resources being accessed and the possession of corresponding attributes of users, a group of users, or entities acting on behalf of users.

An identity-based security policy is based on identities and/or attributes of users, a group of users, or entities acting on behalf of the users and the resources/objects being accessed.

To achieve a high degree of precision and clarity, a policy is often presented as a *formal security model.* That is, the security model specifies *a set of constraints* and *requirements* about functioning of the target system as well as its security system. Not only does the formalism promote precision when defining the security systems, but it enables verification of formal specifications and also verification of each specific implementation.

The design of a secure system, after establishing a security policy, essentially consists of two steps: *the building of a formal representation* of the system, and its *implementation.* Formal representation may be analysed in order to derive some important *system characteristics* and to detect potential *design errors* prior to the practical implementation.

From the point of view of data security, formal representation essentially provides a basis for determining *whether or not a system is secure,* according to the prespecified criteria, stated in the corresponding security policy. If insecure, the model helps to identify and to detect the design flaws and insufficiencies. Formal representations must be mathematically rigorous enough to be able to prove formally the security of the system in order to determine whether it meets the security constraints and requirements.

With the publication of the *Trusted Computer System Evaluation Criteria (TCSEC)* [DoD83], the *DoD Orange Book,* the issues of formal specification and verification in the design of secure systems are gaining more and more importance. The Orange Book requires that a secure system, classified at *B1* level or above, must have a *formal security model.* An interpretation of the *TCSEC* for a network environment has been recently published as an interpretation for *secure database design.* Similar classification schemes, equivalent to the *TCSEC,* have been proposed in Germany [ZSI89] and in the *UK* [COMM89].

Given such a climate in the field of secure systems design, it is necessary to consider how to use a *formal approach* and *formal models* for the design, analysis and verification of security systems. This allows the designer to demonstrate that the system is actually secure by showing formally that the system conforms to a particular security model.

In general, *modelling* and *verification* of security involves at least the following three global stages:

a. *Definition* of the security policy, security constraints and requirements – *descriptive security model.*

b. Formal *specification* of the security model.

c. *Implementation* of the security system according to the formal model and its *verification* against the security policy.

There are essentially two types of verification processes, namely, *design verification* and *program verification.* Design verification consists of showing consistency between the first two items above, i.e. between the security model and its formal specification; whereas in program verification, the relation between the last two items must be proved, i.e. it is necessary to show that formal specification (the formal model) and the implemented security system are consistent.

It is often the case that a single level of formal specification is not enough. Therefore, a formal model may have several levels, each describing security constraints in successively more detailed terms. The constraints on each level must be shown to imply the constraints on the next lower level, or to put it another way, for the constraints on some level it must be proved that they are consistent with corresponding constraints on the higher level.

The upper level of the abstract model describes security constraints and requirements in a very simple way that can be accepted as the basic definition of security for the system. Successively less abstract levels add details and the representation concerns that are necessary to relate the model to the functional specifications. The lowest, least abstract level, is called the *concrete model.*

In practice, one begins with an abstract top level specification and refines it in a number of stages. Typically two types of refinements are possible: *algorithmic refinement* and *data structure refinement.* In algorithmic refinement, a single operation at the higher level is implemented with calls to lower level operations. Data structure refinement maps data items from the higher level to some detailed configurations of items in the lower level.

Functional specification starts with requirements usually stated in the form of an informal description of the behaviour of the system and the definition of its desired security properties. Some formal modelling may also exist at this level of specification, but this is likely to be used to describe precisely only some aspects of the behaviour. The first level of specification that is entirely expressed in formal terms is usually called the *design specification*. This may also have sublevels starting with the top-level specification. Successively less abstract levels add details and significant representation concerns.

The important difference to note is that the model levels attempt only to constrain the functioning of the system. They have quite different objectives and may be expressed in different languages. However, at some point of this process they must be related. This is usually done at the lowest *model level* and the highest *design specification level*. The objects in the model must be associated with objects in the design and the model constraints applied to the design. The design specifications must then be shown to conform to the constraints.

It is therefore important to notice, since the abstract model may be expressed in a language not closely related to the design, that the concrete model may not be easily related to the design. It is possible to include some mechanisms in the concrete model that are not directly concerned with the constraints. This happens in the effort to produce a concrete model that can easily relate to design specifications.

The same formal model may be used for more than one set of specifications, for the same security system or for different systems. In this case, different concrete models can be derived from a common upper-level model. In this way the same global notion of security may be applied to both security systems, while a different concrete model is used for each of them.

Development of the security model as a series of less abstract models can assist in developing the specifications. Since one wants to be able to verify the correctness of the top-level specifications with respect to the concrete model, it is essential that the two are stated within a common framework. Consequently, with each security model level, one can develop an associated partial specification to reflect the structure and objects in the model. In this way, when the top level specification, which should be complete, is produced, it is easier to associate it with the concrete model and in that case verification should be more tractable.

Furthermore, as each partial specification is developed, one can formally verify its consistency with the associated model level. In this way the correctness of the top--level specification can be established in steps concurrently with the development of the concrete model.

For the described process some special languages have been designed: *Estelle* [BUDK87] and *LOTOS* [BOLO87].

Having considered certain aspects of the development of security models, the next stage is the possible *methodology* that can be applied for the design of secure systems based on the use of formal models. Design methodology includes:

1. Informal specification of security constraints – security model.

2. Development/selection of a suitable representation scheme or formalism.

3. Formal specification of security constraints and system functionalities.

4. Validation/verification – whether the system satisfies specified constraints.

A formal model provides a framework and formalism for the specification of security policies, and for the construction and verification of the corresponding security system. The model must be general enough to cover conveniently all kinds of operational environments and various types of users, resources, operations and requirements. But generality of the approach is not sufficient. To understand formal security requirements and to ensure that the security system really meets those requirements, the detailed behaviour of the global system must be described.

Formal models appearing in the literature and briefly described in the next section are usually concerned with only one aspect (function) of the security system. Even so, some of them have been shown to be undecidable [HARR76].

On the other hand, if efficiently analysable, models usually address only a very special class of simple policies. For some models, that are well established and frequently quoted in the security literature (for instance [BELL73]), it has been shown that, other than being formally correct, they are in fact obvious and trivial, and even inconsistent [McLE87].

In Section 5.3 an attempt is made to overcome all these difficulties when defining and using formal models. The approach is similar to the one which may be found in [CLAR87]. It is basically the following: first, the set of security properties (called "evaluation criteria" [CLAR87]) is established. Next, a formal model is defined in the form of a finite state machine with *states* described by the required security properties, and with *transitions* being actions in the system, such as to preserve the security properties. Finally, appropriate specifications of the security properties of the *ODP* system are derived, so that if guaranteed, the target system will be secure, according to the prespecified requirements. How to guarantee these properties is determined by the particular design and implementation of the security system.

Four types of security models have received significant attention over recent years. They are: *access control models, information flow models, integrity models*, and *authentication models*. In this chapter the following models will be briefly reviewed and their applicability to modelling of the *OSI* and *ODP* environment analysed:

    a. *Access control models:* the model of Bell and LaPadula [BELL73], with some comments and criticism by McLean [McLE87] and the schematic protection model for acyclic attenuating schemes by Sandhu [SAND88].

b. *Models based on information theory:* a lattice information flow model by Denning [DENN76], nondeducibility model by Sutherland [SUTH86] and the model of non-interference by Goguen and Messeguer [GOGU84].

c. *Integrity models:* the model of commercial security policies by Clark and Wilson [CLAR87].

d. *Models of authentication protocols:* two models for authenticated communications, i.e. the model by Sidhu [SIDH86] and the model by Varadharajan [VARA89].

5.2 OVERVIEW OF SECURITY MODELS

5.2.1 Access Control Models

This type of formal model essentially models the control of users' access to data or information. Models usually use two types of components: active components, called *subjects,* and passive components, called *objects.* Security policy (in fact, *access policy*) is a set of rules which determine whether a particular subject should be given access to a particular object. The decision may be based on the protection attributes of the subject and object, or on corresponding security levels, or it may be left to the discretion of the owner of the object. These models are, however, inadequate for real understanding of information protection, because of the existence of *covert channels* even in systems that obey a very tight access control policy. Covert channels exist because there are other sources of information in computer systems besides the storage objects whose availability should be controlled, e.g. various error messages that deny access to some objects, sensitive information generated by retrieval of publicly available data, operational statistics, etc.

5.2.1.1 Bell and LaPadula Access Control Model [BELL73]

Elements of the Model. The definition of the model starts by identifying elements which correspond to components of the real system to be modelled. The authors assume the real system to have multiple users operating concurrently on a common database with multi-level *classifications* for both users and data and need-to-know *categories* associated with both users and data. In the model, subjects (processes) may be considered surrogates for the users.

The elements of the model are shown in the following table (PK in the definition of the function F means the subset of the set K):

Set	Elements	Semantics
S	$\{S_1, S_2, \ldots, S_n\}$	*subjects:* processes, programs in execution
O	$\{O_1, O_2, \ldots, O_m\}$	*objects:* data, files, programs, subjects
C	$\{C_1, C_2, \ldots, C_q\}$ $C_1 > C_2 > \ldots > C_q$	*classifications:* clearance level of a subject, classification of an object
K	$\{K_1, K_2, \ldots, K_r\}$	*need-to-know categories:* project numbers, access privileges
A	$\{A_1, A_2, \ldots, A_p\}$	*access attributes:* read, write, copy, append, owner, control
R	$\{R_1, R_2, \ldots, R_u\}$	*requests:* inputs, commands, requests for access to objects by subjects
D	$\{D_1, D_2, \ldots, D_v\}$	*decisions:* outputs, answers, "yes", "no", "error"
T	$\{1, 2, \ldots, t, \ldots\}$	*indices:* elements of the time set; identification of discrete moments; an element t is an index to request and decision sequences
$P(\alpha)$	all subsets of α	power set of α
α^β	all functions from the set β to the set α	
$\alpha \times \beta$	$\{(a,b) : a \in \alpha, \, b \in \beta\}$	Cartesian product of the sets α and β
F	$C^S \times C^O \times (PK)^S \times (PK)^O$ an arbitrary element of F is written $f = (f_1, f_2, f_3, f_4)$	classification/need-to-know vectors; f_1 : subject-classification function f_2 : object-classification function f_3 : subject-need-to-know function f_4 : object-need-to-know function
X	R^T an arbitrary element of X is written x	request sequences
Y	D^T an arbitrary element of Y is written y	decision sequences
M	$\{M_1, M_2, \ldots, M_{nm2^p}\}$ an element M_k of M is an $n \times m$ matrix with entries from P(A); the (i,j)-entry of M_k shows $S_i's$ access attributes relative to O_j	access matrices
V	$P(S \times O) \times M \times F$	states
Z	V^T an arbitrary element of Z is written z; $z_t \in z$ is the tth state in the state sequence z	state sequences

States of the System. The states of the system are defined in such a way as to embody all the information which is considered pertinent to security considerations.

A state $v \in V$ is a 3-tuple (b, M, f) where

- $b \in P(S \times O)$, indicating which subjects have access to which objects in the state v;

- $M \in M$, indicating the entries of the access matrix in the state v; and

- $f \in F$, indicating the clearance level of all subjects, the classification level of all objects, and the needs-to-know associated with all subjects, and objects in the state v.

State-Transition Relation. Let $W \subseteq R \times D \times V \times V$. The system $\Sigma(R, D, W, z_0) \subseteq X \times Y \times Z$ is defined by $(x, y, z) \in \Sigma(R, D, W, z_0)$, if and only if $(x_t, y_t, z_t, z_{t-1}) \in W$ for each $t \in T$, where z_0 is a specified initial state usually of the form (ϕ, M, f), where ϕ denotes the empty set.

W has been defined as a relation. It can be specialized to be a function, although this is not necessary for the development herein. When considering design questions, however, W will be a function, specifying next-state and next-output. W should be considered intuitively as embodying the rules of operation by which the system in any given state determines its *decision* for a given *request* and moves into a *next state*.

Compromise and Security. A compromise state is defined as follows: $v = (b, M, f) \in V$ is a *compromise state (compromise)*, if there is an ordered pair $(S, O) \in b$ such that:

(i) $f_1(S) < f_2(O)$ or

(ii) $f_3(S) \not\supseteq f_4(O)$.

In other words, v is a compromise if the current allocation of objects to subjects (b) includes an assignment ((S,O)) with at least one of two undesirable characteristics:

(i') S's clearance is lower that O's classification;

(ii')   Subject S does not have some need-to-know category that is assigned to object O.

In order to make later discussions and arguments a little more succinct, a security condition will be defined. $(S, O) \in S \times O$ satisfies the security condition relative to f (*SC rel f*) if:

(iii) $f_1(S) \geq f_2(O)$ and

(iv) $f_3(S) \supseteq f_4(O)$.

A state $v = (b, M, f) \in V$ is a *secure state* if each $(S, O) \in b$ satisfies *SC rel f*. The definitions of secure states and compromise states indicate the validity of the following unproved proposition.

Proposition: $v \in V$ *is not a secure state, iff v is a compromise.*

A state sequence $z \in Z$ has a compromise, if z_t is a compromise for some $t \in T$. z is a secure state sequence, if z_t is a secure state for each $t \in T$. $(x, y, z) \in \Sigma(R, D, W, z_0)$ is called an *appearance* of the system. $(x, y, z) \in \Sigma(R, D, W, z_0)$ is a secure appearance, if z is a secure state sequence. The appearance *(x,y,z)* has a compromise, if z has a compromise.

$\Sigma(R, D, W, z_0)$ is a *secure system*, if every appearance of $\Sigma(R, D, W, z_0)$ is secure. $\Sigma(R, D, W, z_0)$ has a compromise, if any appearance of $\Sigma(R, D, W, z_0)$ has a compromise.

Proposition: $z \in Z$ *is not secure, iff z has a compromise.*

Proposition: $\Sigma(R, D, W, z_0)$ *is not secure, iff* $\Sigma(R, D, W, z_0)$ *has a compromise.*

Basic Security Theorem: Let $W \subseteq R \times D \times V \times V$ be any relation such that $(R_i,\ D_j,\ (b^*, M^*, f^*),\ (b, \bar{M}, f)) \in W$ implies

(i) $f = f^*$ and

(ii) every $(S, O) \in b^* - b$ satisfies *SC rel* f^*.

$\Sigma(R, D, W, z)$ is a secure system for any secure state z_0.

Proof: Let $z_0 = (b^{(0)}, M^{(0)}, f^{(0)})$ be a secure state. Pick $(x, y, z) \in \Sigma(R, D, W, z)$ and write $z_t = (b^{(t)}, M^{(t)}, f^{(t)})$ for each $t \in T$.

z_1 is a secure state. $(x_1, y_1, z_1, z_0) \in W$. Thus by (i), $f^{(1)} = f^{(0)}$. By (ii), every (S,O) in $b^{(1)} - b^{(0)}$ satisfies *SC rel* $f^{(1)}$. Since z_0 is secure, every $(S, O) \in b^{(0)}$ satisfies *SC rel* $f^{(0)}$. Since $f^{(0)} = f^{(1)}$, every $(S, O) \in b^{(1)}$ satisfies *SC rel* $f^{(1)}$. That is, z_1 is secure.

If z_{t-1} is secure, z_t is secure. $(x_t, y_t, z_t, z_{t-1}) \in W$. Thus by (i), $f^{(t)} = f^{(t-1)}$. By (ii), every (S,0) in $b^{(t)} - b^{(t-1)}$ satisfies *SC rel* $f^{(t)}$. Since z_{t-1} is secure, every $(S, 0) \in b^{(t-1)}$ satisfies *SC rel* $f^{(t-1)}$. Since $f^{(t)} = f^{(t-1)}$, every $(S, 0) \in b^{(t)}$ satisfies *SC rel* $f^{(t)}$. That is, z_t is secure. By induction, z is secure so that *(x,y,z)* is a secure appearance. *(x,y,z)* being arbitrary, $\Sigma(R, D, W, z_0)$ is secure.

Notwithstanding the formal precision of the Bell-LaPadula model, McLean has shown that the basic security theorem does not guarantee security for the system [McLE85]. He has shown that a counter example, a system which conforms to an alternative policy, the reverse of that of Bell and LaPadula, is also secure, according to Bell and LaPadula criteria.

This shows that real problems can occur when considering security models: *(1)* is the definition of "security" offered in the model a good one? and *(2)* can it be proved that a real system meets the definition? The Bell-LaPadula model is formulated in terms of *secure states* (security restrictions on state properties) and *secure transforms* (definitions of secure sequences of states). The problem with this approach is that *no redundancy* is provided for checking that the model accurately captures what properties are assumed under *"security"*.

This may be resolved by a definition of security in terms of *secure states* and an alternative definition of *secure transforms*. In that case, it must be proved: *(1)* that if the system starts its operations in a secure state and uses only secure transforms, it will end in a secure state, and *(2)* that if the system goes from a secure state to a new secure state, the corresponding transform must have been secure. These two approaches complement the definition of a secure system and show that the two distinct formulations are identical ([McLE87]).

5.2.1.2 *The Schematic Protection Model (SPM)* [SAND88]

The Schematic Protection Model *(SPM)* is basically an access control model with acyclic attenuating properties. An acyclic property specifies that a user may not (directly or indirectly) create itself as a new user in the system. An attenuating scheme requires that the set of access attributes, assigned to a new subject, is a subset of attributes assigned to its creator. This property means that in the dynamic access control model, a newly created subject should not get more access attributes than its creator.

This model matches the desired properties of generality, i.e. it contains many divergent characteristics of specific access control models and schemes, and has applicability and usefulness in the analysis of various access control schemes.

The key to balancing the conflicting goals of generality and analysis in the *SPM* is the notion of *protection type*. The intuitive concept is that instances of the same protection type are treated uniformly by control privileges. A critical assumption in the *SPM* is that entities are *strongly typed*, that is, every entity is created to be of a specific type, and its type cannot change thereafter.

The *SPM* views the security domain of a subject as having two parts: a static type dependent part defined by the *protection scheme* and a dynamic part consisting of *tickets* (capabilities). The scheme is defined in terms of types by the *security administrator* when a system is first set up and thereafter cannot be changed. The idea is that major policy decisions are built into the scheme, while details are reflected in the initial distribution of tickets.

Tickets are privileges of the form Y/x, where Y identifies some unique entity in the system and the *access right symbol* x authorizes the possessor of this ticket to perform some operation on Y. More generally *the right symbol* x may be the authorization for some particular set of operations on Y. Tickets are unforgeable and cannot be generated at will by a subject.

Types and Right Symbols. The first step in defining a scheme is to specify the disjoint sets of *object types* TO and *subject types* TS. Their union T is the entire set of *entity types*. The idea is that protection types are used to identify classes of entities that share some common attribute. For subjects this may be membership in a department or a particular position of authority in a group. For objects this may be a classification such as an internal document or a public document.

The next step is to define the *right symbols* carried by tickets. The set of right symbols R is partitioned into two disjoint subsets: RI the set of *inert rights* and RC the set of *control rights*. Examples of inert rights are the typical *read, write, execute,* and *append* privileges for a file. Because of the role of inert rights, the symbols in RI require no interpretation for analysis purposes.

Every right symbol x comes in two variations x and xc, where c is the *copy flag*. The only difference between the Y/x and Y/xc tickets is that the former cannot be copied from one domain to another, whereas the latter can. It follows that presence of Y/xc in a domain subsumes the presence of Y/x, but not vice versa.

The remaining components of a scheme are defined in terms of functions and relations involving the sets TS, T, and $T \times R$. The SPM requires that T and R be finite sets, so a scheme is defined by finite sets, relations, and functions. The SPM recognizes three operations that change the protection state: *copy, demand,* and *create*.

The Copy Operation. The copy operation moves a copy of a ticket from the domain of one subject to the domain of another, leaving the original ticket intact. This may be understood as copying a ticket from one subject to another, although technically a ticket is copied from one subject's domain to another's domain. In addition to the copy flag, this operation is authorized by a *link predicate* (denoted by $link_i$), defined by control rights and its associated *filter function* (denoted by f_i), which are all components of the scheme.

Link Predicates. A link predicate takes two subjects, say X and Y, as arguments and evaluates to *true* or *false*. If true, it establishes a connection from X to Y that can be used to copy tickets from the domain of X to the domain of Y. Its definition is in terms of the presence of some combination of control tickets for X and Y in the domains of X and Y.

Filter Functions. The final condition required for authorizing a copy operation is defined by the corresponding filter function $f_i: TS \times TS \to 2^{T \times R}$. The interpretation is that $Y/x{:}c$ can be copied from $dom(A)$ to $dom(B)$ if and only if all of the following are true for some i, where the types of A, B, and Y are a, b and y, respectively.

    (i) $Y/xc \in dom(A)$,

    (ii) $link_i$ (A,B),

    (iii) $y/x{:}c \in f_i(a, b)$.

The filter functions are a powerful tool for specifying security policies. They impose mandatory controls that are inviolable and confine the discretionary behaviour of individual subjects. Some sample values for $f(a,b)$ are $T \times R$, $TO \times RI$, and ϕ. In the first case all types of tickets can be copied from a subject of type a to a subject of type b, provided the corresponding link predicate is true. In the second case, only inert tickets for objects can be copied, whereas in the third case no tickets can be copied.

The Demand Operation. The demand operation allows a subject to obtain tickets simply by demanding them. A scheme authorizes this operation by the *demand function* $d: TS \to 2^{T \times R}$. The interpretation of $a/x{:}c \in d(b)$ is that every subject of type b can demand the ticket $A/x{:}c$ for every entity A of type a.

Demand is a method for specifying implicit distribution of tickets. If $a/x{:}c \in d(b)$, then every subject of type b has the ability to access every entity of type a, including those that will be created some time in the future.

The Create Operation. The create operation introduces new subjects and objects into the system. There are two issues here: What types of entities can be created and which tickets are introduced as the immediate result of a create operation?

Authorization. The first issue is specified in a scheme by the *can–create* relation $cc \subseteq TS \times T$. The interpretation is that subjects of type a are authorized to create entities of type b, if and only if $cc(a,b)$.

Create-Rules. The tickets introduced by a create operation are specified by a *create-rule* for every pair in cc. Let subject A of type a create entity B of type b. If B is an object, the create-rule $cr(a,b)$ tells which tickets for B are placed in $dom(A)$ as a result of this operation. If B is a subject, the create-rule must also tell which tickets for A are placed in $dom(B)$.

Summary and Discussion. In summary, the Schematic Protection Model requires the Security Administrator to specify a protection scheme by defining the following components:

    1. A finite set of entity types T partitioned into subject types TS and object types TO.

2. A finite set of right symbols R partitioned into inert rights RI and control rights RC.

3. A finite collection of local link predicates $\{link_i \mid i = 1 \ldots N\}$.

4. A filter function $f_i : TS \times TS \rightarrow 2^{T \times R}$.

5. The demand function $d : TS \rightarrow 2^{T \times R}$.

6. The can-create relation $cc \subseteq TS \times T$. Equivalently, $cc : TS \rightarrow 2^T$.

7. A local create-rule for each pair in cc.

A *system* is specified by defining a protection scheme and the initial protection state, that is, the initial set of entities and the initial distribution of tickets. Thereafter, the protection state evolves by *copy, demand,* and *create* operations. The system is secure if every cc relation satisfies acyclic attenuating properties in transfer of access attributes.

5.2.2 Models based on Information Theory

One approach in the modelling of computer security is to use models based on information theory. There are two types: *nondeducibility models*, which are mainly concerned with *information sharing,* and *noninterference models*, which are based on the quantity of information generated by some process or user.

Nondeducibility models are based on the process called *information flow* which is more appropriate to compartmentalization than to security [McLE90]. Two models of this type will be described in this section: the information flow model by Denning [DEN76] and the nondeducibility model by Sutherland [SUTH86].

The information flow concept focuses on actual operations which transfer information between objects. Such models attempt to explain ways in which information may be compromised in a computer system, at system register, program variable or even at the bit level. Analyses based on such models may be used to discover covert channels. This is not to say that flow models eliminate the need for access control models. Access control models are still useful for specification of *access policies*.

Information flow models treat the system as an abstract *state transition machine*. The current state of the machine refers to the assignment of values to variables. A transition causes information to flow from one variable to another. This is the case when the new value of a variable is dependent on the old value or on values of some other variables. Consider, for instance, the statement: *IF X THEN Y = Z*. Here there is a flow of information from the variable X to Y. This type of *implicit flow* will not be recognized by an ordinary data flow analysis. However it may not be possible to detect *timing channels;* this depends on whether it is possible to specify the necessary timing information.

5.2.2.1 Lattice Model of Secure Information Flow [DENN76]

An information flow model (denoted as *FM*) is defined as the 5-tuple:
$FM = < N, P, SC, \oplus, \rightarrow >$.

$N = \{a, b, \ldots\}$ is a set of logical *storage objects* or information receptacles. Elements of N may be files, segments, or even program variables, depending on the level of detail under consideration. Each user of the system may also be regarded as an object. $P = \{p, q, \ldots\}$ is a set of *processes*. Processes are the active components responsible for all information flows.

$SC = \{A, B, \ldots\}$ is a set of security classes corresponding to disjoint classes of information. They are intended to encompass, but are not limited to, the familiar concepts of "security classifications", "security categories", and "need-to-know". Each object a is bound to a security class, denoted by $\underline{a}$, which specifies the security class associated with the information stored in a. There are two methods of binding objects to security classes: *static binding*, where the security class of an object is constant, and *dynamic binding*, where the security class of an object varies with its contents. Users may be bound, usually statically, to security classes referred to as "security clearances". Each process p may also be bound to a security class, which is denoted by $\underline{p}$. In this case, $\underline{p}$ may be determined by the security clearance of the user owning p or by the history of security classes to which p has had access.

The class-combining operator " $\oplus$ " is an associative and commutative binary operator that specifies, for any pair of operand classes, the class in which the result of any binary function on values from the operand classes belongs. The class of the result of any binary function on objects a and b is thus $\underline{a} \oplus \underline{b}$. By extension, the class of the value of an n-ary function $f(a_1, \ldots, a_n)$ is $\underline{a}_1 \oplus \cdots \oplus \underline{a}_n$. To avoid semantic ambiguities that may arise when two different functions over the same domain have overlapping ranges, it will be assumed that the operator " $\oplus$ " is independent of the function used to combine values. No generality is lost by this assumption, since the effect of a function-dependent operation " $\oplus$ " can be simulated by an appropriate set of processes using a function-independent operation " $\oplus$ ". The set of security classes is closed under operation " $\oplus$ "

A *flow relation* " $\rightarrow$ " is defined on pairs of security classes. For classes A and B, the flow relation $A \rightarrow B$ exists, if and only if information in class A is permitted to flow into class B. Information is said to flow from class A to class B whenever information associated with A affects the value of information associated with B. In this model the concern is only with flows which result from (sequences of) operations that cause information to be *transferred* from one object to another (e.g. copying, assignment, I/O, parameter passing, and message sending). This includes flows along "legitimate" and "storage" channels. The model is not concerned with flows along "covert" channels (i.e. a process's effect on the system load). This shows the general classification of this model into a group of nondeducibility models. These models do not control possible information flows (leakage) along implicit "covert" channels by generation of information during operations of the system. The latter class of models is therefore called noninterference models.

The security requirements of the model are simply stated: *a flow model FM is secure if and only if execution of a sequence of operations cannot give rise to a flow that violates the relation* " $\rightarrow$ " . If a value $f(a_1, \ldots, a_n)$ flows to an object b that is statically bound to a security class $\underline{b}$, then $\underline{a}_1 \oplus \cdots \oplus \underline{a}_n \rightarrow \underline{b}$ must hold. If $f(a_1, \ldots, a_n)$ flows to a dynamically bound object b, then the class of b must be updated (if necessary) so that $\underline{a}_1 \oplus \cdots \oplus \underline{a}_n \rightarrow \underline{b}$ holds for this case also. Assuming that flow relation " $\rightarrow$ " is transitive, it is easily shown that the security of individual operations implies that of arbitrary sequences of operations.

Enforcement of Security

The primary difficulty with guaranteeing security lies in *detecting* (and *monitoring*) all flow causing operations. This is because not all such operations in a program are explicitly specified or indeed even executed! As an example, consider the statement **if** $a=0$ **then** $b := 0$; if $b \neq 0$ initially, testing $b=0$ on termination of this statement is equivalent to knowing whether $a=0$ or not. In other words, information flows from a to b regardless of whether or not the **then** clause is executed. This means that values of some variables may be *deduced* by knowing some other information and not by reading those variables directly (the problem which is covered by access control models).

To deal with this problem, one must distinguish between two types of information flow: "explicit" and "implicit". *Explicit flow* to an object b occurs as the result of executing any statement (e.g. assignment or I/O) that directly transfers to b information derived from operands $a_1, \ldots, a_n$. *Implicit flow* to b occurs as the result of executing or not executing a statement that causes an explicit flow to b when the statement is conditioned on the value of an expression. To illustrate the difference: the statement **if** $a=0$ **then** $b := c$ causes an explicit flow from c to b only when $a=0$ and the assignment to b is performed, but it causes an implicit flow from a to b irrespective of the truth of $a=0$.

To specify the security requirements of programs causing implicit flows, it is convenient to consider an abstract representation of programs that preserves the flows, but not necessarily all of the original structure. An abstract program (or statement) S is defined recursively by:

  (i) S is an elementary statement; e.g. assignment or I/O.

  (ii) There exist S_1 and S_2 such that $S = S_1; S_2$.

  (iii) There exist $S_1, \ldots, S_m$ and m-valued variable c such that
        $S = c : S_1, \ldots, S_m$.

Step (i) declares simple statements as abstract programs. Step (ii) declares sequences of simpler programs as abstract programs. Step (iii) declares conditional structures, in which the value of a variable selects among alternative programs, as abstract programs. Implicit flows can occur only in type (iii) structures.

The conditional structure is used to represent all conditional (including iterative) statements found in programming languages. For example, **if** c **then** S_1 **else** S_2 is represented by $c : S_1, S_2$. Both **if** c **then** S_1 and **while** c **do** S_1 are represented by $c : S_1$, and **do case** c **of** $S_1; \ldots; S_m$ is represented by $c : S_1, \ldots, S_m$. When an expression e selects among alternative programs S_1, ..., S_m, the representation $c := e; c : S_1$, ..., S_m will be used. Structures arising from the unrestricted use of **go to** statements can also be represented by the conditional structure, but to do so requires a control flow analysis of the program to determine the set of statements directly conditioned on the values of a variable.

The *security requirements* for any program of the above form are now stated simply. First, an elementary statement S is secure if any explicit flow caused by S is secure. Specifically, if S replaces the contents of an object b with a value derived from objects $a_1, \ldots, a_n$ ($a_i = b$ for some a_i is possible), then security requires that $\underline{a}_1 \oplus \cdots \oplus \underline{a}_n \to \underline{b}$ hold after execution of S. If b is dynamically bound to its class, it may be necessary to update $\underline{b}$ when S is executed. Second, $S = S_1; S_2$ is secure if both S_1 and S_2 are individually secure (because of the transitivity of " $\to$ "). Third, $S = c : S_1, \ldots, S_m$ is secure if each S_k is secure and all implicit flows from c are secure. Specifically, let $b_1, \ldots, b_n$ be the objects into which S specifies explicit flows (i.e. $i = 1, \ldots, n$ implies that, for each b_i, there is an operation in some S_k that causes an explicit flow to b_i); then all implicit flows are secure if $\underline{c} \to \underline{b}_i (1 \leq i \leq n)$, or equivalently $\underline{c} \to \underline{b}_1 \otimes \cdots \otimes \underline{b}_n$, holds after execution of S. If b_i is dynamically bound to its security class, it may be necessary to update $\underline{b}_i$ by $\underline{b}_i := \underline{b}_i \oplus \underline{c}$.

5.2.2.2 Nondeducibility Model by Sutherland [SUTH86]

This model states that information should flow in the system from objects classified at the high classification level to objects at some lower classification level if and only if some possible assignment of values to the low-level objects in the system security state is incompatible with the possible assignment of values to the state's high level objects. Let H denote the assertion that the system will reach the state that realizes the assignment with respect to the system's high-level objects, and equivalently L for low level objects. Let $p(H)$ and $p(L)$ denote probabilities that assertions H and L are true. The *nondeducibility requirement* states that there is no information flow from H to L if and only if, for all assignments to system objects, probability $p(H) > 0$ and $P(L) > 0 \to p(H|L) > 0$.

This model accommodates the bidirectional concept of information flow by a method of compartmentalization, but counter examples may be found where high-level output may be generated from low-level input. This is the major weakness of nondeducibility models. Good examples of this problem may be found in [DENN87B].

5.2.2.3 Noninterference Models

The Goguen and Messeguer noninterference model [GOGU82] is also based on information theory. This model states that a system is secure if noninterference is guaranteed, i.e. if a system's low-level output is independent of its high-level input. This independency is in the sense that for any system with output function $out(u,I)$, whose value is the output generated by input history I to user u, $out(u,I) = out(u,I^*)$, where I^* is I purged of all inputs from users with security levels that are greater than u's level. This model implies (requires) that a user may not interfere with any confidential information that is out of his processing history. The output function assumes that the input history I is a deterministic sequence of states.

The problem of protecting high-level output is even more serious for systems with non-deterministic history [McCU87]. In such systems, a system provides noninterference if, for every legal trace of the system and every alteration which can be made to that trace by deleting or inserting high-level inputs, there is a legal trace that is equivalent to the first trace, except perhaps with respect to high-level outputs. This concept is called *generalized noninterference*. However, for generalized noninterference, there must be an assumption (which is not generally true) that a program or a user cannot generate high-level output if it is given solely low-level input. This has been mentioned as not being generally true [DENN87].

5.2.3 Integrity Models

Another important goal of a formal security model is to ensure the *integrity of information* to prevent fraud and errors. The security community has primarily concentrated on the *confidentiality aspect;* however, recently there has been increased interest in the integrity issue, especially after the model proposed by Clark and Wilson [CLAR87].

Integrity is a property of those processes (subjects) and information (objects) that meet an a priori expectation (specification) of a level of quality that is considered acceptable for a particular application. Therefore, a metric (model) for integrity must consist of *(1)* a specified set of rules (integrity requirements), *(2)* a measure of trust or confidence (in subjects, resources or information involved in system operations), and *(3)* an acceptable authority to determine, verify and enforce the integrity requirements and specifications.

5.2.3.1 Clark and Wilson Model

The Clark and Wilson model is based essentially on the notion of *well-formed transactions* and *separation of duties.* The well-formed transaction allows only constrained manipulation of information, thereby preserving or ensuring its integrity. The separation of duties attempts to ensure *external consistency* of information objects, that is, the correspondence between the information object and the real world it represents.

The essence of the model, which is concerned with integrity of computer systems, consists of two types of rules, called *certification rules* and *enforcement rules.* Those rules are the following:

C1: *(Certification)* All *Integrity Verification Procedures (IVPs)* must properly ensure that all *Constrained Data Items (CDIs)* are in a valid state at the time the *IVP* is run.

C2: All *Transformation Procedures (TPs)* must be certified to be valid. That is, they must take a *CDI* to a valid final state, given that it is in a valid state to begin with. For each *TP*, and each set of *CDIs* that it may manipulate, the security officer must specify a "relation", which defines that execution. A relation is thus of the form: *[TPi, (CDIa, CDIb, CDIc,...)]*, where the list of *CDIs* defines a particular set of arguments for which the *TP* has been certified.

E1: *(Enforcement)* The system must maintain the list of relations specified in rule *C2*, and must ensure that only manipulation of any *CDI* is by a *TP*, where the *TP* is operating on the *CDI* as specified in some of the integrity enforcement relations.

E2: The system must maintain a list of relations of the form: *[User ID, TPi, (CDIa, CDIb, CDIc,...)]*, which relates a user, a *TP*, and the data objects that *TP* may reference on behalf of that user. It must ensure that only executions described in one of the relations are performed.

C3: The list of relations in *E2* must be certified to meet the segregation of duty requirement.

E3: The system must authenticate the identity of each user attempting to execute a *TP*.

C4: All *TPs* must be certified to write to an append-only *CDI* (the log) all information necessary to permit the nature of the operation to be reconstructed.

C5: Any *TP* that takes an *Unconstrained Data Item (UDI)* as an input value must be certified to perform only valid transformations, or else no transformations, for any possible value of the *UDI*. The transformation should take the input from a *UDI* to a *CDI*, or the *UDI* is rejected. Typically, this is an edit program.

E4: Only the agent permitted to certify entities may change the list of such entities associated with a *CDI* and list of users associated with a *TP*. An agent that can certify an entity may not have any execute rights with respect to that entity.

Clark and Wilson did not define the notion of integrity, but their approach was to ensure that certain objects (data or programs) or modifications to previously existing objects are the results of actions by authorized users, effected through sufficiently trusted programs, as to guarantee the integrity of the result. They propose to accomplish this by requiring that *CDIs* can only be manipulated by a restricted set of *TPs*, in accordance with rules which ensure that all such transformations are *"well-formed"*. In some systems which operate in a distributed environment, it may be particularly important that the well-formed transaction be carried out as a single atomic activity.

Unfortunately, the Clark and Wilson inductive model is not very useful, for it cannot be assumed that a *TP* has knowledge of the entire (distributed) system [JUEN89]. Since a *TP* cannot have a global view of what constitutes a valid data input, but can only process data in accordance with the information it has available, defined in a local security policy, it follows that a valid output of one *TP* may be judged invalid by another *TP*, especially if they run in different security domains.

The Clark and Wilson induction must therefore be modified to state that, if all the *IVPs* and *TPs* are certified as valid *with respect to a particular domain,* and if all the *CDIs* are valid with respect to that same domain, and if only *TPs* that have been certified valid are allowed to access the *CDIs*, then all of the *CDIs* will remain valid with respect to that domain only. Since it depends on certain properties of TPs, it may be concluded that the integrity of a process (and data it manipulates) is probabilistic, not a binary property, and can only be defined relative to a specified integrity (security) domain [JUEN89].

5.2.4 Models of the Authentication Protocols

Authentication protocols provide authenticated communication between two or more parties in a network environment. The essence of these protocols includes private communication, authentication of parties, message authentication and digital signatures. Models of those protocols usually treat the sender and the receiver symmetrically and make no assumptions about any specific time ordering of events.

In both models described in this section, the protocol is first specified using a finite state machine concept. Then some important properties of the protocol are verified. The finite state machine model may also be used for automatic verification of correctness and other important properties of the authentication protocols.

5.2.4.1 Sidhu's Model of the Authentication Protocols

The finite state machine model in [SIDH86] is applied to two authentication protocols, based on symmetric and asymmetric encryption, from [NEED78].

The two authentication protocols are designed with two properties in mind: *(1)* the sender and the receiver have symmetrical roles, and *(2)* no assumption is made about any specific time ordering of events. The first property of the protocol is needed because the lack of it would require that an entity or a process in the role of sender and receiver must use completely different protocols to communicate with another process. The second property helps in getting around the difficult problem of process synchronization in a distributed environment. The solution to this problem is to build into the protocol all possible time ordering of events that can conceivably take place between two communicating entities in the network.

The author shows that the two authentication protocols from [NEED78] possess the following properties:

- completeness;

- deadlock freeness;

- livelock or tempo-blocking freeness;

- termination;

- boundedness;

- absence of non-executable interactions.

Completeness means that the protocol accepts all inputs, i.e. there are no unspecified receptions in the directed graph representation of the protocol. *Deadlock freeness* means that the protocol never gets into an overall system state such that no more transmissions are possible and the system stays in that state indefinitely. *Livelock* or *tempo-blocking freeness* means that the protocol does not get into any looping through a set of system states. The *termination* property implies that the protocol always reaches a well-defined final state when started from the initial state. *Boundedness* means that the maximum number of messages in each channel is always less than or equal to the maximum capacity for that channel. The *absence of non-executable interactions* means that the protocol does not contain any reception, transmission or an interaction path that cannot be realized under normal operating conditions. Note that no claim is being made that the protocol properties (1)-(6) are all independent.

5.2.4.2 Varadharajan's Model of the Authentication Protocols

The authentication protocol used for formal analysis is independent of any specific algorithm used and resembles peer entity authentication mechanisms described in ISO/TC97/SC20/WG1 [ISO87B] and the Needham–Schroder protocol [NEED78]. It assumes the existence of a network authority called the key distribution centre *(KDC)* which plays an important role in distributing the necessary keys between the two parties to have a secure communication.

The protocol may be considered as a collection of communicating processes, one process for each entity in the protocol. Each entity in the protocol is represented as a finite state machine. The inputs and outputs of these machines are messages directed to other machines. A state transition is caused by *send-message* and *receive-message* events.

In addition to the communicating entities, the network consists of channels to hold the messages in transit. A separate channel is assumed between each pair of the processes. One can also consider a slightly different arrangement whereby only a single buffer is provided for all undelivered messages. In such a situation, the identity of the receiving entity of a message is determined from the message contents.

Some of the typical formal properties of the protocol which were studied by Varadharajan include the following:

- The protocol always accepts all inputs whatever path it takes – *completeness.*

- The protocol does not get into a state where no more transitions are possible and the system stays in that state indefinitely – *deadlock freedom.*

- The protocol does not get into looping of a subset of system states – *livelock freedom.*

- The protocol always reaches a well-defined final state when started from the initial state – *termination.*

- The maximum number of messages in the channel is bounded – *boundedness.*

The execution of a protocol can be viewed as a sequence of states. Temporal logic seems to be a natural technique that can be used to reason over sequences of states. In general, temporal logic is an extension of classical propositional or predicate logic, with additional temporal operators that state the time-dependent behaviour. The ordinary logic is used for reasoning about properties that are time independent, while temporal operators specify the time-dependent behaviour. In particular, one can reason whether a property P will be true at some future instant. Note that it is also possible to reason about the past behaviour using past temporal logic operators.

Varadharajan has shown that simple authentication protocols possess some of the desired formal properties. These include completeness, deadlock freedom, livelock freedom, termination and boundedness. The model checker provides an effective way for automatic verification of such properties. Interpretation of such properties within the protocol context may be used for analysis of the significant key distribution aspects.

However, such analysis becomes difficult as the number of states increases. This is the state explosion problem associated with this type of state machine analysis. Therefore, this type of formal model is used mainly for analysis of single security services, and implemented only by specific mechanisms and protocols.

5.2.5 OSI Security Systems and Applicability of Existing Formal Models

The basis for a formal analysis of the *OSI* security framework is the concept of a *security domain*. A security domain is a homogeneous security environment defined by a specific *security policy*. Since there can be many security policies imposed by the administrators of distributed open systems, each of these policies defines a separate security domain. This means that all entities within a single security domain are subject to a single security policy, administered by a single authority with the same type of available security services and mechanisms. A single security domain may be a large host machine with its local users, a local area network, all the computing facilities within some department, a wide area network used by a corporation, etc. Security domains may be interconnected by various computing structures, in the most general case by a large *OSI* system.

A security domain is therefore a subset of users and resources of the global *OSI* environment, conforming to the same security policy. *The security policy*, as defined by *ISO*, is the set of criteria for the provision of security services. A security policy states, in general terms, what is and is not permitted during the general operations of the open system in question.

The conceptual model of the *ODP* security architecture can consist of a number of co-operating security domains. This will be the basis for later formal analysis of *ISO/OSI* Security Architecture, so the security domain may be defined formally by the following definition:

Definition 5.2 *(Security Domain): A security domain, as a homogeneous security environment, consists of the following logical components :*

1. *A unique security policy, i.e. a set of criteria and requirements for provision of security services.*

2. *A single (logical) Security Administrator, to enforce and control implementation of the security policy in the local environment.*

3. *A single (logical) Security Manager, a set of tools and modules needed for management of security services and mechanisms, system resources and SMIB components.*

4. *A set of uniformly available modules for provision of security services and mechanisms needed to enforce elements of security policy.*

5. *Other security resources and functions, necessary for   security-relevant
   functions, such as auditing, verification, recovery, etc.*

All details of components of security domains, i.e. Security Management Centres, will
be specified in Chapter 7.

In order to analyse the applicability of the formal models briefly described earlier in
this chapter, the following approach will be used. First, relevant *functions (operations)*
of the *OSI* system will be synthesized, and after that significant *security constraints*
for each of these functions will be defined. Then the applicability of *OSI* security
services to each of the relevant functions will be analysed in order to meet the security
constraints. Finally, on this basis, the applicability of the described formal models
will be considered.

Analysis of the five security services suggested by *ISO* (Section 2.1.2) reveals that the
OSI security architecture implicitly assumes the following types of users (entities),
data, and processes in the *OSI* system:

A. *Users.* Users are classified into two types: those allowed to use the *OSI* system,
therefore registered in the *SMIB* (and subsequently called *legal users*), and those who
are not allowed to use the *OSI* system (called *intruders* or *illegal users*). Legal users are
further structured in two types: ordinary, *regular users,* and *security administrators,*
the special users authorized to access the *SMIB*. The *OSI* security architecture defines
security labels, which may be a tool for finer classification of legal users, but this is
not relevant for the current analysis.

B. *Data.* Data appears in the *OSI* security architecture in various forms; as *messages*
transferred along communication lines and data in host systems (records in databases,
application data, etc.). There are two implicit types of data in the *OSI* system relevant
for security analysis: *regular data* and *control data*. Regular data are the resources
of the *OSI* system which must be protected. Control data is information needed by
various security structures (services, mechanisms, Security Managers, etc.) in order
to enforce security in the open system. Control data within each security domain
is *stored* in the *SMIB* and exchanged between security domains by special security
management protocols.

C. *Processes.* Processes, like users (entities) in *OSI* systems, are classified into *legal* and *illegal* processes. Legal processes are further classified into regular processes,
called *application processes,* which in this context need protection, and *security processes,* whose function is to provide security in the *OSI* system. This second category
includes all software and hardware implementations of security services and mechanisms, security management modules, various security agents, etc.

The first characteristic of all *OSI* security services is that they protect only the *legal
users* and their *resources* against *illegal users.* No distinction is made between legal

users in terms of *mutual trust* or *level of competence.* The second characteristic is protection of resources (data) *in transfer.* All security services in the *OSI* security architecture, which are not directly concerned with communication aspects, are in fact designed to support these activities (authentication, access control or non repudiation). Finally, the object of *OSI* security services is *data (messages)* and not *information* conveyed. Therefore, an important characteristic of the *OSI* security services is that they protect only the "structure" of messages (their format, content, origin (sender), target (receiver), etc.) and not the information (meaning) conveyed or the impact of the receipt of messages.

Therefore the applicability of the models described to the *OSI* security architecture is limited. The model by Bell and La Padula and the SPM are primarily access control models and they may be used only for verification of an access control security service. Even in this case, that service must be further extended and defined more precisely, since in the current form it does not possess all properties, rules and operations required by both of those models.

Information flow models are concerned with the flow of information between two users with different security classes. As mentioned earlier:

a. Security classes of entities are not defined by the *OSI* security architecture (although they may be imposed by *labelling* of users).

b. Information dissemination is not a primary concern of the *OSI* security architecture, but only the *transfer of messages,* although the former may be imposed by the later.

In order for this type of model to be applied to the *OSI* security architecture, the architecture needs substantial extensions, interpretations and additional definitions. Even in that case, the scope of information flow models would be rather limited, since they could only be applied possibly to three services of *OSI* security (entity authentication, data confidentiality, and non-repudiation).

Authentication models may be directly applied to the entity authentication service, provided that this service is implemented by one of the protocols described in [NEED78]. They appear to be the most applicable to *OSI* security services from all described models, since they were designed for verification of only one security service, and only for specific implementation of that service. This situation reveals in fact the conflicting goals in modelling of security systems: generality of models and their applicability [SAND88].

Conclusions

The following conclusions may be reached concerning the applicability of the described formal models for verification of the *OSI* security architecture:

1. Most of the existing formal models are concerned with the functioning of a single system with sequential scheduling of operations or with some specially designed computer networks [GLAS87].

2. Some models deal with aspects that are not so relevant for the *OSI* security architecture (information flow), and others with a limited number of security services.

3. The most applicable models are those concerned with particular implementations of specific security services.

If one of these existing models is used for verification of the *OSI* security architecture, then that architecture must be further extended, defined and elaborated, which may result in it being well beyond the scope of its primary purpose. Even in that case the scope of applicability of these models is limited to one or two security services.

The main reasons for this situation are that some of the existing security models are concerned with aspects which are only part of the *OSI* security architecture, some are concerned with security services not covered by the *OSI* security architecture, and none of them is concerned with distributed computing structures, such as *OSI*.

Most of the existing models are defined for specific operational environments, with specific operations, security constraints and problems, while *OSI* is a general, distributed, global environment. Most of the existing models are designed to verify particular security services and their implementations, and not concepts of security architecture, such as the *OSI* security architecture.

The most important and useful properties of all the existing models are, in fact, their approach and the achieved results. They can be used as principles for modelling the *OSI* security architecture, which is described in the text that follows. A new approach is suggested for modelling a general distributed open environment, and it will be used for the specification and verification of security requirements in the *OSI* and *ODP* security architectures.

5.3 SPECIFICATION OF SECURITY REQUIREMENTS
FOR ODP SYSTEMS

5.3.1 The Structure of a Secure ODP System

The analysis in this section is based on a general concept of functional systems. Such systems consist of two abstract sets: a set of *objects* and a set of *relations* between objects. Objects have an internal structure and properties, so that a dynamic internal state is defined by state variables relevant to the context. The relations between objects are in fact *associations,* modelling interactions between associated objects. Through interactions it may be possible to initiate *actions* with objects. In this way actions change the internal state variables of objects and thus the whole system changes its global state.

When modelling *ODP* systems on this basis, the whole system will be considered as a collection of active objects interacting with each other and a collection of passive objects, being used by active objects. Any relationship between two or more active or passive objects in the system may be considered an *association*. If the object is active, it will be called an *entity*. Entities may initiate actions in the *ODP* system which consequently change system states. The entity can also respond to some initiating interaction, coming from some other entity. The entity may be a person (user of the system), database process, communication process, directory or some other functionally compact group of subfunctions able to act as a relatively independent party in a global system environment.

The entity may consist of subfunctions capable of carrying out useful activities on other entities or objects. These capabilities are indicated to other entities or objects by some form of a parameter vector, consisting of components called *capability attributes*. The capability attributes provide a means for selecting the common subset of functions to be performed between two or more entities. The capability attributes also reflect the internal security structure of the entity.

The entity needs certain resources to perform some actions. The resources are passive by their nature and are owned, at least temporarily, by entities. These are various types of resources, for example: application data, files, disk devices, communication channels, printers, etc. For the purpose of formal modelling, it will be assumed that entities use resources only via the appropriate service functions of the corresponding owner entity.

The entity is identified by its *identity vector* containing the name(s) of the entity and other attributes used for identity validation. In the interaction the entities are referred to by their names, while in some other protocols, several identification attributes may be used [FIAT87].

The state variables reflect the internal temporal and dynamically changeable configuration of the entity (object). Since this section is devoted to modelling of secure *ODP* systems, security must be maintained at all times. The secure system has thus invariant security properties, satisfying corresponding security assertion rules or procedures. The assertion rules may be functions of the security property attributes, indicating whether the system is secure or not. In this section those security properties for secure *ODP* systems will be defined.

Security in any computing structure can be defined as the *property of the structure to perform correctly all its operations and to guarantee the correct status of all resources, in accordance with strictly and formally defined rules, specifications, and principles*

[MUFT92B]. Some authors extend this concept to *dependable operations*, where dependability simply means *continuous availability* and *quality of services* provided by that structure [RUSH86].

A *secure computing structure* will be defined to have the following four security properties:

Definition 5.3 *(Authenticity): The property that the identity of each element of the system may be unambiguously established and validated, i.e. that each element of the system is always the one claimed or required.*

Definition 5.4 *(Integrity): The property that all resources in the system are always available in a "high quality" form, i.e. that the content, meaning, structure, and function of each resource are always available and preserved in the correct form.*

Definition 5.5 *(Confidentiality): The property that existence, sources, targets, content, meaning or structure of system resources are not made available or disclosed in any way to unauthorized entities.*

Definition 5.6 *(Authorization): The property that all actions in the system are always initiated, executed and terminated in accordance with requirements and constraints of the security policy.*

Comments:

1. Interpretation. The first property of a secure computer system guarantees that only legal entities (users or programs) may use the system, i.e. its resources. The next two properties are concerned with resources: they guarantee that they are always available, their content, meaning or function (in case of programs) are always correct and also protected, even from legal, but unauthorized users. Integrity, with appropriate interpretation, also includes availability. Confidentiality also includes anonymous activities in the system. Finally, authorization classifies legal users and available, but confidential, resources into authorized mutual relations.

2. Mutual relations. With additional or alternative interpretations, some of the four properties may appear as "overlapping". For instance, if authorization is provided, then confidentiality may be assumed, since violation of confidentiality is never in accordance with authorization. If originality of entities is assumed under authenticity, then this property may include integrity, if applied to resources. The proposed structure with four security properties is balanced between a small number of properties and their precise definition.

3. Granularity. The four security properties may be further "synthesized" or some additional properties may be added, but this is more a matter of semantic interpretation. For instance, all four properties may be synthesized into *dependability* [RUSH86], *confidentiality* may be assumed as provision of integrity of the content (illegal disclosure), *reliability* or *availability* may be added or interpreted as special aspects of integrity, etc. The four properties offer a balance between a minimal number of distinguished properties and their still acceptable understanding and interpretation.

4. Terminology. Some terms used in Definitions 5.5–5.8 have not yet been precisely defined (like identity, validation, unauthorized entities, etc.), but they will be defined shortly.

Following the approach by McLean [McLE87], two definitions of a secure system will be given: the one in terms of *secure states* and another in terms of *secure transforms*.

Definition 5.7 : A computing structure is *secure*, if in all its states the four properties: authenticity, integrity, confidentiality, and authorization are preserved.

Definition 5.8 : A computing structure is *secure*, if all its transforms preserve the four properties: authenticity, integrity, confidentiality, and authorization.

Of course, procedures to verify the four properties of the states and of the transforms are different.

The system designed in accordance with the model defined later in this section will be proved to be secure on the basis of the following two properties:

1. If the system is transformed from a *secure state* to some new state by some *secure transform,* then the new state will also be *secure.*

2. If the system is transformed from a *secure state* to some new *secure state,* then it must have been transformed by some *secure transform.*

As given above, each *ODP* system consists of *entities* and *resources*, while functioning of the system is represented by *actions* (*operations*), performed under principles of open systems in the distributed environment. In a *secure ODP system*, entities and resources have certain (security) characteristics, affected by system operations, but with the four properties preserved for each system state and for each operation.

Let $ID = \{id_1, id_2, \ldots\}$ be a finite set of elements, which may be used to identify resources of the *ODP* system, and which will be called *resource identities*. In the case of entities, these elements may be intrinsic to the entity being identified, or else extrinsic and private information assigned to the legitimate entity and (presumably) not known to an impersonator. Various elements may be used as entity identities, such as character strings, passwords, knowledge of an algorithm, location, possession of some special devices, etc.

Let $C = \{c_1, c_2, c_3, \ldots\}$ be a finite set of security parameters (characteristics) which may be used to enforce that *(a)* activities of each entity, and *(b)* use of each resource is always performed in accordance with the security policy. The elements of this set will be called *security capabilities* and they may include categories of entities and resources, membership in groups, query set sizes, types of entities and resources, computing capabilities, history of activities, various security attributes, etc.

If $P(A)$ denotes a power set of the set A, i.e. the set of all subsets of the given set A, and with the assumption that each entity may have several identities, the following definition defines the security profile of an entity:

Definition 5.9 *(Security Profile): The security profile of an entity is defined as an element of the Cartesian product $P(ID) \times P(C)$, i.e. the security profile is the ordered pair in which the first element is some subset of entity identities and the second element is some subset of its security capabilities (parameters).*

The security profile of a resource is the set of identities and its capabilities associated with a resource which determines the status, usage and activities of that resource (entity) in accordance with the defined security policy. Notice that in the given definition, $P(C)$ may be an empty set, while $P(ID)$ may not; it must have at least one element from the set ID. The set of security profiles will be denoted by SP. For a resource denoted by i, the security profile will be denoted by p_i and according to Definition 5.9, $p_i = [(id_{i,1}, id_{i,2}, \ldots, id_{i,m}), \ (c_{i,1}, c_{i,2}, \ldots, c_{i,n})]$.

Definition 5.10 *(Security Management Information Base (SMIB)): The SMIB is a special resource in the ODP system which contains security profiles of all system resources. Therefore, $SMIB \subseteq SP$.*

Definition 5.11 *(Security Manager (SM)): The Security Manager is the unique entity in each security domain which has the "SM" attribute as one of its distinguished security capabilities in its security profile, denoting that it is the only entity which has direct access to the SMIB.*

Definition 5.12 *(Security Administrator (SA)): The Security Administrator is the unique person in the security domain, who has the characteristic that one of his/her security capabilities in the security profile is "SA", denoting that this is the only person who can*

- *define new security profiles in the SMIB for other entities (definition and registration of new users);*

- *delete/modify existing security profiles in the SMIB for other entities;*

- *control the content and usage of the SMIB.*

The model which will be described in Section 5.3.2 assumes that security profiles, as defined so far, may be updated in two ways:

a. *externally*, by the Security Administrator, *initially* when defining a new security profile, or subsequently, as *updates* of an existing security profile, both in accordance with the defined security policy;

b. *internally*, by the Security Manager, as results (consequences) of system operations and their influence to relevant security profiles, again as specified by the defined security policy.

The initial definition of security profiles may be considered *static*, while later updates and internal modifications, as consequences of system operations, may be considered *dynamic*. This flexibility differs from some analogous models and situations in closed systems and so it is more suitable for systems operating under open principles.

The security profile is associated with the resource primarily on the basis of its type, status and security characteristics. For specific activities in which a resource is involved, in [VOYD83] called *associations*, this resource may be assigned some security parameters additional to its security profile. These can be session keys, algorithms for various security services, parameters characterizing the association, etc. In principle, these security parameters are defined for a specific association, they are valid during the lifetime of that association, they may influence the values of security parameters in the security profile, but, generally, they are not needed when an association becomes inactive.

Let $A = \{a_1, a_2, a_3, \ldots\}$ be a finite set of security parameters (characteristics) which may be used to define a security regime in an association. The elements of this set will be called *security characteristics* of an association (association security profiles) and they may be security services, security mechanisms, relevant parameters, available facilities or operating characteristics of the association. Each entity, when establishing an association and later during its usage, selects desired security characteristics for that association. This concept may be synthesized in the following two definitions. Let $SMIB_i$ denote the instance of the global *SMIB*, belonging to the ith security domain in the *ODP* system. Then $P(SMIB_i)$ is some subset of security profiles of entities from the ith security domain. These entities may be involved in an association with entities from other security domains.

Definition 5.13 *(Association): An n-ary association (an association with n resources involved) is an element of the set $P(SMIB_1) \times P(SMIB_2) \times \cdots \times P(SMIB_n)$, i.e. association is an ordered n-tuple of security profiles from the global SMIB.*

Note: Since the set $P(C)$ may be empty in each ordered pair from SP, the definition above does not define *secure association*. The same is true even if *all* second components in ordered pairs from SP are not empty, since no security characteristics for the association have been defined. For that purpose, the following definition is needed:

Definition 5.14 *(Secure Association): Let* $p_i \in SMIB$ $(i = 1,2)$ *be security profiles of two resources involved in an association. If each of these two profiles have associated relevant association security profiles, i.e.* (p_i, a_i) $(i = 1, 2)$, *then such an association is called a secure association between two resources.*

Note: As defined above the security characteristics of an association may be different for two resources. If they are harmonized, then instead of $[(p_1, a_1), (p_2, a_2)]$, the notation $[(p_1, p_2), a]$ may be used. For n users, the notation for secure association would be $[(p_1, a_1), (p_2, a_2), \cdots, (p_n, a_n)]$ or $[(p_1, p_2, \ldots, p_n), a]$.

5.3.2 Formal Specifications of Secure ODP Systems

This section is based on [MUFT92B]. It presents a formal model of security policy; therefore a security system designed and implemented according to these requirements may be evaluated at a very high level by any evaluation and certification criteria ([ITSEC90], [DoD83]).

5.3.2.1 Approach and Scope

As mentioned earlier a secure ODP system is viewed as a collection of *security domains*, mutually and dynamically related by communicating processes in the open, distributed environment. All definitions of Security Administrators, Security Managers, $SMIB$, and entity security profiles apply to individual security domains. *Secure associations* may be established between two or more entities belonging to the same or to different security domains. In the first case security measures may be more easily applied, since all parties are within the same security environment, i.e. under homogeneous security conditions. In case of different security domains, the problem may be more complicated, since the parties may be under very different security conditions.

Security requirements for ODP systems will be specified by using a finite-state machine approach. The *states* of the machine will be defined by resource security profiles and security characteristics of active associations. *State transitions* will be security relevant events in the ODP system. The criteria for security are the four properties from Definitions 5.5–5.8: authenticity, integrity, confidentiality, and authorization. As mentioned earlier, security of the ODP system will be verified in the following way:

a. the initial state will be defined as a secure state;

b. each transition will have security-preserving properties;

c. every new state will also be required to be a secure state.

Combination of *(a)* and *(b)* will prove that each *new state* in the system will also be a secure state, while combination of *(a)* and *(c)* will prove that each *transition* in the system is secure.

This concept will be suitable for modelling of secure *ODP* systems, since the following assumptions will be significant:

1. Security-relevant transitions may or may not be deterministic, so that *probabilistic ODP protocols* may also be modelled in this way.

2. State transitions may happen *in parallel*, i.e. no sequential state machine is assumed. In this way concurrent processes in a distributed environment may be modelled.

3. *OSI* type systems may be modelled by the concept of *n*-ary secure associations, established between heterogeneous security environments.

5.3.2.2 Secure States and Secure Transitions in Local Security Domains

States and transitions of a secure system for operations in a local *ODP* environment may be shown as a finite state diagram as in Figure 5.1.

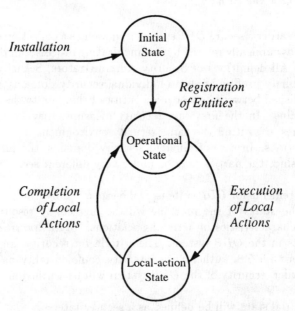

Figure 5.1. State Transition Diagram of a Secure System in a Local ODP Environment

In subsequent text, each transition from an initial to the new state will be represented by a squared box containing: the sequence number of the transition, current state, operation (transition), and the new state. Therefore, each box corresponds to one transition (arrow) in Figure 5.1 and the text after the box describes the security properties of the corresponding states and the transition.

1	*None* $\longrightarrow$ *Installation* $\longrightarrow$ *Initial state*

A secure *ODP* system is in the *Initial* state after *installation* of all security modules and the definition of the *SA's* and *SM's security profiles*, both secret (private) and public, in the *SMIB*. The prerequisite for this state is the determination of all relevant aspects, parameter constraints and requirements of the local security policy. There are no other resources registered in the *SMIB*, since there are no associations established.

Identification elements in the *SA's* security profile must be defined in such a way to guarantee the *authenticity* of the Security Administrator. Capabilities in the *SA's* profile must *authorize* him to access the *SMIB* for the following activities: definition of new users and their security profiles, deletion or updating of existing users or their security profiles, and reading of all (security relevant) information from the *SMIB* (for control purposes). *Integrity* of the *SA's* security profile entered in the *SMIB* must be also guaranteed. *Confidentiality* of secret elements of the *SA's* security profile must be guaranteed. (*Confidentiality* of the *SA's* security profile in the *SMIB* is provided by access control, which prevents any entity accessing the *SMIB*.)

Therefore, for the operation *Installation* of the security system, the following property must hold:

Property 1: Operation *Installation* is secure if it has the following security properties:

1.1. *Authenticity* of the Security Administrator must be verified before performing the *Installation* operation.

1.2. *Integrity* of the *SA's* identity and security profile entered in the *SMIB* must be guaranteed.

1.3. *Confidentiality* of secret elements of the *SA's* security profile is needed.

1.4. *Authorization* to access *SMIB* should be given to the Security Administrator in his security profile.

As a consequence, the *Initial* state is secure if operation *Installation* has the required security properties 1.1-1.4.

2	*Initial state* $\longrightarrow$ *Registration of entities* $\longrightarrow$ *Operational state*

The only activity which may be performed in the *Initial* state is *Registration* of new entities. This operation may be performed only by the Security Administrator. As the result, identities and security profiles of new entities are entered in the *SMIB*. No associations are established yet. The new state will be called *Operational* state, since it provides possibilities for registered entities to initiate various operations in the *ODP* system.

Security profiles entered in the *SMIB* must guarantee *authenticity* of new entities. Since elements of those profiles are entered by the *SA*, there may be a possibility of *SA* to impersonate other legal entities. In order to eliminate this threat, the new set will be defined, denoted by $ID^* = \{id_1^*, id_2^*, id_3^*, \ldots\}$, associated with each entity as the set of its *secret identities*. The previously defined set of identities, denoted by $ID = \{id_1, id_2, id_3, \ldots\}$, may now be called *recorded identities*.

Corresponding elements, i.e. the elements of the set ID^* and elements of the set ID, belonging to the same entity, must be related in the following way:

a. Given secret identity id_i^*, it is easy to calculate the recorded identity id_i;

b. Given recorded identity id_i, it should not be possible (other than by a random guess) to derive the corresponding secret identity id_i^*;

c. (For reasons which will be explained shortly), identification and authentication procedures, based on recorded identities, should give no information about the corresponding secret identities;

d. The values of secret identities and procedures for their usage should strongly resist trial-and-error attempts.

The first two properties are called non-invertibility, i.e. recorded identities should be *non-invertible* to secret identities, and the third property is called *zero-knowledge* procedures. The fourth property implies that secret user identities should be chosen randomly from a large space.

Besides recorded identities, two types of elements of a user's security profile must also be defined: *public elements*, entered in his security profile in the *SMIB*, and corresponding *secret elements*.

Relations between recorded and secret identities must guarantee the *authenticity* of each entity. *Integrity* of recorded identities and security profiles entered in the *SMIB* must be guaranteed. Their *confidentiality* is not needed since the *SMIB* can be read only by the *SA* (through the *SM*), and no information confidential even to the *SA* is recorded in the entity security profiles. Two types of *authorization* must be given to each entity in this state:

- to update only his own security profile, but in such a way that *authenticity* of entities may be verified by the *SA* and the *integrity* of updates is guaranteed,

- authorization to access resources in a local domain under specifications and restrictions of the local security policy.

Integrity and *confidentiality* of secret user profile elements are needed. Together with his secret identification elements, public elements of the *SA's* security profile are also given to the user. Their *integrity* must be guaranteed.

The same operation, *Registration of entities*, may also be executed with *Operational* as an initial and as a target state. This is the case when adding new legal users into an existing *SMIB*.

Under the described constraints, operation *Registration of entities* must have the following property:

Property 2: Operation *Registration* of entities is secure, if it has the following security properties:

2.1. *Authenticity* of new entities must be guaranteed.

2.2. Recorded identification elements of security profiles of new users in the *SMIB* must be *non-invertible* to their corresponding secret elements.

2.3. Procedures for the use of security profiles must be *zero-knowledge*.

2.4. Procedures for the use of security profiles and values of secret identities must be *trial-and-error resistant*.

2.5. *Integrity* of both public and secret elements of new security profiles, plus *integrity* of *SA's* public elements, must be guaranteed.

2.6. *Confidentiality* of secret user profile elements is needed.

2.7. *Authorization* of entities to update only their own security profiles, provided Conditions 2.1, 2.5, and 2.6 hold.

As a consequence, the *Operational* state is a secure state if derived from the *Initial* state by the operation *Registration of entities* with the required security properties 2.1-2.7.

3	*Operational state* $\longrightarrow$ *Exec of local actions* $\longrightarrow$ *Local-actions state*

In the *Operational* state, an entity may initiate various activities. Since *ODP* is primarily considered as a distributed environment, two types of such activities will be distinguished on the basis of whether *communication associations between two or more security domains are established or not.* This means that the main criterion for actions in a local or in a global environment is *establishment of associations* between two (or more) security domains. All actions within a single domain (even involving standard communication functions) are considered as local actions.

If only resources within a single security domain are involved, this type of activity will be called *Execution of local actions.* This operation may be initiated in the *Operational* state and takes the system into the *Local-actions* state. All effects of operations in the local environment relevant for security may be synthesized to *modifications of security profiles* in the local *SMIB* according, of course, to security policy and established authorization privileges of initiators. These may be the creation of new security profiles, updates or deletion of existing security profiles. Of course, these modifications may be performed directly in the *SMIB,* or they may appear as consequences of various activities of entities in the *ODP* system. In this context, functional details of those activities are not relevant.

Modifications of security profiles in the *SMIB,* direct or indirect, may be performed only by *authenticated* entities with appropriate *authorizations.* In this context *integrity* and *confidentiality* of resources and security profiles involved in those actions must be guaranteed to conform to the security policy.

Therefore, activities in the local security domain are those which do not establish associations with any other security domain. If these activities modify security profiles in the local *SMIB,* then the following property must hold for them:

Property 3: The operation *Execution of local actions* is secure if it has the following security properties:

3.1. *Authenticity* of the initiator (entity) of the local action must be verified.

3.2. *Integrity* of resources and security profiles must be guaranteed.

3.3. *Confidentiality* of resources and security profiles should be provided.

3.4. *Authorization* of the initiator to perform the local action is needed.

As a consequence, the *Local-actions* state is a secure state if derived from the *Operational* state by the *Execution of local actions* operation with the required security properties 3.1-3.4.

4	*Local-actions state* $\longrightarrow$ *Compl. of local actions* $\longrightarrow$ *Operational state*

Upon *Completion of local actions,* the system returns to the *Operational* state. Since all the activities in the *Local-actions* state have been performed with security conditions 3.1-3.4., the only security property needed in this operation is *non-repudiation*. In particular, this means that for all executed actions, *authenticity* of their initiators may be verified, *integrity* of data involved in the operation is guaranteed, as well as its *confidentiality*. In addition, it should be possible to *identify* each local action performed, as well as individual *participation* of each entity involved in each action. The difference between these security properties for the *Execution of local actions* operation and for the *Completion of local actions* operation is that in the former those properties are required in advance, as conditions to perform local action, while in the latter these properties should be provided as consequences of the local action (non-repudiation).

For the *Completion of local actions* operation, the following property is required:

Property 4: The operation of *Completion of local actions* is secure if it has the following security properties which may be verified any time after completion of local action (these properties together constitute a non-repudiation security service):

4.1. *Authenticity* of all participants involved in each local action may be proved.

4.2. *Integrity* of resources used in local actions should be guaranteed.

4.3. *Confidentiality* of resources used in local actions must be provided.

4.4. Each executed local action may be identified and individual participation in that action may be proved (*authenticity*).

As a consequence, the *Operational* state is a secure state if derived from the *Local-actions* state by execution of the *Completion of local actions* operation, if that operation has the required security properties 4.1-4.4.

5.3.2.3 Secure states and secure transitions in global ODP systems

Cooperations in local security domains between two or more users involve the creation and usage of associations. The same is the case between remote security domains. The associations between entities in a local domain can be modelled equivalently as associations between two different security domains.

Associations may be established only in the *Operational* state of each local environment and they must be secure according to Definition 5.14. Therefore, a definition of the secure *ODP* system may be the following:

Definition 5.15 *(Secure ODP System): An ODP system is secure if all its local domains are secure and if all established associations are secure.*

The communication aspects of open distributed systems will be analysed in two stages:

    a. establishment of secure associations;

    b. use of secure associations.

Each of these stages has an initiation step and termination step, organized as separate operations of the system.

Establishing, Modifying, and Terminating Secure Associations

Establishing, modifying, use and termination of secure associations may be shown in the form of a finite state diagram as in Figure 5.2.

Figure 5.2 can be described as follows:

Before some secure association is established, each peer-entity involved must go through the *Negotiation* state, where security profiles of all entities and association security characteristics are established, exchanged, negotiated, verified, and, finally, accepted.

The system changes into the *Negotiation* state from the *Operational* state by the *Association-requested* operation. In that operation the initiator sends to his peer entity all security parameters needed for establishment of the desired secure association. If the partner accepts the proposed security characteristics of the association, the system changes from the *Negotiation* state into the *Association active* state by the *Association-accepted* operation. If the association is rejected by the peer entity, the system returns back into the *Operational* state by the *Association-rejected* operation. If in the reply the peer entity suggests alternative security parameters for the association, then the system remains in the *Negotiation* state by the *Association-negotiated* operation.

During the lifetime of an active secure association all peer entities involved may require modifications, extensions, or additional verification of the association security parameters. This action is initiated in the *Association-active* state by the *Association-modified* operation. The system transfers back into the *Negotiation* state. Further actions from this state are equivalent to the association establishment stage. *Association-negotiated* operation includes modifications of existing security parameters, definition of additional security parameters, or additional verification of existing parameters.

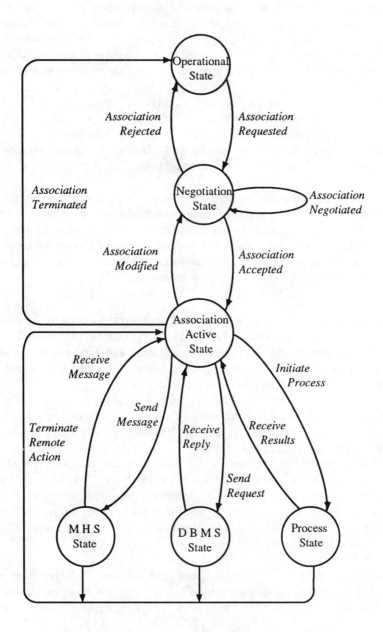

Figure 5.2.   State Transition Diagram of a Secure System
in a Global ODP System

If the active secure association is not needed any more, it may be terminated in the appropriate way. The secure system transfers from the *Association-active* state back into the *Operational* state by the *Association-terminated* operation. During that operation, some special parameters or "closing sequences of confirmation messages" for non-repudiation security service may be required by some of the parties.

The major state in this stage, from which all further actions of the secure *ODP* system are initiated, is the *Association-active* state. In this state security profiles of all peer entities involved are exchanged and mutually verified and the common, desired security parameters of the association are established. In such a way secure association for further operations of the *ODP* system is established.

This has been a brief description of the sequence of operations (and subsequently the states of the secure system) needed in order to establish a secure association. It starts in the *Operational* state, and through possibly several iterations of the *Negotiation* state, eventually reaches the *Association-active* state. The four security properties (authenticity, integrity, confidentiality, and authorization) may be considered for the whole sequence and not for its individual operations.

In addition to *authenticity* of all individual entities, established initially during signing on in their local environments, *mutual authenticity* must be also verified. This means that each party involved in the request, negotiation and acceptance of a secure association may require authentication of other entities. In [ISO88] this security service is called *peer-to-peer authentication*.

Integrity of all elements of the exchanged messages during request, negotiation and acceptance of a secure association must be guaranteed. According to the Definition 5.4, this means that during the exchange of messages, their content, meaning and structure must always be available and preserved in the original form. In addition, source and targets of each message must also be preserved. This means that threats like insertion of false messages, playback of previously recorded messages, impersonation or delivery to wrong destinations must be eliminated. *Timing integrity* of each message (origination time, transmission delay, delivery time, ordering in a sequence of arrival, etc.) must also be guaranteed.

Confidentiality of all message elements (messages, selected fields, headings, etc.) must be provided. Sometimes confidentiality of entities involved in an association may also be required, the security service which is known as *anonymous communications*.

Authorization of all parties involved in the process of requesting, negotiating or accepting secure associations must be verified. When requesting a new association, an initiator must be authorized to access a remote security domain. When negotiating a secure association, each party must ensure that the desired security properties of the association may be met by parameters of his security profile and the security characteristics of his local security domain. Finally, when accepting a secure association, each party must verify whether the parameters of the security profiles of local resources (to be used in the association) are adequate for the security profile of his peer entity.

The same rules apply to the *Association-modified* operation.

If some of the required security properties of the secure association cannot be satisfied, the requested association will be rejected. All previous procedures must be organized in such a way that they do not leave to the intended partner:

- any information useful for illegal determination of any of the secret security parameters of the peer entity (*zero-knowledge*);

- any obligations, information, computing capabilities, etc., which are not balanced by the equivalent properties or resources received by the other peer entity (*cooperation of suspicious partners*).

Previous discussion on establishing, using, and terminating secure associations in the *ODP* system may be summarized into the following six properties of the secure *ODP* system:

Property 5: Operation *Association-requested* is secure if it has the following security properties:

5.1. *Authenticity* of all participants and *mutual* (peer-to-peer) *authenticity.*

5.2. *Integrity* of all exchanged messages, including: content, meaning and structure of messages must be *preserved,* sources and targets *guaranteed* and *timing properties* preserved.

5.3. *Confidentiality* of all elements (messages, sources and targets) must be provided, together with *confidentiality* of peer entities involved.

5.4. *Authorization* of the initiator to access the remote security domain is needed.

As a consequence, the *Negotiation* state is a secure state if derived from the *Operational* state by execution of the *Association-requested* operation with the required security properties 5.1-5.4.

Property 6: Operation *Association-negotiated* is secure if it has the following security properties:

6.1. *Mutual authenticity* of peer entities;

6.2. *Integrity* and *confidentiality* of all exchanged messages and involved partners, as in 5.2 and 5.3,

6.3. *Authorization* of the remote peer entity to access the local security domain is needed.

As a consequence, the *Negotiation* state will remain secure, as long as the operation *Association-negotiated* has the security properties 6.1-6.3.

Property 7: Operation *Association-accepted* is secure if it has the following security properties:

7.1. *Mutual authenticity* of peer entities.

7.2. *Integrity* and *confidentiality* of all exchanged messages and involved partners, as in 5.2 and 5.3.

7.3. *Authorization* of each peer entity to participate in the desired secure association and *adequacy* of security parameters of local resources for the authorized access by remote peer entities.

As a consequence, the *Association-active* state will be a secure state, if it is derived from the *Negotiation* state by the *Association-accepted* operation with the security properties 7.1-7.3.

Security properties of the operation *Association-modified* are equivalent to properties of the operation *Association-negotiated*, except that the former applies to an existing secure association, while the latter applies to a new association. Therefore, this operation, in order to be secure, must meet the security requirements 6.1 and 6.2. Security requirement 6.3 is not needed, since this operation is performed in the state when an association has already been established. Therefore, the following property holds for the *Association-modified* operation:

Property 8: Operation *Association-modified* is secure if it has security properties 6.1, 5.2, and 5.3. Consequently, the *Negotiation* state is a secure state, if it is derived from the *Association-active* state by the operation *Association-modified*, with the security properties 6.1, 5.2, and 5.3.

Property 9: Operation *Association-rejected* is secure if it has the following security properties :

9.1. All procedures in *Association-requested* and *Association-negotiated* operations must be *zero-knowledge*.

9.2. All exchanges in *Association-requested* and *Association-negotiated* operations must be performed as protocols for cooperation of *mutually suspicious* users.

As a consequence, the *Operational* state is a secure state, if derived from the *Negotiation* state by the *Association-rejected* operation with the security properties 9.1 and 9.2.

Security properties of the *Association-rejected* operation are in fact stated as properties of the *Association-requested* and *Association-modified* operations. Therefore, they might have been included in the Properties 5 and 6. In that case, *association-rejected* operation would be a simple closing of a dialogue, which must always be a security preserving operation and with no additional security properties. However, inclusion of security requirements 9.1 and 9.2 in Property 9 provides *verification* for noninterference, nondeducibility or memoryless security systems.

Property 10: Operation *Association-terminated* is secure if it has the following security properties:

   10.1. Properties 9.1 and 9.2 as with *Association-rejected* operation.

   10.2. Non-repudiation by peer entities involved, as in *Property 4* (for local actions).

As a consequence, the *Operational* state is a secure state, if derived from the *Association-active* state by the *Association-terminated* operation with the security properties 10.1 and 10.2.

Use of Secure Associations

Entities may use secure active associations for various operations. In *OSI* type of systems, all those operations may be modelled just as *send/receive* sequences. But, since distributed processing operations in end-systems are also of particular interest, especially with respect to their security, three types of communicating aspects will be distinguished, as consequences of communications via active associations. These three communicating aspects are (refer again to Figure 5.2):

   1. Transfer of *messages*, with no further consequences in remote systems, as in *MHS* (electronic mail) type systems (this will be called *Send-message* operation).

   2. Transfer of *queries* to remote database management systems with database processing at remote locations and with query sets as replies (this will be called *Send-request* operation).

   3. Initiation of *remote processes* with results of their operations as replies (this will be called *Initiate-process* operation).

All three operations together will be called *Initiate-remote-action* operations.

Each of these operations transfers the secure system to the new state, subsequently called *MHS* state, *DBMS* state, and *Process* state. If there are no replies expected, operation *Terminate-remote-action* will take the system back into the *Association active* state. In case of replies, the corresponding operations may be called:

a. *Receive message*, with *MHS* as the initial and *Association active* as the target state.

b. *Receive reply*, with *DBMS* state as the initial and *Association active* as the target state.

c. *Receive results*, with *Process* state as the initial and *Association active* as the target state.

All these three operations return the secure system back into the *Association active* state.

When sending a message to a remote security domain (via an already established secure association), security requirements should be concerned with three logical components of that operation: *(a)* both peer entities, *(b)* secure association itself, and *(c)* the message to be transferred. For peer entities and for the association (during its lifetime), the same security requirements as initially for that association, must hold. They must be verified from time to time. These are security *Properties 5, 6,* and *7* for secure associations. For each message, sent to a remote domain, its *authenticity* (the identification of the message), *integrity* and *confidentiality* must be guaranteed. In addition, the *authorization* of the sender to send messages to a remote domain may depend on the type of message, so it also must be verified.

These are security requirements for the communication type (*Send-message*) operation. With such an operation it is assumed that no remote resources are affected. But if the remote action (with the database or some process) is needed, security must include additional requirements concerned with the particular resource in the remote domain. First, the remote resource must be *authenticated,* and access not only to a remote resource must be allowed, but also *authorization* to access a specific remote resource (database or process) must be established.

From this discussion, the following two security properties for operations of sending various types of messages to a remote security domain may be established:

Property 11: Operation *Send-message* is secure, if it has the following security properties:

11.1. All security requirements from *Properties 5, 6,* and *7* (security of the association).

11.2. *Authenticity, integrity,* and *confidentiality* of each message must be guaranteed.

11.3. *Authorization* of the sender to send messages to a remote security domain is needed.

11.4. Non-repudiation by peer entities involved, as in *Property 4* (for local actions).

As a consequence, the *MHS* state is a secure state, if derived from the *Association-active* state by the *Send-message* operation with the security properties 11.1-11.4.

Property 12:   Operation *Send-request* (or *Initiate-process*) is secure, if it has the following security properties:

12.1. All security requirements from *Property 11* (for sending messages to a remote security domain).

12.2. *Authentication* of a remote resource.

12.3. *Authorization* of the sender to access the remote resource.

As a consequence, the *DBMS* (or *Process*) state is a secure state, if derived from the *Association-active* state by the *Send-request* (or *Initiate-process*) operation with the security properties 12.1-12.3.

Receive-message is the operation equivalent to the *Send-message* operation, so the *Property 11* may also be required for that operation in order again to reach the secure *Association-active* state.

Receive-reply is the operation initiated by the *Send-request* operation to a remote *DBMS*. The data in the *Receive-reply* operation is the query set to be delivered to the initiator. In addition to security requirements applicable to *Send/Receive-message* operations (*Property 11*), for this operation it must be verified that by presenting the reply to the initiator, the security of the system will not be violated. In particular, the query set must be "outside" of the scope of any (previously established) tracker, information-type dependence with any other sensitive resource, or information-type "memory" of the receiver. These are the requirements to prevent information inference, and hence the violation of the receiver's *authorization* profile. These requirements should all be reflected as appropriate security parameters in the initiators's security profile, generated and updated dynamically during his previous operations. Therefore, for the *Receive-reply* operation the following security properties hold:

Property 13:   The operation *Receive-reply* is secure, if it has the following security properties:

13.1. All security requirements needed for the *Send/Receive-message* operations (*Property 11*).

13.2. DBMS *authorization* requirements for prevention of information inference (trackers, information dependence, information memory).

As a consequence, the *Association-active* state is a secure state, if derived from the *DBMS* state by the *Receive-reply* operation with the security Properties 13.1 and 13.2.

Receive-results is the operation which follows the execution of remote processes (initiated by the *Initiate-process* operation). Data in the *Receive-results* operation are the results of the execution of some process in the remote domain. Since that process is peer entity, security requirements for cooperation of peer entities in this case are needed in addition to security requirements for *Send/Receive-message* operations (*Property 11*). They can all be stated in the form of the following property:

Property 14:   The operation *Receive-results* is secure, if it has the following security properties:

14.1. All security requirements needed for the *Send/Receive-message* operations (*Property 11*).

14.2. *Integrity* of resources must be preserved against the "memory" of the initiated process ("memoryless" processes).

14.3. *Authorization* requirements for cooperation of suspicious users must be provided: *zero-knowledge* procedures, equivalent (*authorized*) exchange of sensitive information, equivalent (*authorized*) modifications of computing capabilities.

As a consequence, the *Association-active* state is a secure state, if derived from the *Process* state by the *Receive-results* operation with the security Properties 14.1-14.3.

If the cooperation with the remote security domain is *unidirectional* (no replies expected), after the *Send-message, Send-request* or *Initiate-process* is completed, the security system returns automatically to the *Association-active* state. In this case, communication security requirements (*Property 11* applied to the *Receive-message* operation), DBMS (*Property 13*) or process security requirements (*Property 14*) are not needed. Since transitions to the *MHS, DBMS* or *Process* states were secure, and consequently so are those states themselves, without any reply to the initiator, the automatic transition back to the *Association-active* state is again secure. So will be the *Association-active* state. (The only interesting security property for completion of remote operations is *non-repudiation*, which is included as the security requirement 11.4).

Violation of Security and Recovery

Properties 1 to 14 define characteristics and operational requirements for a secure ODP system. Security mechanisms, security services, and security management in the ODP system must be designed and implemented in such a way that all fourteen properties hold at all times of system operations.

But it may not be expected that any secure system will guarantee the validity of all fourteen properties at all times of system operations. No system is absolutely secure. Therefore, it must be taken into account that there will be some violations of security properties and security operations. These violations may be expected in any stage of system operations, therefore must be taken into consideration in any state of the secure system model. Accepting potential security violations, the secure system must be able to *discover* all the violations, to *analyse* them, and to *recover* back into some secure state, i.e. to eliminate causes and consequences of the violation.

Therefore, security violation and recovery may be modelled by two additional states, as in Figure 5.3.

The secure system transfers to the *Security violation* state from any other state if security violation is detected. Since security requirements are given in Properties 1 to 14, security violation means that some of the required properties of the system are not satisfied. In other words, it has been detected that the system does not possess or does not comply with some of the defined security properties. This operation will be called *Security-violation detection*. It transfers the secure system from any (current) state to the *Security violation* state. In order to be secure, that operation must be able to detect violations of all security requirements, stated in Properties 1 to 14. Therefore, the following new property for the secure system must be required:

Property 15: The operation *security-violation detection* is secure, if it always detects every violation of security Properties 1 to 14.

As a consequence, the *Security-violation* state will be a secure state if derived from any other state by the *Security-violation detection* operation conforming to the Property 15.

This in fact means that the secure system will remain secure if all security violations are detected.

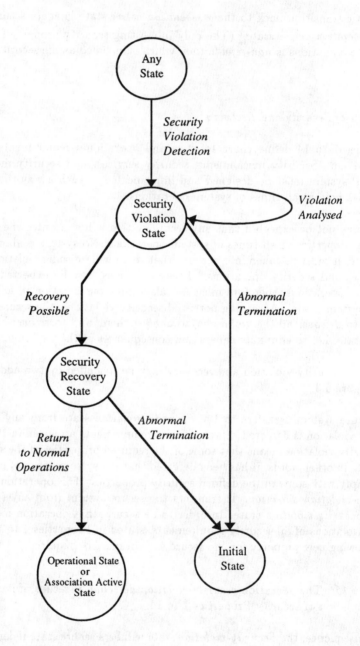

Figure 5.3. Security Violation and Recovery States of a Secure ODP System

The secure system may transfer out from the *Security-violation* state by three operations (as shown in Figure 5.3):

- *Violation-analysed* operation;

- *Recovery possible;* and

- *Abnormal termination.*

The difference between *Security-violation* detected and *Violation-analysed* operations is that in the former only inconsistency in security properties is detected, while in the latter two aspects are analysed:

a. What were the reasons for violation of security?

b. What corrective measures are needed in order to again establish the security of the system?

In addition, if possible, some conclusions and redefinitions of the security system are derived, in order to eliminate the possibility of the same problems in the future.

If *Violation-analysed* operation is successful with the two goals stated above, the system transfers to the *Security recovery* state by the *Recovery possible* operation. In the *Security recovery* state the system re-establishes its security parameters and security status, and transfers to normal operations, either to *Operational* or to *Association-active* state.

Property 16: The *Recovery possible* operation is secure, if it always detects *(a)* what were the reasons for violation of security, and *(b)* what corrective measures are needed in order to establish again the security of the system.

As a consequence, the *Security-recovery* state will be a secure state if derived from the *Security-violation* state by the *Recovery possible* operation conforming to the Property 16.

If *Violation-analysed* operation was not successful, *Abnormal termination* operation is executed and the system returns to the *Initial* state. In that state, the Security Administrator will analyse the causes and consequences of security violation and organize appropriate corrective actions. The same is the case if in the *Security recovery* state the system determines that recovery is not effectively feasible. After determining what were the reasons for violation and what corrections are needed, recovery may still fail due to unavailability of appropriate decisions, parameters, procedures or corrective data.

5.3.3 Conclusions: Synthesis of Security Requirements

Definition 5.15 defines a secure *ODP* system as a collection of secure local domains, cooperating via secure associations in such a way that:

a. each association is established and used with the required security properties;

b. the status of all resources in all security domains is always preserved in the secure state, either in case of local manipulations with those resources or with remote accesses through secure associations.

Explicit security requirements for:

- establishing secure local domains;

- local manipulations with resources in security domains in a secure way;

- establishing, using, modifying or terminating secure associations;

- using remote *ODP* resources in a secure way;

- detection and recovery from security violations.

are stated in Properties 1 – 16. Therefore, the conclusion may be that any *ODP* system is secure if Properties 1 – 16 are valid for that system at any time of its operations.

This model is particularly suitable for all aspects of security management, as required by [ISO88] and described in Section 1.4. The intrinsic properties of this model are *monitoring, logging, audit,* and *recovery* activities. Furthermore, particular properties, or the whole model, may be applied at different levels of the secure *ODP* system, starting from individual user stations, local computing environments, security domains, up to the global *ODP* systems.

6

ASSESSMENT OF SECURITY

6.1 INTRODUCTION

An assessment of network security means making a statement qualifying its functionality and effectiveness. Such a qualification can be required with different purposes
and at different levels.

Primarily one will be interested in the security of a specific application on the network;
for instance, security of the electronic mail service or some banking application. In
fact, it is the application, the data involved with it, and its users that dictate the
security requirements of the application or the whole network. These requirements
are part of the security policy. With the security policy as a starting point, a risk
analysis can be performed. After that, the services and the mechanisms that prevent
or limit damage have to be selected and implemented. The risk analysis also might
result in modifications of the security policy.

Another approach can be followed if one is not interested in the security of a specific
application, but simply wants to classify network security domains into different categories. A network security domain is a complete network or a part of a network that
has to obey the same security policy and has the same security administration. A network security domain will be referred to simply as a domain. The category in which
a domain is classified depends on the security services that are present in the domain
and the mechanisms that are used to implement these services. When two or more
domains of different security classifications have to cooperate, one can conclude from
their classifications what kind of services are available in all domains, so it is known
in advance what type of security their combination (association) can offer. However,
it is very hard to predict what the quality of the security will be.

For the purpose of selecting security services and mechanisms, as well as for the classification of networks in security classes, there must be a methodology for rating of

services and mechanisms. This rating should make it possible to choose in each particular situation the most suitable services and mechanisms. This selection can be done before a network is put into operation, but it can also be done on a dynamic basis between domains by negotiations at the moment of establishment of an association.

6.2 SECURITY POLICY AND RISK ASSESSMENT

A security policy can be defined as a statement by the top management that defines in very general terms what is and what is not to be permitted in the area of security during general operation of the system being secured [ISO88].

Security policies that are defined in very general terms can be of use in a variety of different situations. However the policy has to be refined to cater for specific applications. The result of the refinement process is the given policy restated in very precise terms drawn directly from the application. It is this application-specific policy that is needed when considering the security of an application.

The security policy must be implemented by taking the appropriate security measures. For the network (communications) component of an application, it means that one has to make the right choice from available network security services and mechanisms. The technique that can be used for this purpose is a risk analysis, followed by a cost–benefit analysis of possible counter measures. The result will be a selection of services and mechanisms to be used in the network.

In the following it is assumed that an application is to be installed in the network. A security policy for that application has been defined and a risk analysis has to be performed. The basic steps that have to be taken in that process are given in Figure 6.1.

The risk analysis has to start by establishing what has to be protected. If the security policy is sufficiently specific, this follows immediately from the policy. Otherwise one must first derive an application-specific policy from the general high level policy.

The next step is the establishment of vulnerabilities and threats, and the sources of those threats. A vulnerability means any situation that could lead to a breach of security. A threat is the specific action that will profit from a vulnerability and will cause a loss of security. Making a list of vulnerabilities and threats for an application or a network is a difficult step that requires strict methodology, creativity and imagination. There exists a close relationship between vulnerabilities and threats. Without a vulnerability there is no threat and without threats there is no vulnerability. It should be noted that when one is making a list of threats and their sources, one has to think of intentional acts as well as of accidental acts that might harm the security of the system or a network.

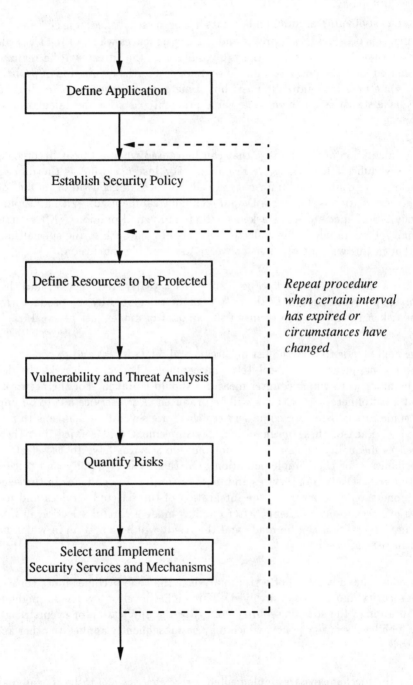

Figure 6.1 Selection Procedure for Security Services and Mechanisms

After a list of vulnerabilities and threats has been established, it is necessary *to quantify* as much as possible these threats and the consequences when a threat is realized. This means that, for each threat, the probability that the threat will be realized must be evaluated, and the possible damage estimated. For the estimation of probabilities one can sometimes look into the past, but some probabilities are so small that one does not have statistics on them. The same problem exists for the calculation of possible damage.

The calculation of the damage that can be caused when a threat becomes reality can be very difficult for intangible resources. For instance what is the damage when a disclosure of confidential information leads to a loss of goodwill or public confidence ? When estimation is difficult a Delphi technique can be used. With a Delphi technique a number of specialists are asked for their individual opinions. After that a second round follows in which the collected answers are fed back to the specialists. The idea is that in this way the opinions converge to a reliable conclusion.

When a threat is expected to be realized with yearly frequency F, and the expected damage per realization is D, the risk R can be calculated by the product $R = F \times D$. The risk R is expressed in terms of the amount of money lost per year.

The next step is to take the list of threats and related risks and to consider all threats whose consequences are absolutely unacceptable. For all such risks the decision has to be made as to which counter measures should be taken. For the network, it means that a list of necessary services will be produced. Each service has to be implemented by some mechanism. For some services there are several mechanisms to provide that service. Each of these mechanisms may implement that service, but there are differences in quality and price. So not only do services have to be selected, but also mechanisms for their implementation. On this basis of quality and price compared with risk, a selection of services and mechanisms has to be made. In the selection process one should be aware of the integration of the selected services and mechanisms into one secure environment. After one has made a careful selection in this manner, an implementation can be made and the result will be a system in which it is known which risks are still present.

An additional advantage of a risk analysis is that one becomes more conscious about the security and the risks involved. This higher level of awareness might lead to an adaptation of the specific security policy for the application or even strengthening of the high level security policy, which may be subsequently applied to other applications as well.

After the mechanisms are implemented a risk analysis has to be repeated every time there are changes in the environment, in the network or in the applications. Even if there are no changes, a risk analysis should be carried out at regular intervals, because opinions on threats and the risks involved may change.

6.3 CLASSIFICATION OF NETWORKS BASED ON SECURITY SERVICES

Classification of domains into a small number of classes based on the security services that are present in these domains offers a framework for verifying and testing the security within a domain and makes it easier to establish the security of interdomain associations and their applications. The classification should be made in such a way that the result is a comprehensive and clearly structured arrangement of security classes. The intention should be to define classes with certain ordering among them. Security services aimed at the same kind of protection (e.g. confidentiality or integrity) should be placed together in the same class. This has the extra advantage that within a group the same mechanisms can be used as much as possible.

On the basis of the *OSI* security services [ISO88], a global classification can be made, in which four groups of security services may be defined. To prevent confusion with other classifications, such as in the Orange Book [DoD83] which defines classes *A* to *D*, and other schemes [ITSEC90] which use *E* and *F*, here the classes will be denoted with *G1*, *G2*, *G3* and *G4*. A more precise classification would give classes *G 1.1*, *G 1.2*, *G 2.1*, *G 2.2*, *G 2.3*, *G 3.1*, *G 3.2*, *G 3.3*, *G 4.1* and *G 4.2* (see Table 6.1).

In this classification scheme, class *G 4.2* contains all *OSI* security services and class *G 1.1* contains only the authentication service. Classes in group *G 2* and classes in group *G 3* are extensions of the classes in group *G 1*, but in different directions. The reason is that in this case it is not meaningful to arrange groups of services in a strictly hierarchical order as has been done in the Orange Book. It is possible to have confidentiality without integrity or the reverse. The classification has been made based on the following considerations: The number of classes should be limited in order to make the approach easier to understand and apply. There can be no security without authentication and some form of access control, so authentication and access control will be included in the first class. Confidentiality and integrity are complementary services, so they may be applied separately or they may be combined. Therefore, they will be classified in separate classes, but their combination is in the class *G 4.1*. Applications may require all security services, so the last class contains all *ISO/OSI* security services. Table 6.1 gives an overview of which *OSI* security services belong to the classes *G 1.1* to *G 4.2*.

Classes in Table 6.1 can be summarized as follows:

Class G 1 : Authentication and access control

Class G 2 : Authentication, access control and confidentiality

Class G 3 : Authentication, access control, integrity, and non-repudiation

Class G 4 : Authentication, confidentiality, integrity, and non-repudiation.

Table 6.1.   Classification of OSI Security Services

OSI Security Service	1.1	1.2	2.1	2.2	2.3	3.1	3.2	3.3	4.1	4.2
Peer Entity Authentication	X	X	X	X	X	X	X	X	X	X
Data Origin Authentication	X	X	X	X	X	X	X	X	X	X
Access Control Service		X	X	X	X	X	X	X	X	X
Connection Confidentiality			X	X	X				X	X
Selective Field Connection Confident.			X	X	X				X	X
Connectionless Confidentiality				X	X				X	X
Selective Field Connectionless Confid.				X	X				X	X
Connection Integrity with Recovery						X	X	X	X	X
Connection Integrity without Recovery						X	X	X	X	X
Selective Field Connection Integrity						X	X	X	X	X
Connectionless Integrity						X	X	X	X	X
Selective Field Connectionless Integrity						X	X	X	X	X
Traffic Flow Control							X	X	X	X
Non-repudiation, Origin					X		X			X
Non-repudiation, Delivery					X		X			X

The next table (Table 6.2) gives an overview of the mechanisms which are necessary for implementation of security services in different classes.

The conclusion is that encipherment and authentication exchange mechanisms are present in every security class. This means that if those mechanisms are not available, there can be no security in this scheme.

The above network security classes can be arranged in a lattice structure, as shown in Figure 6.2. An arrow from X to Y means that class X is a subclass of the class Y.

The refined scheme arranged in a lattice structure may look like Figure 6.3.

Table 6.2.   Security Mechanisms for Implementation of Security Classes

Security Mechanism	1.1	1.2	2.1	2.2	2.3	3.1	3.2	3.3	4.1	4.2
Encipherment	X	X	X	X	X	X	X	X	X	X
Digital Signature	X	X			X		X	X	X	X
Access Control			X	X	X		X	X	X	X
Message Authentication Codes						X	X	X	X	X
Authentication Exchange	X	X	X	X	X	X	X	X	X	X
Traffic Padding				X					X	X
Routing Control			X	X					X	X
Notarization					X			X		X

So far, only *OSI* security services have been considered for classifications. Each of the security classes can be extended with one or more services selected from the extensions mentioned earlier.

The possible extensions are:

- subliminal channel service;

- secure group communications;

- anonymous communications.

This gives the possibility that a network has for instance security class *G 3.3*, plus secure group communications. In this way security services in the network may be indicated by specifying the security class and its extensions. But, so far, there has been no any consideration of the *quality of implementations*. The services may be implemented with strong or with weak mechanisms. To quantify the quality of the services, a *rating system* for services and mechanisms is necessary.

A rating system for security mechanisms may be established in the following way: Each mechanism gets a rating on a scale of 0 to 10 (0 means no security at all, 10 means absolute security). If a service depends on the cooperative use of more than one mechanism, the rating of the implemented service will be equal to the rating of the mechanism involved with the lowest rating. In the same way a rating can be appended to a security class by taking the lowest rating of the services available in the subset defined by that security class. The result will be that one can indicate the security of a network by giving the security class and the rating. So a network has for instance security class *G 3.3*, with a rating of 6.

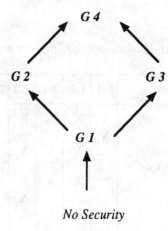

Figure 6.2. Lattice Structure of Network Security Classes

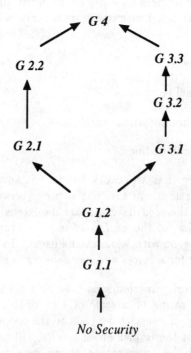

Figure 6.3. Refined Lattice Structure of Network Security Classes

6.4 RATING AND SELECTION OF SERVICES AND MECHANISMS

6.4.1 The Approach

As mentioned before, a domain can offer a large number of security services. Subsets can be created from the set of all possible services. Which services are needed in a subset is determined by the applications that use that subset. Services are provided by means of mechanisms. The quality of the mechanisms used to provide a service determine the quality of the service.

Rating should make it possible to represent the quality of a mechanism by a number on a certain scale, and by means of these scaled mechanisms each service could get a number. This number that qualifies the service could be considered as the security level of that service. A higher number means a higher security. When the security level of a subset of services has to be established, the following rules can be applied.

1. The security level of a subset of services is equal to the rating of the service with the lowest rating in that subset.

2. When a service is provided by a number of cooperating mechanisms, the mechanism with the lowest rating determines the security level of the service.

Because the basis of the security rating lies in the mechanisms, it is necessary to rate the mechanisms first. For each mechanism two parameters are needed. The first determines the rating on a security scale, the other gives a measure for the cost of the mechanism. Cost can be real money, but it can also mean something difficult to express in money, such as complexity or difficulty of use. Because most of the time higher security means higher costs, and to avoid unnecessary costs, the best thing one can do is to choose mechanisms of the same security rating to implement a specific subset of services. When a certain type of mechanism is necessary for more than one service in a subset of services and more mechanisms of that type are available, it is advisable to use the same mechanism for all services, unless the costs (for example processor time) make this unacceptable.

6.4.2 Rating of Mechanisms

When one has to compare products that differ in a large number of properties, one can try to make a decision more simple by placing the product somewhere on a linear scale. To get the position on the scale one has to combine the result of the assessment of all relevant properties into one single number. It is a technique that can be used for all kinds of products. The problem is to determine what properties are important and to give a value for each property. The method which will be used is described in [ELOF83].

The original method starts with formulating the requirements for a security product, and their importance. The importance of some requirement i is expressed by a number k_i, which can be considered as a weighting factor. The higher k_i, the more important the requirement is. Eloff uses a scale from 1 to 4 for values of k_i. After the requirements have been weighted in this way, one has to verify all those requirements for the product under investigation. Each required property denoted by i is validated in the real product by a number x_i, where $x_i = 0$ means the requirement is not met at all, $x_i = 1$ means the requirement is met only partially, and $x_i = 2$ means the requirement is completely fulfilled. After that, the weighted mean of the values of x_i is calculated. In order to get as a result a number between 0 and 10, and because each x_i has a value of 2 as a maximum, the weighted mean is multiplied by a factor $K=5$. The result will be the *rating coefficient R*. R can be calculated by the following formula:

$$R = \frac{\sum_{i=1}^{N} k_i \times x_i \times 5}{\sum_{i=1}^{N} k_i}$$

There are some problems in applying this method without modification in the process of selection of security mechanisms.

The first problem has to do with the handling of critical properties. When making a list of required properties, each property gets a weight. A property of critical importance gets the highest weight. But it is still possible that a reasonable weighted mean is reached when a critical requirement is not completely fulfilled. For instance, when rating an encryption algorithm, a critical requirement is that security does not depend on the secrecy of the algorithm. Suppose this requirement is given weight 3, and suppose that there is an algorithm which is dependent on its secrecy. So, this requirement is not fulfilled. If there are two other requirements with weight 3 and 2 and those requirements are both fulfilled, then the result of the rating would be $R = 6.3$. It would be a reasonable rating, but with an unacceptable algorithm.

Because of this problem, the suggestion is to change the method in such a way that critical requirements are not part of the calculation, but are verified beforehand.

The second problem has to do with quantitative properties. The presence of certain properties is a qualitative measure, but some properties can be expressed very well as a number. For instance the time (measured in seconds) necessary to successfully cryptoanalyse a ciphertext of a given length is a number. If there is no limit on this number, but only the principle "the higher, the better", then it can never be fully verified that a requirement is completely fulfilled. Therefore, in such a situation the requirements have to be specified in the form of a limit. In this case the requirement could be specified as "cryptanalysis time of a ciphertext of 1 Kbytes takes more than *100* years". When the criteria (*100* years) is taken high enough, it can be used to rate the mechanisms. All mechanisms that have an expected cryptoanalysis time more than *100* years get the same high rating, other mechanisms get lower ratings.

The third problem is the handling of varying conditions. It is only possible to validate a mechanism under very specific conditions. When for instance a mechanism can be implemented in software or in hardware, then this has to be considered as two different mechanisms. When the key length plays a role, the same mechanism with different key lengths should be considered as different mechanisms.

It should be noted here that the result of a rating process is not an absolute value that is valid under all circumstances. It depends on the environment and the application and has subjective elements in it. An example rating can be helpful, but for each new situation a careful validation has to be performed.

6.4.3 Rating and Selection of Cryptographic Algorithms

6.4.3.1 General Methodology

When a method is applied to select a cryptographic algorithm, the first thing that has to be done, is to establish a list of required properties. The requirements can be split into two groups, requirements as a consequence of the *security* (that must be high) and requirements as a consequence of the *costs* (they must be low). Two figures have to be calculated: firstly the security rating *RSEC* in which only the security requirements are taken into account, and secondly the rating *RCOST* in which the cost aspects are being used. *RCOST* plays no role in the determination of the security level. It is used for selection purposes only. Note that the formulation of the cost requirements should be in such form that a high value means low cost.

The following list of security and cost requirements and weights can be constructed:

Security Requirements	Weight
1. Security must not depend on the secrecy of the algorithm	*critical*
2. Time to cryptoanalyse the ciphertext of 1K	
must be greater than 100 years	*3*
3. Chaining possible	*3*
Cost Requirements	**Weight**
4. Speed greater than 64 Kbits per second	*3*
5. Key easy to generate	*1*
6. Key exchange does not need a secret channel	*3*

Suppose that the encryption algorithms to be evaluated are *DES* and *RSA*. Then the distinction must be made between *DES/CBC* and *DES/ECB* and also between software implementation and hardware implementation. For the *RSA* the length of one block has to be chosen, in this case, say, *200* digits has been assumed. Also the assumption has been made that the *RSA* is implemented in software.

Then the following tables can be constructed.

Table 6.3 A.   Security Rating of Cryptographic Algorithms

Requirement	k_i	DES ECB soft.	DES ECB hard.	DES CBC soft.	DES CBC hard.	RSA 200 dgts
1	*critical*	Y	Y	Y	Y	Y
2	*3*	2	2	2	2	2
3	*2*	0	0	2	2	0
RSEC		6	6	10	10	6

Table 6.3 B.   Cost Rating of Cryptographic Algorithms

Requirement	k_i	DES ECB soft.	DES ECB hard.	DES CBC soft.	DES CBC hard.	RSA 200 dgts
4	*3*	1	2	1	2	0
5	*1*	2	2	2	2	2
6	*3*	0	0	0	0	0
RCOST		4.6	5.8	6.2	7.5	5.4

When these tables are used for selection it is clear that *DES/CBC* implemented in hardware should be selected. Based on the criteria used, it has the same high security rating as *DES/CBC* implemented in software, but it has a higher cost rating. (Higher cost rating - preference, means lower costs). From these tables it also follows that the *RSA* should be preferred rather than *DES/ECB* implemented in software.

When this method is being used to determine security then the requirements that have to do with the costs must be neglected. Only the first table is important for security. From its columns it can be noticed that there is no difference in security level when implemented in hardware or in software. Also the ease of sending a public key in *RSA* does not contribute to a greater security. For *DES/ECB* (implemented in hardware or software) and for *RSA* this table gives a security rating of 6, but *DES/CBC* (implemented in hardware or in software) gives a security rating of 10. This means that *DES/CBC* should be preferred as the encryption algorithm, and that its security should be rated at 10.

6.4.3.2 Rating and Selection of Mechanisms for Entity Authentication

Four basic mechanisms will be evaluated: simple password, variable password, encryption, and handshaking (also called challenge/response mechanism). Some of these mechanisms can only be used meaningfully in combinations, and the following alternatives are feasible.

   a. Simple password mechanism without encryption.

   b. Simple password mechanism with encryption.

   c. Simple password mechanism with a challenge/response and encryption.

   d. Variable password mechanism without encryption.

   e. Variable password mechanism with encryption.

   f. Variable password mechanism with challenge/response and encryption.

Encryption here means that the password is encrypted on the communication lines. Of course the password should never be stored in a system in a clear form. For storage of a password a one-way encryption function should be used.

For entity authentication the following security and cost requirements can be listed:

Security Requirements	Weight
1. The password is encrypted during transmission	*3*
2. Replay is not possible	*2*
3. The user can memorize the secret information which is needed to operate the mechanism	*2*
Cost Requirements	**Weight**
4. Processor time used for authentication is minimal	*1*
5. No additional messages needed for authentication	*1*

With these requirements the following tables can be constructed:

Table 6.4 A.   Security Rating of Entity Authentication

Requirement	k_i	a	b	c	d	e	f
1	3	0	2	2	0	2	2
2	2	0	0	2	2	2	2
3	2	2	1	1	0	0	0
RSEC		0	6	10	4	10	10

Table 6.4 B.   Cost Rating of Entity Authentication

Requirement	k_i	a	b	c	d	e	f
4	1	2	1	1	2	1	1
5	1	2	2	1	2	2	1
RCOST		5.0	6.5	8.0	5.0	7.5	7.0

From these tables it can be concluded that several mechanisms give a security of 10, but due to the cost requirements, method *c*, the simple password mechanism supplemented with a challenge/response mechanism and encryption, should be selected.

6.4.3.3 Rating and Selection of Mechanisms for Message Stream Integrity

For message stream integrity three mechanisms are possible: sequence numbers, time stamps, and a challenge/response mechanism. To be successful these mechanisms have to be supplemented by stream encryption.

It is assumed here that the initial value for the sequence numbering for a message stream is random. Also it is assumed that the time-stamp mechanism verifies two things: first, that the time difference between the time in the stamp and the real time is within a certain margin, and second that the time stamps in the mechanism form a monotonic nondecreasing sequence.

For the challenge/response mechanism a challenge for the other party and a response to the last challenge from the other party are included in each message. It means that when one partner has sent a message (which contains a challenge), that partner must wait for a message from the other side (which must include the response).

The following security and cost requirements are applicable here:

Security Requirements	Weight
1. Undetected insertion must be impossible	*3*
2. Undetected deletion must be impossible	*3*
3. Undetected replay must be impossible	*3*
Cost Requirements	**Weight**
4. Extra processor time is minimal	*1*
5. The number of things to remembered between messages is minimal	*1*
6. No dependency on synchronous clocks in the network	*1*
7. No extra limitations on the protocol	*3*

This gives rise to the following tables:

Table 6.5 A.   Security Rating of Mechanisms for Message Integrity

Requirement	k_i	Seq. no.	Time stamp	Chall/Resp
1	*3*	2	2	2
2	*3*	2	0	2
3	*3*	2	1	2
RSEC		10	5	10

Table 6.5 B.   Cost Rating of Mechanisms for Message Integrity

Requirement	k_i	Seq. no.	Time stamp	Chall/Resp
4	*1*	2	2	2
5	*2*	2	2	2
6	*1*	2	0	2
7	*2*	2	2	0
RCOST		10	6.1	8.6

From these tables it can be concluded that a message sequence number mechanism and the challenge/response mechanism have the same security level, but owing to the cost of the protocol restrictions of the challenge/response mechanism, the sequence number mechanism should be selected. Note that both methods have to be supplemented by stream encryption.

7

DESIGN
OF THE COMPREHENSIVE
INTEGRATED
SECURITY SYSTEM (CISS)

7.1 INTRODUCTION

In Chapter 4, Section 4.2, several extensions of the standard *OSI Security Architecture* have been suggested. All have been considered as potential topics of this book. Some of them, like formal modelling, have been covered in Chapter 5. Most of the others will be described in this chapter through the design of the *Comprehensive Integrated Security System (CISS)*. This security system includes most of the extensions mentioned in Section 4.2. It is functional and flexible, so that it covers a broad range of security aspects and it is applicable to various types of applications and environments. Some considerations of its implementation and usage in existing *OSI and other applications* and some *prototype implementation guidelines* will be given in Chapter 8.

7.2 CONCEPTUAL MODEL OF THE EXTENDED OSI
SECURITY ARCHITECTURE

Security architecture in the *ODP* environment may be treated in four different, but complementary aspects:

    a. The *organizational aspect* of the security architecture is concerned with the logical components of the comprehensive security system, their functions, mutual interactions, and relations to the underlying environment.

b. *The functional aspect* of the security architecture is concerned with functions of the *ODP* system, their structure and organization, and the most appropriate arrangement of these functions in order to implement security services.

c. *The management aspect* of the security architecture is concerned with organization and management of the global security system in order to make it operational, efficient and effective.

d. *Implementation* of the security architecture is concerned with the implementation aspects of various functions (modules) of the security system.

The following four subsections are introductory to each of these four different aspects of designing, establishing, and using security architecture in the *ODP* environment. Most of this chapter is concerned with the structure, organization and management of the global *ODP* security system, while functional aspects, relevant for implementation, are treated in the next chapter (Chapter 8).

7.2.1 Organizational Approach to ODP Security Architecture: Comprehensive Integrated Security System (CISS)

The main goal of this book is to design, with all the necessary details, a global security system for a general *ODP* environment. The system should provide a large number of security services, each implemented with several alternative mechanisms, and should be applicable to a broad range of open environments and applications, as well as being functionally convenient for use in any situation. Therefore, the desired properties, and at the same time design goals, of such a security system may be the following:

1. To provide as many *security services* as possible.

2. To include many *security mechanisms* with different *efficiency* and *strength* and to provide a possibility to implement security services with *alternative combinations* of security mechanisms.

3. To provide all types of *management functions* in order to make the installation, monitoring, optimization or restructuring of the security system functional and flexible.

4. To be operationally *efficient* and *transparent* to users and applications, and *flexible* for modifications, improvements and expansions.

5. To be *applicable* to any type of operational environment, varying from a single *PC, LAN,* small or large mainframe system to the most general *OSI* and *ODP* system.

6. To be easily *applicable* to all kinds of users, programs, data, and applications.

7. To be designed, structured and established *formally,* in a modular way, so that the structure of the system, its properties and operations may be formally specified, tested and verified.

A security system with these stated properties will be called a *Comprehensive Security System.*

In addition to the functional diversity of its components, their combinations, operational environments and user requirements, the *Comprehensive Security System* must be compact, well-defined, implemented as a limited set of modules, to provide usage and management simplicity. This means that basic components of the security system must be general enough, so that with a variety of combinations and their integration, different versions of the *Comprehensive Security System* may be created. Generality means rich functionality of individual components, their operational efficiency and flexibility in setting up various combinations and versions of the *Comprehensive Security System.* This essential property, i.e. the creation of various versions of the *Comprehensive Security System* by *synthesis* of its individual functions while maintaining full secure operations within applications, means that the global security system must be securely *integrated* from individual components.

Such a security system, with comprehensive functions and properties, and with the general, integrable components, being simple, flexible, efficient, and broadly applicable, will be called a *Comprehensive Integrated Security System (CISS).*

A *Comprehensive Integrated Security System* may be designed with a "layered" architecture, consisting of five functional layers, as shown in Figure 7.1. This principle of modular design of a security system breaks its complexity into subcomponents, allows alternative implementations, and provides structured relations between its components for easier rating and verification of the system. In order to achieve synergy, individual autonomous components of the security system are mutually interrelated and functionally composed to achieve an optimal structure, operational efficiency with functional security effectiveness. Since all the necessary details of the *CISS* system are described in Section 7.3, only a brief description of each component is given in this introductory section.

The structure of the five layers of the *CISS* and mutual interrelations between its basic components are shown in Figure 7.1.

The Basic Layer: Elementary Modules

The lowest ("basic") layer of the *CISS* consists of *elementary (mathematical) modules,* used for implementation of various security mechanisms. The parameters needed by these modules are recorded in individual *segments* of the security management information base (SMIB). Components of this layer are "basic" in a sense that they

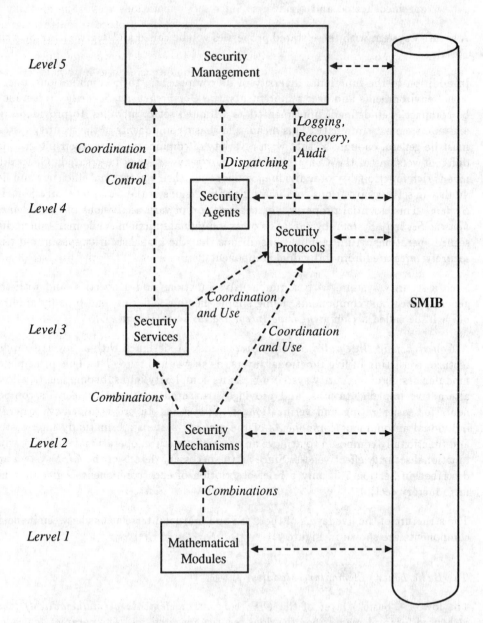

Figure 7.1. Conceptual Model of the CISS

do not have any functional subcomponents or data attributes appearing as subfunctions or portions of other *CISS* components.

It is well known that most of the asymmetric cryptographic algorithms require mathematical operations with large numbers. Since these operations are also needed in certain types of special protocols (for instance zero-knowledge protocols, contract signing protocols, etc.), they must be implemented as general purpose mathematical modules, applicable for any situation or algorithm. Some of these elementary modules include random number generator, test for primality, exponentiation in a finite field, etc., all operating with large numbers.

Another component of this "basic" layer are the six logical segments of the *SMIB* [MUFT88C]. *SMIB* is a repository of all control information and parameters necessary for normal functioning of the security system. These parameters are also needed at the higher conceptual layers of the *CISS* system, as shown in Figure 7.1, so the *SMIB* belongs logically to each of the *CISS* layers.

This conceptual model of the security system has *six individual segments,* constituting a logical structure of the *SMIB.* In practice, various implementations may have a more detailed structure of *SMIB* segments. The segments may be implemented as a centralized or distributed database in the ODP environment. The conceptual segments are the following:

1. An *Identification* segment for entities and other network resources.

2. A segment with (static) *security profiles* (recorded profiles of users, programs, and all other network resources for extended security services), to be called the *Extended security* segment.

3. A segment with appropriate parameters for *active* network users and their associations – dynamic security profiles includes threshold parameters, membership in closed groups, secure teleconferences, etc., to be called the *Secure Associations* segment.

4. An *Extended Access Control* segment, containing the specification of access control parameters for network users and resources.

5. A *Security Log* for recording security relevant information and for restructuring the secure states of the *ODP* system on recovery.

6. A *Confidential* (private) segment for active entities.

This organization of the logical segments of the *SMIB* follows from its formal definition given in Chapter 5, Section 5.3.1. The *SMIB* contains the security profiles of the network entities of the form:

$$p_i = [(id_{i,1}, id_{i,2}, \ldots, id_{i,n}),\ (c_{i,1}, c_{i,2}, \ldots, c_{i,m})],$$

where id_i are various parameters used for identification and authentication of entities, and c_i are various security capabilities. In the proposed *Identification* segment only one identification element is suggested; if more of them are used, because they are needed in some special protocols [FIAT87], they should all be recorded in the *Extended Security* segment. Capabilities are recorded in the *Extended Access Control* segment.

When establishing secure associations, the security profiles in the form (p_i, a_i) $(i = 1, 2, \ldots, n)$ are established. These profiles (for active network users) are kept during the lifetime of an association in the segment, with dynamic security profiles. In addition, all accesses in the network are controlled by access control parameters recorded in the *Extended Access Control* segment.

Secret security identities and parameters of network users should be recorded on some private media (available only to the individual user).

The Second Layer: Security Mechanisms

The next layer of the CISS consists of individual security mechanisms. They provide the tools to implement the individual functions of the security system, i.e. the security services. These mechanisms are general in a sense that they are implemented by combinations of elementary (mathematical) modules. For their operations they use their own security parameters recorded in appropriate segments of the *SMIB*. Security mechanisms are functionally general in a sense that each mechanism may be used for implementation of several security services.

The Third Layer: Security Services

Security services needed in the *CISS* are, first, those required by *ISO* [ISO88], but also some additional security services appearing in the literature [MUFT88D]. Each security service is designed and implemented as an autonomous, self-contained functional module, which may be called (used) by appropriate parameter lists and protocols. All security services are implemented in a form of security library, interfacing to the upper conceptual layers (agents and applications) by corresponding *Application Programming Interfaces (API)*. Prototype implementations of security services will be described in Section 8.3.2.

The Fourth Layer: Security Agents and Protocols

Security mechanisms are used to implement various security services. But since services are just *functions* of the security system, they are not physically implemented, but rather *provided* to users, by appropriate combinations and sequences of security mechanisms.

This functional layer is primarily needed for combinations and use of security mechanisms and security services. Logical components of the *CISS* on this layer are called *agents*. There are also special *protocols* for their cooperation, either between themselves or with the "outside" world. *CISS* agents and protocols will be described in Section 7.3.

Therefore, this layer of the conceptual model of the security system consists of security agents and protocols, as basic components of the *Comprehensive Integrated Security System*.

The Fifth Layer: Security Administration and Management Tools

Finally, the top conceptual layer consists of modules belonging to various aspects of security administration and management. They include all *operational functions* of the Security Administrator, all functions for *security management*, as recommended by *ISO* [ISO88], plus some *additional functions*, suggested as results of the original research. These modules are used for installation, monitoring, tuning, and restructuring of the *CISS*. Some examples of those modules will be given in Section 8.3.

7.2.2 Functional Structure of the ODP Security Architecture

One possible approach to the design and implementation of security architecture is *separation of functions* of the *ODP* system by their types. Clark and Wilson [CLAR87] implicitly distinguish two types of areas: the secure *ODP* system and the outside environment. According to Clark and Wilson, security and integrity controls must be placed "at the border" of the protected *ODP* system:

C5: *"Any Transformation Procedure (TP) that takes an Unconstrained Data Information (UDI) as an input value must be certified to perform only valid transformations, or else no transformations, for any possible value of the UDI. The transformation should take the input from a UDI to a Constrained Data Information (CDI), or the UDI is rejected"* [CLAR87].

When data is entered into an *ODP* system, two additional types of operations may be distinguished: *data processing* functions (in host systems) and *data communication* functions. Different security services should be applied in each of these two functional areas.

Therefore, three general types of functional areas in the *ODP* system, i.e. two types of "functional borders", may be established:

1. *transaction source area* (user data entry and query dissemination area), (outside of the *ODP* system);

2. *data processing* and *storage* area (host systems);

3. *data communications* area (OSI environment).

The transaction source area contains all data entry and other input/output functions, the processing area contains all elements of the network that possess processing power (usually host computers), and the data communications area contains all data communication facilities (communication nodes, lines, communication software modules, etc.). The global structure of the three functional areas is given in Figure 7.2.

Based on the above separation of functions in the *ODP* system, a useful notion for development, implementation, and use of security systems is that of a *security perimeter* [BRAN87]. A security perimeter is a homogeneous set of tools and measures, established "around" some computing environment, in order to protect it from the "outside" world. The overall goal of *ODP* security would be to handle data within each perimeter and to communicate data from one perimeter to another, all in a secure way. In principle, in the *ODP* system, one or several security perimeters may be established, depending on the underlying assumptions and design solutions. This notion is equivalent to the concept of the security domains mentioned in Chapter 5: a security perimeter indicates the limits of the domain and its border with another domain or the non-secure environment.

If a security perimeter is established around the entire (closed) system, as one extreme case, then it is assumed that no sensitive or valuable data are ever communicated outside the system, no threats are believed to exist in the communication network, or security is provided through *non-ODP* methods. In that case, just internal security services are needed. (Some closed networks are presently being operated in this manner.) This is acceptable as long as everyone and everything inside the perimeter is "trusted" and complies to the same security policy. Trust also implies that intentional threats or accidental undesirable events are considered to be minimal and undesirable disclosures, modifications, or losses of data can be controlled, because of the closed environment.

Another extreme situation would be to establish a security perimeter around each user process or individual application. This approach would provide high granularity security, since in this case each user process or a particular application would have its own protection methods. In this case nothing within the *OSI* communication architecture needs to be trusted. (This is the case of most of the current *OSI* applications – *X.32, X.400, X.500*, etc; each of them has one or more security methods recommended.) However, this approach requires that all desired security services be implemented in every user process, in every program or application. Although possible, this approach is contrary to the goal of *OSI* for performing services in the layers of *OSI* rather than in each user process. Inter-domain security services and management are also needed in this scheme. Duplication of security functions may cause problems in terms of their efficiency, compatibility or consistency.

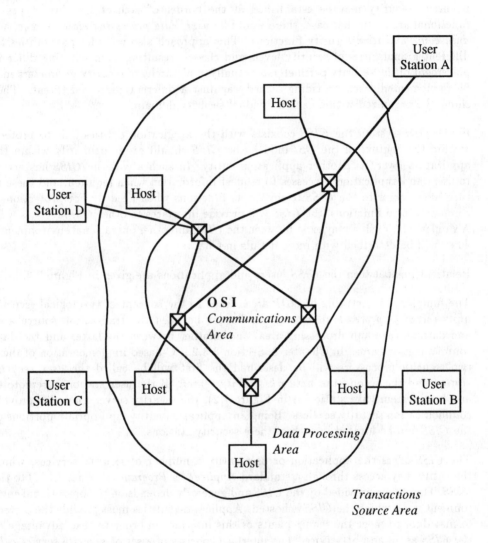

Figure 7.2. Functional Structure of the ODP System

In a real situation, a security perimeter may be established conceptually to be between these two extremes. For that, the described functional structure of three areas may be used: security may be established at the border of each of the three types of functional areas. In that case, there would be *user, data processing, data storage,* and *data communication* security functions. This approach also provides possibilities for different granularities of security levels and classes, resulting from selecting different placement of the security perimeters. Actually, a hierarchy of security perimeters may be implemented, each providing security against a different perceived threat. They should be organized within each individual security domain.

In the *ODP* system the *CISS* coexists with the application entities it is to protect. Within the context of the *OSI* model, the *CISS* should reside primarily within the application layer, as another application entity. In such a way the *CISS* has access to users and application processes to request information when required, and these in turn have access to the *CISS* to invoke its functions when needed. For protection of communication functions, the *CISS* will provide interfaces to other *OSI* layers as well. A similar relationship may exist between the *CISS* and other operational environments. They will be described with more details in Chapter 8.

Relationships between the *CISS,* users and applications are given in Figure 7.3.

The functional structuring of *ODP* areas leads to the concept of two logical security units (*security processors*), one at the border between the transaction source area and data storage and processing area, and another between the latter and the data communications area. In Chapter 8, Section 8.3.2, PC-based implementation of these two security processors will be described the first will be called the *user security station* and the second the *network security server.* If the user station is remote to any host system (like station *A* in Figure 7.2), the security server may also provide communication security services. Being an application entity, appropriate portions of the *CISS* will be located in each of these security stations.

The *CISS* offers the application or user entity a number of security services, which the entity may access through a standard *Application Program Interface (API)* to the *CISS.* The *API* is provided by the *CISS* and generally depends on the operational environment upon which the *CISS* is hosted. Application entities must provide the correct format data to meet the requirements of this interface in order to take advantage of the *CISS* as an add-on service. The interface consists of a set of *security service calls* and associated *parameters* used by the application and *CISS.* If the *CISS* is located remotely to the application, security of communications between applications and the *CISS* must also be provided.

In practice, some components of the *CISS* may be implemented as a trusted, tamper-proof hardware modules, and associated software. Such an implementation would give significant improvement in physical security over the equivalent software-only system, especially with regard to the security of the *SMIB* data, upon which the integrity of the system critically depends. The protection of agents within the module also

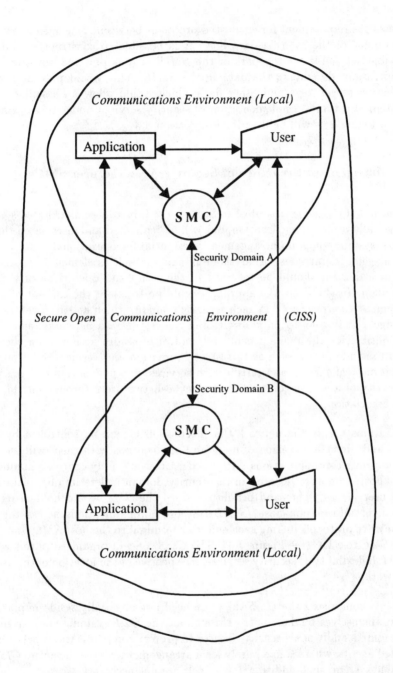

Figure 7.3. Relations of CISS to Users, Applications and Security Management Centres

eliminates the requirement for encrypted protocols between some agents, owing to the inaccessibility of the internal data bus. It is possible to construct a module using battery-backed *RAM* for the part of the *SMIB* that is powered down on detection of an intrusion, destroying the data in the *SMIB*. This would prevent compromise of the users' secret keys and other data which would allow an assaillant to defeat the system. Prototype implementation of security services under these principles, as shown in Figure 7.4, will be described in Section 8.3.

7.2.3 Management Structure of Security Architecture: SMCs

Components of the *CISS* described in Section 7.2.1, in a large distributed system, will not physically reside in one location, but will be replicated and distributed throughout the *ODP* system. Such an arrangement is essential for operational control, efficiency and management purposes. Analysis of threats, as well as elements of local security policy in a domain should be reflected in the setup and operations of the *CISS* in that domain. In this case, the approach would be to adopt the concept of a *Security Management Centre (SMC)* in each security domain, which acts as a central security "exchange", analogous to packet-switching centres in data networks, and which will be responsible for the management and control of secure activities on the network. This will include duties such as third-party provision and verification of public keys, notarization, registration and certification services, and association policing to ensure the integrity of a secure communication between two users throughout the duration of that association.

All operations within the network that need security will be controlled by the local *SMC(s)* and direct association of users and applications with them will be made via the appropriate communications *API*. Each *SMC* would fully control a number of user stations hosted upon it (located in its security domain), determining authentication, general user access rights and privileges which the *SMC* would hold in its security management information base *(SMIB)*. Secure communications across the network would involve protocols linking each end-user terminal to the host *SMC*, and protocols linking *SMC* to *SMC* (see Figure 7.4). The *CISS* concept organized in this way would provide full flexibility of security services, irrespective of the location of the user within the network.

The agents comprising the *CISS* therefore need not physically reside in one location, but may themselves be distributed throughout the *ODP* system. Such an implementation requires additional security services to protect communications between remote replicated agents, whereas in a purely local arrangement, where the entire *CISS* resides in a single system, such additional protocols are not necessary.

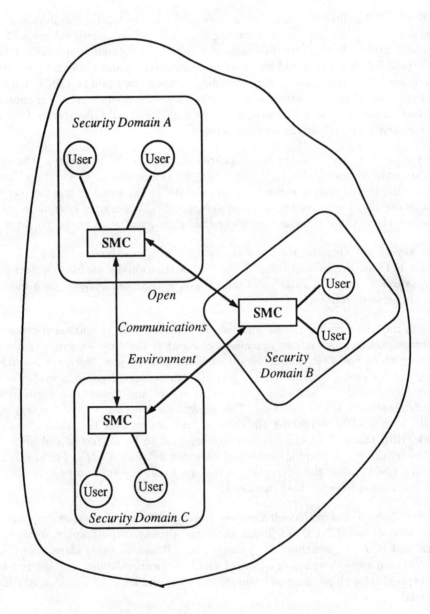

Figure 7.4. The Structure of Security Management Centres

7.2.4 Implementation Aspects of the ODP Security Architecture: Security Components of the ODP System

In Section 7.2.2 three functional areas were structured in the *ODP* system and security was suggested to be implemented "at the borders" of these functional areas. This particularly means that security functions would be implemented as specialized "*security servers*". For users, it would be "*user security server*", and the same with the other two types of functional areas: corresponding components could be called "*data storage and processing*" *security server* and *communications security server*. For short, in this context, these three security servers will be called *user security server, host security server,* and *communications security server*.

This idea of security servers has appeared already in the literature. The so-called *Trustworthy Network Interface Unit (TNIU)* for the *Newcastle Connection* Unix-based secure distributed system is described in [RUSH83]. The problem was the establishing of a secure distributed system based on unsecure *UNIX* operating systems in individual components of the system and with unreliable communications between them.

The key to the proposal for the security system is to enforce security of communication between insecure systems. Therefore, a trustworthy meditation device, called a *Trustworthy Network Interface Unit,* or *TNIU,* is placed between each host system and its network connection.

The initial and very restrictive purpose of *TNIUs* was to permit secure and reliable communications only between machines belonging to the same security partition. Controlling which hosts can communicate with one another is a *Reference Monitor* function, but because a communication network can be subverted or tapped, the *TNIUs* must also provide a separation function to isolate and protect the legitimate host-to-host communications channels. This separation function is provided cryptographically, with *TNIUs* encrypting all communications sent over the communication network. Host machines in their system are assumed to be untrusted and may attempt to thwart the cryptographic protection provided by their *TNIUs*. For this reason, in the described system the encryption is managed very carefully to prevent clandestine communication between host machines.

Some improvements of that idea may be based on the application of cryptography at each user station [CNUD90]. Today there are already cryptographic algorithms, like DES and RSA, implemented on a single chip. Based on these chips, more complex processors may be designed in a form of small hardware modules, containing a number of cryptographic chips, internal memory (for data and keys) and appropriate interface controllers.

The concept of user security processors requires various cryptographic keys, such as:

- user public and secret keys;

- keys related to user groups (threshold schemes or secure teleconferences);

- the computer (station) key;

- the public key of the Security Administrator.

At the user side, all these keys and other secret information should be stored in the user's equivalent of a personal "smart card".

There are a number of very good reasons to use smart cards to hold user keys and the relevant secret parameters:

1. The amount of data that must be memorized by a user or stored on a magnetic strip card in the comprehensive security system is too big.

2. The security properties and advantages of smart cards are well-known.

3. The built-in "intelligence" of smart cards makes it possible to execute some of the necessary cryptographic functions inside the smart card.

A smart card may have several functions and purposes:

a. it may be used as a *token,* for user identification and authentication, having information, such as: the name of the owner, the crypto-identifier of the owner, his language code, his authority level, application and version number, the start and expiration date, etc.;

b. it may be used for the storage of user secret data or key information, such as: the secret and public *RSA* key of the user, information to verify the authenticity of the public *RSA* key of the Security Administrator, etc.

At the host side, the necessary cryptographic keys and other security parameters should be stored in the host security server. This server may be integrated with the communications security server. The following cryptographic functionalities are required from such a global server:

a. the (safe) storage of the various necessary *RSA* keys;

b. the (safe) distribution of the public components of these keys;

c. capabilities to add link-protection to outgoing messages and to remove it from incoming messages.

The host security server may be used not only to provide the necessary cryptographic computing power to the host computers in the *ODP* system, but also for safe storage of the various *RSA* keys and other security parameters at the host side. This means that this server should be used to store some of the segments of the *SMIB*.

Of course, other solutions of this kind exist in this area, but common to all of them is the concept of functional areas, and each of the servers is purposely designed to assist at the borders of each of these areas.

Regardless of the approach (functional, operational, or management), the global security system must be designed and implemented in its totality. The next section contains all the details of the design of the *Comprehensive Integrated Security System (CISS),* whose global structure was briefly outlined in Section 7.2.1.

7.3 DESIGN OF THE COMPREHENSIVE INTEGRATED SECURITY SYSTEM (CISS)

The *Comprehensive Integrated Security System,* because of its functional complexity and topological distribution, should not be designed as a monolithic system. Rather, it should be decomposed into global functional elements, here referred as *Security Agents.* Security agents are the results of modelling techniques of the security system in the *ODP* environment. The agents not only perform their specific, logically related functions, but they also mutually cooperate to provide functioning of the total security system. These interactions between agents and interactions with the "outside" world must use *security protocols.*

The concept of security agents and their mutual protocols is designed to provide a model from which a comprehensive and complete set of security services may be developed. By appropriate combinations, parametrization, and sequencing of security mechanisms, agents may provide a complete set of functions of the security system by interaction to the "outside" world (users, applications, OSI layers, other security modules, etc). Besides operational security facilities, security agents provide the basis for other security relevant functions, constituting security management facilities, as shown in Figure 7.1.

The concept of a generic security system is attractive to users or applications which may wish to transmit sensitive data across networks. The producer of an application program will typically not know the sensitivity of the application data, so he may not build security into his program or application in advance. When an application handles data, it is the data that may be sensitive, not the application program itself. The application is often, or usually, written without regard for security. It is desirable however, that the application be suited for use with sensitive data and that security may be provided as an occasional value-added service. It can be assumed that security will not be required at all times within an application. The provision of a security system, whereby the security may be switched on and off, means that the overheads and expenses associated with security can be avoided for non-sensitive public domain type data.

One of the fundamental properties of the *CISS* is its ability to be used as a comprehensive, autonomous security server, as it may provide security to multiple applications at the same time. Because the format of the data used by various applications tends to vary from application to application, the *CISS* also provides an interface for communications with the "outside world": users and the operational environment (applications, host OS, OSI stack, LANs, etc.).

In the *OSI (ODP)* environment (OSI reference model) the *CISS* will be functionally located as another application layer entity. Applications and users should communicate with the *CISS* via a dedicated interface module, which is part of the *CISS*. The interface module for user communications will be designed as a general *user agent* which should be used by each user who needs the *CISS*. The *CISS* interacts with the operational environment through another special component functioning as the *operational environment agent.*

Unless a protocol between an application and the *CISS* (through the *User or OPEN Agents*) exists, users and applications may not use the *CISS*. This means that, after the *CISS* is installed, each standard application in the *ODP* system must be appropriately modified to interact with it. The same applies to the user interactive facilities. The output of one (local) instance of the *CISS* must be in a form comprehensible to the receiving *CISS* arrangement at the other end of the network. The *CISS* should be applicable to any business or communications applications. Such applications do not usually have security functions built in, so the option of using the *CISS* to provide security should be attractive. Of course, it must be carefully verified and guaranteed that the application (or an illegal user) cannot bypass *CISS* at any time. Similar principles can be used in the *CISS* modules as are used for detecting viruses and other illegal software modifications.

The *CISS* is conceptualized as a collection of communicating and cooperating agents. Each agent carries out a strictly defined task. These tasks are combined in order to provide security services. The agents are independent (autonomous) of each other, so that various combinations of agents may be used. The same series of agents may provide different services by being combined in different orders.

An agent is defined to be a logical component of the security system, designed to implement a particular function or group of functions. The functional modularization of the system in this manner makes possible the general definition of a flexible security architecture. These agents will be involved with the interactions between users and applications, and the interaction between applications. These agents, their interactions and overall management are central functions in the *Comprehensive Integrated Security System*. The main criteria for structuring the ten agents in this text was the design of functionally homogeneous modules.

The ten security agents of the *CISS* are the following:

1. User Agent (UA): The agent for interactions between users (people) at one side and the *CISS,* used both for user operational and user management functions.

2. Security Administrator Agent (SAA): The agent for exclusive interactions with network management personnel, first, with the Security Administrator (a tool for performing all Security Administrator operational and management functions), plus the agent for security policy controls by management.

3. Security Services Agent (SSA): The agent for provision, coordination and management of security services.

4. Security Mechanisms Agent (SMA): The agent for provision, coordination and management of individual security mechanisms.

5. SMIB Agent (SMIBA): The agent for exclusive access to the *SMIB.* This agent performs all operations on the *SMIB* on behalf of all other components of the *CISS* system.

6. Agent for Operational Environment Interactions (OPENA): The agent responsible for interactions with the operational environment, primarily in a local environment (applications, host OS, OSI layers, LANs, etc.).

7. Association Agent (AA): The agent responsible for establishing and maintaining security of the overall peer-entity associations (end-to-end protection).

8. Inter-Domain Communications Agent (IDCA): The agent responsible for secure communications between heterogeneous security domains.

9. Monitoring Agent (MA): The agent for continuous monitoring of all security relevant events, access (via the *SMIB Agent*) to the security log segment and management of all operations upon that segment.

10. Recovery Agent (RA): The agent responsible for all security violation detection and *CISS* error recovery.

The overall structure of the *CISS* agents, their interrelations, and interactions with the "outside world" are shown in Figure 7.5.

7.3.1 Basic Modules, Security Mechanisms, and Security Services

7.3.1.1 Mathematical Modules

The primary functions of the *CISS* system are security services, and they are implemented (structured) as sequences of the corresponding security mechanisms. As already mentioned in Section 7.2.4, the basis for implementation is the set of atomic mathematical algorithms which are quite general in terms of the number of digits in the numerical values and calculations. The algorithms used for prototype implementations of the security system, described in Section 8.3, may handle numbers *up to 500 decimal digits,* and with such numbers they may perform all the necessary

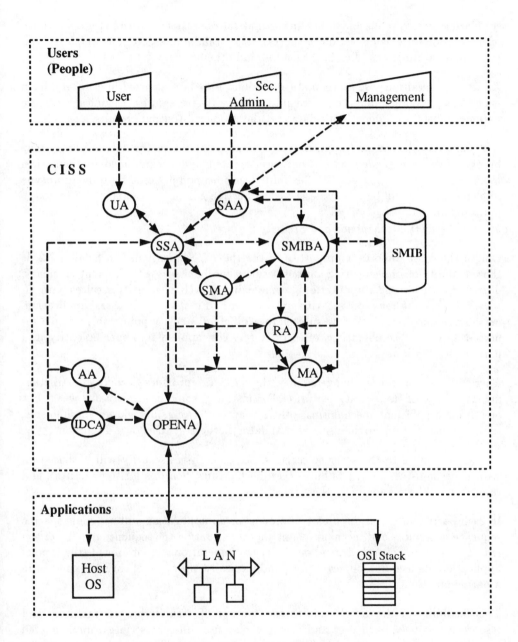

Figure 7.5. Interrelations between CISS Agents

standard cryptographic and other mathematical operations: arithmetic operations, operations in finite fields, various tests (primality, randomness, etc.), as well as special mathematical functions: Jacobi, Legendre, and others.

All these general-purpose mathematical modules may be organized in a library, from which basic modules may be linked into other software security modules, with the parameter lists containing input data and the produced (output) results.

Although very general and applicable, this concept of the mathematical library may be even further extended with other, user-created and programmed mathematical modules, to further improve *CISS* flexibility. Specific modules used for some prototype implementations will be briefly described in Section 8.3.

7.3.1.2 Security Mechanisms and Security Services

One of the most important properties of the the *CISS*, mentioned in Section 7.2, is the possibility of implementing various security mechanisms, with different efficiency, degree of security and computational complexity, as well as security services with *alternative combinations* of security mechanisms. Finally, each user, application, network resource, etc., may be subject to a different security policy, in principle reflected as various combinations of security services, applied to a specific entity in a particular situation.

Therefore, besides conceptual generality, the *CISS* also provides *flexibility* in structuring and usage of its security features. For instance, some users may use weak, but operationally efficient mechanisms, others may use strong, but slower mechanisms, some will use certain mechanisms as mandatory, others at their own discretion.

The same applies to the security services: for some users security will be based on strong mechanisms, for others on weaker mechanisms. Services for some entities and resources will be mandatory, others selective.

In each particular situation, a user, a process or an application will use some specific sequence of services and mechanisms, in another situation the sequence may be different. This will, in general, depend on the type of operational environment, the type of application, its users, resources it uses, and naturally, the types of threats expected in a particular situation.

This flexibility of the *CISS* leads to the concept of *security profiles* for users and resources. Namely, each user and resource may use different services, implemented by different mechanisms with different sized parameters. These variations must be represented somehow for the determination of user security capabilities and for negotiation with other users. One possible representation of user security profiles may be as structures (sequences) of binary data (vectors). Each component of the structure designates some specific service and binary sequences in those structures that determine the security mechanisms, their characteristics and conditions for their use.

These aspects of the *CISS design* require much more detail and depend on available technology, but for conceptual purposes, some illustrative examples will be included in this section. Some additional information about prototype implementations of the *CISS* system may be found in Section 8.3.

Table 4.1 contains the list of security services suggested for the extended *OSI* security architecture. Each of these services may be implemented with different security mechanisms. Here some suggestions for implementation of some of the security services by different mechanisms are listed:

- *Entity (and Peer-to-peer) Authentication:* simple password, variable password, inverted password, handshaking, zero-knowledge protocols, digital signature, etc.

- *Data Confidentiality:* DES, FEAL, RSA, etc.

- *Data Integrity:* MAC-16, MAC-32, MAC-64, MAC-128, MD2, MD4, MD5, digital seal, etc.

- *Access Control:* access control matrix, access control list, conditional access, etc.

- *Non-repudiation:* confirmation mechanisms, security log, digital signature, special protocols, notary services, etc.

- *Secure Group Communications:* multisignatures, conferences, threshold schemes, etc.

- *Prevention of Data Inference:* trackers, security log, conditional access, etc.

The security profile of each entity determines the use of the security services and the corresponding mechanisms in each particular situation. Assuming that when logging on to the system each user must go through the entity identification and authentication service, other services are determined by the corresponding user security profile.

Security profiles are therefore sequencing data leading the *CISS* system through various stages and operations for each user and his particular session.

An example of such processing is given in Figure 7.6. In that figure, implementation of *OSI* and some other security services is suggested by alternative security mechanisms.

A user always goes through the *Entity Authentication* security service (path (1) in Figure 7.6). After that, a user may choose, for instance, *Data Confidentiality* security service (path (2)), *Data Integrity* service (path (3)) or both (path (2) and (4)), he may involve in some *Secure Group Communications* (path (9)), etc. *Data Confidentiality* may be with *Recovery*, in which case *Security Log* may be needed (path (6)), or *Data Integrity* may be with *Recovery* (path (7)). If a user, after signing on, wants to access some network resources, he must go through the *Access Control* (path (5)). If, for instance, *Data Inference* for that access should be prevented, path (8) will be followed.

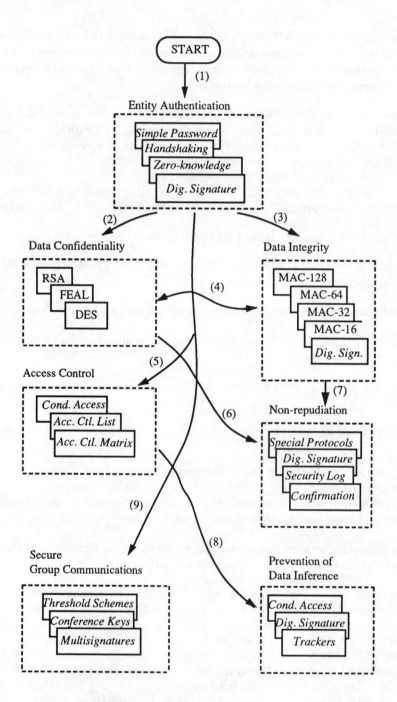

Figure 7.6.   Sequencing Data for CISS Operations

Obviously, various combinations of security mechanisms and services from Figure 7.6 may be selected. Some options may be "in-built" into the user security profile, but some may be selected by the user himself. The user security profile may be structured in a form of groups of bits, with the first bit denoting the applicability of the service, and the other bits in a group (positionally) denoting the mechanisms used for implementation of the particular security service.

For a user (*USER-ID = SMITH*) with mandatory *Entity Authentication*, who has selected to be involved in a secure group communication with confidential data transfer and non-repudiation, the following security profile may be established. It indicates the particular security mechanisms selected for implementation of the desired security services (abbreviations: *E.A.* – Entity Authentication, *D.C.* – Data Confidentiality, *D.I.* – Data Integrity, *A.C.* – Access Control, *N.R.* – Non-repudiation, *G.C.* – Group Communications, *D.Inf.* – Prevention of Data Inference):

User-Id	E.A.	D.C.	D.I.	A.C.	N.R.	G.C.	D.Inf.
SMITH	1 0 1 0 0	1 0 0 1	0 0 0 0 0	0 0 0 0	1 0 1 1 0	1 0 1 0	0 0 0 0

7.3.2 SMIB: The Structure of Segments and their Usage

The *SMIB* is the "heart" of the *CISS* and is one of its most important components from the security point of view. The design of the *SMIB* must be based on general *ODP* security requirements and its segments must be protected to the highest level of security.

The *SMIB* is the repository in which the *CISS* maintains all data pertinent to its security functions, including such data as identities of authorized users, authentication data, user entity capabilities and privileges, security parameters of all network resources, access control privileges, various processing and recovery logs, etc. The conceptual model of the *SMIB* means that individual segments are identified and structured, their mutual dependencies and relations are indicated, and their usage for providing all security relevant parameters to other components of the *CISS* is globally described.

The conceptual model of the *SMIB* may be designed as an extension of the standard addressing structures used in various operational environments. These may be, for instance, the *X.500 Recommendations* for *OSI* systems, addressing and name resolution structures in the *TCP/IP* protocol, etc.

In this section, simply as an example of the design of the *SMIB*, the *X.500* has been selected. The reason is that *X.500* addressing scheme has also been accepted by the *TCP/IP* recommendations (appropriate Requests For Comments (RFC)), so the two most popular WAN protocols, OSI and TCP/IP, both use a similar addressing structure. This structure has been chosen for the *CISS* because of its broader applicability. The *X.500* DIT structure is shown in Figure 7.7.

7.3.2.1 SMIB as Extended X.500 Directory Information Base

Accepting the recommended set of object classes and their mutual relations for identification purposes, the complete *SMIB* structure may be developed as an extended *X.500* model. Hardware devices (components) of the *ODP* system may be identified as an object class *Device*. Users (people) of the *ODP* system may be identified by object classes *Person, Residential Person, Organizational Person* or *Organizational Role*. The *Application Process* object class is used to define entries representing application processes, and the *Application Entity* object class is used to define entries representing application entities. These entities are primarily *data sets*. The conclusion about the *X.500* recommendation is that its object classes and their attributes are quite suitable to be used for *identification purposes* of all security-relevant elements of the *SMIB*. Attribute **commonName** may be used as an entity identity.

The *Directory Information Tree* of the standard *X.500* object classes in Figure 7.7 is structured in seven levels. Entities participating in the *ODP* operations are on levels *6* and *7*. Active network objects (users and processes) are all on level *6*, while passive objects are on level *7*. This structure will appear later very convenient for the extensions of the *X.500* model with security-relevant object classes or attribute types.

In addition to the entity identification security service, which is based on an attribute **commonName,** the *X.500* recommendation, through the *X.509,* also includes the entity authentication security service. Therefore, the *X.500* model has some elements (object classes, attributes, and protocols) for security. So, the complete *SMIB* may be designed by:

- accepting all *X.500* elements for identification purposes;

- accepting *X.509* recommendations for the authentication service;

- extending *X.500* Directory Information Base to include other attributes and object classes (segments) needed for design and usage of the *SMIB*.

The *X.500* recommendations suggest many attribute types to be used for the description of objects. Among them, the following may be relevant for security purposes:

Object (Entity) Identification: For identification of objects (entities) *Relative Distinguished Name (RDN)* and *Distinguished Name (DN)* should be used. RDN is a set of attribute value assertions, each of which is true, concerning the distinguishing values of the entry. On the bottom of the hierarchy of attributes there is always the **commonName** attribute which is used as the entity identity. The Distinguished Name of a given object (entity) is defined as being the sequence of the *RDNs* of the entries which represents the object and all its superior entities.

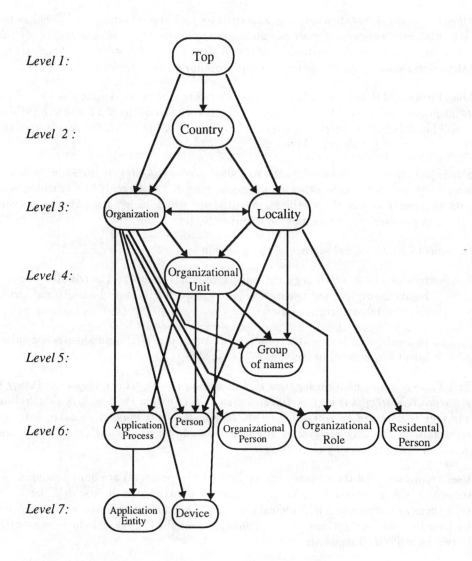

Figure 7.7. X.500 DIT Structure

Object (Entity) Authentication: For authentication of objects (entities) *X.509* has two elements: *user password* (for simple authentication procedure) and elements of some public-key cryptographic system: *secret* and *private key* (for strong authentication). (More details about *X.509* authentication procedures are given in Section 4.2.5.)

UserPassword is just one attribute type, therefore it may be included as part of the *Identification segment* of the *SMIB*. Since a password is only needed for active entities, it will be included in objects on level *6* in Figure 7.7. Object *Person* already contains that attribute. (See also the Appendix.)

Strong authentication is based on the so–called *user certificates:* it is the public key of a user together with some other information, rendered unforgeable by encipherment with the secret key of the certification authority which issued it. (All the relevant details of the user certificate may be found in Section 3.2.5.)

In terms of *SMIB* logical segments, the question is whether:

a. to store in a *SMIB* segment only a minimal number of attributes and elements needed for authentication, and create certificates "in real time", when establishing associations, or

b. to create certificates in advance, store them in *SMIB* permanently for subsequent (repetitive) usage.

The *X.509* recommendation suggests the second approach: *"It is a major advantage of a certificate system that user certificates may be held within the directory as attributes and may be obtained by users of the Directory in the same manner as other Directory information. The user certificates are assumed to be formed by "off-line" means, and placed in the Directory by their creator".*

User certificates and their usage (the authentication protocol) are quite complex. Although *X.509* recommends to treat certificates as attributes, it would be better to keep them as a separate *SMIB* logical segment. Therefore, attributes and parameters for identification and authentication of entities, described so far, should be structured in two logical *SMIB* segments:

a. *X.500 Identification* segment (which for security purposes includes only entity identity and password and therefore provides possibilities only for entity identification and simple entity authentication), and

b. *User Certificates* segment (which contains user certificates and may be used for strong authentication).

There are seven types of *X.500 Identification* segments for different object classes, relevant to security (number 8 to 14 in the Appendix). User certificates are included as (optional) attributes in the *Extended Security* segment.

Simple and strong authentication procedures as suggested by *X.509* may be considered as rather "classical" security mechanisms for an entity authentication security service. In research papers and the literature several alternative mechanisms with better properties may be found. An especially interesting class of authentication mechanisms are the so-called *zero-knowledge protocols.* A good overview of some of these authentication mechanisms may be found in [FUMY90]. These mechanisms require two sets of authentication parameters: *secret* user authentication parameters and their corresponding *public* user authentication parameters. While with a simple authentication scheme the correspondence between user secret password and its recorded counterpart is a *non-invertible* transformation, in zero-knowledge protocols the correspondence is established through special *zero-knowledge* transformations.

For practical purposes, owing to their *secrecy* and a *large number* of secret user authentication parameters, these parameters are usually recorded on some private digital device (chip-card, smart card, etc.) and privately held by their owners. The structure and content of this set of secret authentication parameters depend on selection, design and practical implementation of the *CISS.* These parameters may be considered as another logical segment of the *SMIB.* In Section 7.2 this segment was called the *Confidential (private)* segment. A possible structure of this segment is suggested in the Appendix.

Corresponding public parameters, related to user confidential parameters, should be organized and recorded in a separate *SMIB* segment. In Section 7.2 this segment was called the segment with static security parameters. Since this segment is used for mechanisms and services beyond current *ISO/OSI* security recommendations, it will be called the *Extended Security* segment. For the moment we can say that it may contain user certificates for strong entity authentication.

In Sections 4.2.1, 4.2.2 and 4.2.3 additional communication security services, user security services in end-systems and security management services were suggested (see Table 4.1). They are: threshold schemes, secure teleconferences, anonymous communications, subliminal channel, etc.

In [MUFT88C] some global security parameters needed for these services were considered: *threshold* value for threshold schemes, *identity* for secure group communications, etc. All these parameters should be a part of the *Extended Security* segment of the *SMIB.* (See *Extended Security* segment in the Appendix.)

In addition to these (static) *SMIB* segments, each active user in the network (after signing-on to the session) must define some (temporary) security parameters, additional to parameters from his *SMIB* security profile. These parameters are related to secure associations, they define security profiles of active user associations, and, therefore, they last while corresponding associations are active. These dynamic security parameters will be organized as a separate *SMIB* segment, called a *Secure Associations* segment.

Security parameters which may belong to this segment depend on the selection of security services, mechanisms, algorithms, and their specific implementations, and some of those parameters, suggested in [MUFT88C], may be:

   a. secret cryptographic *session key;*

   b. the *seed* for the random number generator;

   c. an *initialization vector,* for message chaining;

   d. another secret *cryptographic key* for subliminal channel security service;

   e. *conference key,* in case of secure group communications;

   f. *message sequence number;*

   g. *time stamp* (synchronized network global time).

Each entry in this *SMIB* segment may be normalized to each user, in which case there would be one entry for each user in the segment, or each entry may be normalized to each active association, in which case there would be multiple entries for each user, one for each of his/her active associations. An object class *Secure Association,* as suggested in the Appendix, is established for each active association.

With the object classes established and described so far, all except *access control* and *non-repudiation* security services may be implemented. Access control requires specifications in the form of special parameters, called *access rights (or capabilities),* which allow active entities to access passive network resources and specify the conditions and ways of their usage. Non-repudiation is a security service eliminating the possibility that a user repudiates his participation in an association; he cannot repudiate the contents of messages he has sent or received. Access control rights are usually structured in the form of a matrix; rows denoting entities, columns denoting resources, while the matrix elements denote the access rights. The non-repudiation security service requires some form of a system log in which all security relevant information will be recorded. Both of these two forms (access rights matrix and security log) are designed as separate *SMIB* segments.

7.3.2.2 Definition of the Extended Access Control Segment

X.500 recommendations, in particular *X.501,* describe (in Annex F) the access control security service for the *Directory Information Base (DIB).* It only contains guidelines, which may be used as a starting point for designing an *SMIB* segment to provide an access control security service.

The two principles that guide the establishment of procedures for managing an access control security service are:

a. There must be means for protecting information in the Directory from unauthorized *detection, examination,* and *modification,* including protecting the *Directory Information Tree (DIT)* itself from unauthorized modification.

b. The information required to determine users' rights to perform a given operation must be available to the *DSA(s)* involved in performing the operation in order to avoid further remote operations solely to determine these rights.

Presently, *X.501* identifies four levels of protection:

1. protection of the entire subtree of the *DIT;*

2. protection of an individual entry;

3. protection of an entire attribute within an entry;

4. protection of selected instances of attribute values.

From the above information it may be concluded that the subjects (active components) of the access control security service are the *network entities.* These may be persons (network users), application processes or hardware devices. Therefore, for identification purposes of active components the scheme suggested by the *X.500 Identification* segment is quite satisfactory. Six types of these segments (numbered *8* to *12* and *14* in the Appendix, on level *6* and *7* in Figure 7.7) are considered as active components of the access control service.

Network objects which may be used by subjects, and therefore must be protected by the access control, are the *application entities* (software resources) and the *devices* (hardware resources). Both of these two types of resources have their corresponding object classes (number *13* and *14* in the Appendix and located at level *7* in Figure 7.7). Therefore, network devices, which may be used as network resources, but may also initiate various actions, are at the same time subjects and objects for the access control service.

A previous reference in *X.501* indicates that the application entity is not a satisfactory level of granularity for access control, since this service must be applied, not only to individual entries in the *DIT* (corresponding to individual application entities), but also to the *attributes* and selected instances of *attribute values.* This extends the notion of objects of the access control security service to individual attributes, which need protection as a whole or selectively, based on their particular values. Being elements used to describe all other objects of a *DIT,* a new object class, called *ATTRIBUTE - SET* will be defined. It is a subclass of all object classes at level *6* and *7* in Figure 7.7, and therefore of any other object class in the *DIT* from the same figure. *ATTRIBUTE* type is defined by *ATTRIBUTE* macro, clause *9.5.3* in the *X.501* recommendation, and in its Annex C (Attribute data types). *ATTRIBUTE - SET* object class is defined by *ATTRIBUTE - SET* macro (clause 9.4.7). Since attributes themselves are objects for access control protection, they must be defined as a separate object class. The

ASN.1 notation of this new object class is given in the Appendix (number *18,* object class *20*).

Besides active network components (subjects) accessing passive network components (objects or network resources), the third component of the access control security service are the *access rights*. *X.501* suggests use of the following access rights: *detect, compare, read, modify, add, delete, naming*. Other papers, for instance [GRAH72] suggest, in addition, access rights: *create, block, wakeup, stop, execute*. A definite list of these access rights is not the goal of this text, it may be established by a thorough analysis, interpretation and synthesis of access rights that appear in the literature.

Most of the papers dealing with access control treat that security service as a simple access control procedure, but in [BUSS81A] a complete model of this security service is designed. At a conceptual level, access control is treated as a collection of 4-tuples from the set $S \times O \times R \times C$, where: S is a set of subjects, O is a set of objects, R is a set of access rights, and C is a set of conditions which must hold in order that subject $s \in S$ may access object $o \in O$, and use it according to the access right $r \in R$. This interpretation leads to the definition of a new object class, containing the described 4-tuples. It may be noticed that while subject and object identities are simple attributes, access rights and corresponding access conditions (appearing in pairs) are attribute sets. At least one element (pair): (*access right, access condition*) must appear in that attribute set.

With this access control scheme, not only simple control of accesses may be performed, but with appropriate interpretations, conceptual modifications, and design extensions of the described scheme, some other security services from the Extended OSI security architecture (Table 4.1) may be implemented. This can be achieved by appropriate interpretation of the *access condition* parameter. Namely, since the access condition is a predicate, whose value is *true* or *false*, that predicate must be implemented as a *condition checking module* (in *X.500* called *Attribute Value Assertion*). So, the *access condition* parameter is in fact *the name of the module* for value assertion. These modules, from a simple access control scheme, may be replaced by more general modules in the Extended access control scheme in order to establish the Extended *OSI* security architecture.

The *ASN.1* description of the new, *Extended Access Control* object class (segment of the *SMIB*) is given in the Appendix (number *19*).

7.3.2.3 Security Log Segment

This segment is needed for the integrity of cryptographic keys [DENN83], for the overall integrity of system resources, possibly for the non-repudiation security service, and also for monitoring and control purposes. All these functions may be achieved by the appropriate design and usage of the *Security Log*. Its use for integrity or cryptographic keys is described in detail in [DENN83]. Other aspects, especially the non-repudiation security service, may be achieved in a similar way, by recording appropriate security relevant elements in the *Log*. This *SMIB* segment may also be used for some security management functions from [ISO88], like *audit management* or *recovery*. Details of the use of the *Log* have been described in [MUFT88C].

The following events should be recorded in the *Log*:

1. registration of the new public key of each network user;

2. compromise of the public key of each user;

3. public keys certificates;

4. digital signatures and digital seals.

Each entry in the *Log* may have the following attributes:

- the type of the event: *LOG.TYPE*;

- entity identity: *LOG.ID*;

- public key: *LOG.PK*;

- signature certificate: *LOG.CERT*;

- digital signatures: *LOG.SIGN*;

- digital seals: *LOG.SEAL*;

- time of the recording: *LOG.TIME*.

The *time attribute* in the *Log* must be signed by the network security administrator *(SA)* when entering in the *Log*, so that the correct time sequence of entries is guaranteed.

Security Log is a new *SMIB* segment, needed for the Extended *OSI* security architecture. Its conceptual structure in the *ASN.1* notation is given in the Appendix (item number *20*, object class *22*).

The conceptual model of the *SMIB*, as an extended *X.500 DIB*, is shown in Figure 7.8. This figure is based on relevant details of Figure 7.7. Description of all *SMIB* segments from Figure 7.8 in *ASN.1* notation is given in the Appendix. Figure 7.8 shows all object classes of the *SMIB* and global relations between them.

Identification Elements of the Extended AC-Segment

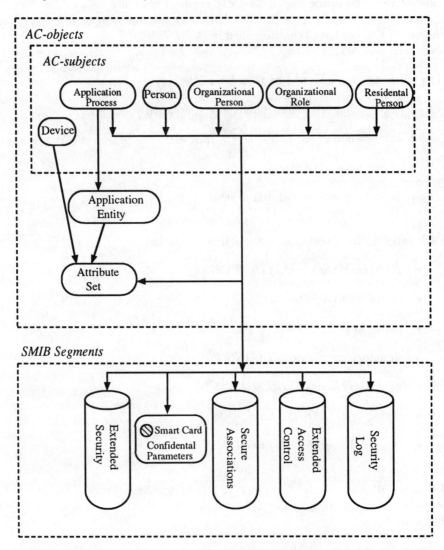

Figure 7.8. SMIB as Extended X.500 DIB

7.3.3 Security Agents

7.3.3.1 User Agent (UA)

The *User Agent (UA)* of the *CISS* comprises "one third" of the interface of the *CISS* to the "outside world". The *CISS* can communicate *(a)* with regular users (people), *(b)* with some management bodies, and *(c)* with the components of the operational environment. These interactions may also be combined, for instance in the case when the application has requested a security service from the *CISS*, and the *CISS* requires some information directly from the user who initiated the application, such as a password, etc.

The main functions of the User Agent are the following:

1. To interface between the user entity and the *Security Services Agent (SSA)* of the *CISS.*

2. To interpret all data from the user entity and ensure its validity before presenting it to the *Security Services Agent (SSA)*, and to determine the location and nature of errors, and inform the *SSA* accordingly. Also, to process all data coming from the *SSA* into a form suitable for interpretation by the user entity before presentation to the user entity.

3. To maintain *a library* of user entity request statements (temporary log), from which the *UA* will determine request/response validity, and suitable responses to the user entity, according to a strict set of rules, thus limiting the number of possible user actions. This particularly applies to prevention of data inference, context-oriented (dynamic) protection schemes, and prevention of information generation.

4. To accept a request from the *SSA* when the service requested required further information from the user, and to act upon this to interrogate the user in a suitable manner for this information.

5. To assist users in performing their security management tasks. Those are functions by which each user as the owner of individual resources defines access rights and privileges for other users of these resources.

6. To provide information and help to users.

The *UA* is conceived as a separate entity from the *SSA,* because the *UA* must be capable of interfacing with many user entities, thus freeing the *SSA* from the complexities of multiple interfaces.

7.3.3.2 Security Administrator Agent (SAA)

The *Security Administrator Agent (SAA)* has five main functions.

First, it is responsible for interactions with the Security Administrator, allowing only the Security Administrator to provide modifications to the existing *SMIB* segments (registration of new users, definition of security profiles, monitoring of *CISS* operations, etc.). There must be very strict protocols and authentication for this type of operation within the system.

The second function of the *SAA* is the responsibility for the strict imposition of the system security policy upon the individual operations of, and interactions between, the other agents of the *CISS*. The main function of the *SAA* in this aspect is to provide a complete interface and a set of information for the management to control the security policy in the ODP system. Within this context the *SAA* should be used to provide the Security Administrator with various reports, indications and information concerning the implementation and usage of the security within the operational system.

The third function of the *SAA* involves communications (and control) of the *SMIB Agent* to read and write information into the *SMIB* and to modify existing information as new users are added to the system, existing users removed, security policy updated, user capabilities and privileges modified, and mechanisms and services are added/modified.

The fourth function of this Agent is to invoke certain security services through interactions with the *SSA* on behalf of the Security Administrator or network management.

Finally, the fifth function of the *SAA* is cooperation with *Monitoring* and *Recovery Agents* in order to ask for services from them or reports on the current status of their actions.

Therefore, the main functions of the *Security Administrator Agent* are the following:

1. To interface between the Security Administrator and the CISS (operational control).

2. To interface between the system management and the CISS (managerial control).

3. Cooperation and coordination with the *SMIB Agent*.

4. Invocation of security services through the *SSA* on behalf of the Security Administrator and network management.

5. Cooperation and coordination with the *Monitoring* and *Recovery Agents*.

The *SAA* may be invoked externally either by the Security Administrator or by authorized management personnel, in which case these two functions must be clearly separated by appropriate authorization, or it may be activated internally by switching from the *UA*. In the latter case, after turning on a station, all users would receive the same interface from the *UA*, but the Security Administrator and management personnel would be able to switch to the *SAA* by using the appropriate procedure and authorization.

In Figure 7.5 the invocation of the *SAA* is separated from the invocation of the *UA*.

7.3.3.3 Security Services Agent (SSA)

The *Security Services Agent (SSA)* is the central control and operational agent of the *CISS*. It is responsible for:

1. Accepting and checking the validity of all *CISS* service requests from various other agents: User Agent, Security Administrator Agent, Operational Environment Agent, Association Agent, Inter-Domain Communications Agent, Monitoring or Recovery Agent. This is an important function which is necessary to prevent invalid calls from trying to confuse or subvert the *SSA* into performing functions which are not permitted by the security policy. This validation is accomplished by the *SSA* checking all requests for security services against the user entity capabilities and privileges stored in the *SMIB* and the sequence of operations carried out at that time. Any request not expressly permitted for that user entity by the *SMIB* will be refused.

2. Selecting the appropriate security mechanisms pertinent to the function to be performed under the supervision of the *Security Mechanisms Agent (SMA)* by additional assistance of the *SMIB Agent*, passing the relevant sub-function control data to the *Security Mechanisms Agent* and sequencing the application of security mechanisms correctly to perform the requested security service.

3. Ensuring the correct routing of the information data to and from, and in the correct sequence among, the security mechanisms. It is possible to implement two completely different security services with the same set of security mechanisms, by merely using them in a different order. For example, two security mechanisms implementing a compression (hash) function such as *DES* in block chaining mode, and an *RSA* encryption/decryption scheme could be used for *(1)* a hybrid file encryption system for a confidentiality service, *(2)* file and message signatures for non-repudiation and integrity checks, and *(3)* checking signatures for authenticity and integrity.

4. Checking with the *SMIB* the capability of the user entity, and determining whether the user entity has the privilege to execute the requested service.

5. Cooperating with the *Operational Environment Agent, Associations Agent,* and *Inter-Domain Communications Agent* (in both directions) to provide the requested security services to the "outside world" in a local or remote domain.

6. Key management functions (generation, verification, storage and secure distribution of cryptographic keys): includes generating and distributing the session keys for communicating parties, when requested. This ensures secure instances of the session keys and also a secure and a standardized way of key distribution. The generation and delivery of the key pairs, the secret key and the public key to the right owner, and the public key to the directory, are also responsibilities of the *SSA*.

7.3.3.4 Security Mechanisms Agent (SMA)

The Security Mechanisms Agent must:

1. Accept control commands from the *SSA*, and select and control the security mechanisms to perform the service requested, including sub-function selection of multi-function mechanisms. For example, a *DES* card could perform normal block encryption, block chaining mode encryption and so on.

2. Return to the *Security Services Agent* the status information including details of function performed, status of operation (success, failure), etc.

3. Cooperate with the *SMIB Agent* in order to receive parameters and certain initial values for parametrization (tuning) of the required security mechanisms.

4. Cooperate with the *Monitoring* and *Recovery Agents* in order to use their services or to provide them with the required information for their functions.

7.3.3.5 SMIB Agent (SMIBA)

The *SMIB Agent* is responsible for interfacing the *SMIB* to the other *CISS* agents, including: accepting and processing all requests from the *Security Services Agent* for information from the *SMIB*, including such data as user entity identity checks, user entity authorisation, user entity capabilities and privileges, object entity validity, object entity authorisation, object entity security status, etc. In order to provide reporting information, this Agent must interact with the *SAA*.

Since all accesses to the *SMIB* must go through this Agent, all monitoring information and recovery procedures must also use this Agent.

7.3.3.6 Agent for Operational Environment Interactions (OPENA)

Besides the *User Agent* and the *Security Administrator Agent* this is the third agent for interactions with the "outside world". While the first two are in charge of human entities, this Agent is a primary interface of the *CISS* to the operational environment, including local applications, operating systems, or *LAN* modules. From Figure 7.5 it may be noticed that this Agent is also an interface for secure associations and interdomain communications.

In fact, external communications of the *CISS* are structured in the following way:

    a. There will be some applications (processes) autonomously accessing local resources in a secure way. They will do it through the *OPEN Agent* which will, in this case, cooperate with the local operating system only.

    b. Some applications will need to establish associations with other applications, but in the same security domain. This kind of secure relation may need negotiations as of what security services and mechanisms to use. Such associations will be established by the *Associations Agent* through the *OPEN Agent.*

    c. In the case where secure associations are established between entities in different security domains, some additional negotiations are needed. This is carried out by the *Inter-Domain Communications Agent* in association with the *OPEN Agent* for local operations.

Therefore, the functions of the *OPEN Agent* are very complex and diverse, depending on the particular situation described above. In principle, this Agent is responsible for "single-party" security activities in a local environment, plus the assistance to the *AA* and *IDCA* for secure remote associations, within the same or different security domains. The *OPEN* Agent, therefore, is responsible for:

    1. Accepting security service requests across the application programming interface *API* (to be described in Section 7.3.5) from the local environment and interpreting, validating and routing the requests to the *Security Services Agent*. Application software packages without the necessary *API* will not be able to call the *CISS* in the first place. Those packages with the *API* which make *CISS* request calls in error will receive back an appropriate error code by the *OPENA*.

    2. Ensuring that all output from the *CISS*, including control and information data, is routed back across the *API* at the same entry point which originated the request and the control/information data, to prevent "short-circuiting" of *OSI* layers or *OS* modules.

It should be noted that this Agent is specific to the system implementation of the *CISS*. In general, this Agent will provide the interface to whatever underlying network architecture is in use, and hence the reason why it was designated the *Operational Environment Agent (OPENA)*.

7.3.3.7 Association Agent (AA)

The *Association Agent (AA)* is responsible for the security control of associations between remote end-user entities throughout the duration of the connection. It is assumed that both entities are within the same security domain. (Otherwise the *IDCA* would be involved.) This Agent is responsible for sending the appropriate data when the connection is set up, such as keys, initial vectors, time stamps and so on, for exercising supervisory control during the connection, and for clearing down the association from the security facility aspects. In addition, detection of denial of service attacks should be one of its functions, by sending and receiving random supervisory packets, subject to the current quality of service conditions.

7.3.3.8 Inter-Domain Communications Agent (IDCA)

The secure connectivity of entities within a single security domain is assured by the *Associations Agent,* as in that case all communicating entities are subject to a common security policy. Secure inter-domain communications, however, present a special problem. The communicating entities in the two domains require the use of "translation" protocols to ensure a seamless continuity of security around the association. The *Inter-Domain Communication Agent (IDCA)* is responsible for recognizing inter-domain associations, and invoking additional protocols as necessary. But, inter-domain harmonization (translation of security requests) may or may not be possible.

For example, the remote entity may require some encryption mechanisms unavailable in the local environment. In this case, harmonization of security facilities would be impossible. The *IDCA* will, either in the negotiation stage or later, note that decryption by the local security mechanisms is not possible, and it will flag the appropriate error. If that happens in the communications stage, the *IDCA* will notify the *RA* which will return the appropriate flags to the calling application. The application will then either terminate the association, or re-request the remote entity to communicate in another security mode.

If the remote entity, however, is using say an *M-bit* algorithm, whereas the local processor is capable of decrypting only *N-bit* code, then communication is possible, provided the data is reblocked according to the appropriate run length before encoding/decoding. The *IDCA* is responsible for requesting the appropriate mechanisms via the *SSA* to attempt the translation. The formal analysis of this kind of system is difficult, but is representative of the sort of real problems that will be encountered when interconnecting diverse real networks.

7.3.3.9 Monitoring Agent (MA)

The *Monitoring Agent (MA)* is responsible for accepting and processing all data gathered by the *Security Services Agent* and passing it to the *SMIB Agent* for logging in the *SMIB,* including such data as security service requested, date and time, calling user *ID*, calling process, status (success failure), etc. It is envisaged that the *MA* will itself internally request one of the *CISS* encryption mechanisms, to encrypt the log ready for storage. The only entity with access to the security log will be designated persons (Security Administrator and high level management personnel), who will possess the decrypting keys for the security log, allowing managerial access to the log for the preparation of audit reports for security management and resource optimisation purposes. The Security Administrator will possess access rights to the security log data, and such access rights will be stored in its security profile in the *SMIB.*

The *MA* can also be an AI-based module that will detect problems even before they occur, and take the necessary actions for preventative or remedial measures.

7.3.3.10 Recovery Agent (RA)

The *Recovery Agent (RA)* is responsible for recovery from all *CISS* faults and eventual operational errors. Faults and errors may be caused either by hardware failure of units both within the *CISS* and external to it, and also by certain combinations of situations with which the *CISS* cannot cope, owing to ambiguity of requests for example. The *RA* will perform the important task of detecting these errors, and placing the *CISS* into such a state as to maintain the security integrity of the system, so that the *CISS* is not left in a state where it is vulnerable to attacks.

Faults outside the *CISS* could in certain circumstances also produce system errors. For example, an incorrectly constructed or incomplete data structure could be ambiguous, and the *CISS* may "hang". Internal error recovery routines will automatically re-request the data, but in the absence of a response, the *CISS* will transfer itself into a stable, secure state. The *CISS* has in effect, recovered "internally" from the error, but cannot, of course, influence events outside the *CISS*. Obviously, in a distributed security system, the boundaries cannot be clearly defined. The external errors should be recovered mainly by the application itself.

In the case of a fault developing with either the *SMIB* or the *SMIBA*, the *CISS* protocols will probably be designed so that the *CISS Recovery Agent (RA)* returns fatal errors to the *OPENA, SSA* or *SMA* for all requests, until the detected problem is corrected. Thus, a failure of the *SMIB* terminates all security activities of the user. This differs from faults which may develop with other *CISS* components, which may not return severe errors, but merely limit the operational effectiveness of the system to those functions not requiring the damaged facility.

7.3.4 Security Protocols between Agents

The ten agents of the *CISS* must communicate one with another, and with the outside world, via a rigid set of protocols. This is necessary to ensure that security policy is enforced without the possibility of illegal requests being serviced, and also to allow formal analysis of the system. These protocols must be designed for communications within a single security domain and also between security domains. They must be able to transfer regular data, user requests and security replies, as well as special information, such as cryptographic keys.

The matrix of agent interactions is shown in Figure 7.9. The agents at the side are calling agents and the agents at the top are called agents. (The leading diagonal is obviously blank, because agents do not require to talk to themselves.) Some of the other elements are also blank, representing agents which do not need to communicate with each other directly. For example, the *User Agent* never requires exchange of data with the *Association Agent*.

The remaining elements are numbered sequentially purely for reference purposes, and there are *44* agent interactions in total.

In order to cooperate, agents must mutually communicate. There are two possibilities to implement security protocols (inter-agent communications).

The first possibility is that cooperating agents send *direct* instructions to one another and receive the return status and other reports when instructions have been carried out. Agents should accomplish this by using some kind of a *message handling system*. Instructions and their operands are included in messages sent from one agent to another. The precise form of messages, their structure and fields, field syntax and field semantics depend on which two agents are communicating and which role each agent plays in the communication. Some global formats of inter-agent communication messages will be given later in this section.

A communicating agent plays one of two roles while communicating – it is either a client or a server. A server agent gives instructions to another agent (request for service). These instructions and their operands are included in the message sent to another agent. A client agent carries out instructions received from a server agent. The operations it performs will be carried out on operands (system objects) specified in the instruction message. When the instructions have been carried out, the client agent sends a suitable report back to the server agent.

The communications role played by an agent is valid only for a single communication with a single other agent. An agent can play the client role while communicating with one agent and act as a server agent in communication with another agent. For instance, an agent *A* instructs an agent *B* to carry out some instruction *X*. While carrying out the instruction *X,* the agent *B* requires the cooperation of another agent

Agents	UA	SAA	SSA	SMA	SMIBA	OPENA	AA	IDCA	MA	RA
UA	-	-	01	-	-	-	-	-	-	-
SAA	-	-	02	-	03	-	-	-	04	05
SSA	06	07	-	08	09	10	11	12	13	14
SMA	-	-	15	-	16	-	-	-	17	18
SMIBA	-	19	20	21	-	-	-	-	22	23
OPENA	-	-	24	-	-	-	25	26	27	-
AA	-	-	28	-	-	29	-	30	-	-
IDCA	-	-	31	-	-	32	33	-	-	-
MA	-	34	35	36	37	38	-	-	-	39
RA	-	40	41	42	43	-	-	-	44	-

Figure 7.9. The Matrix of CISS Agents Interactions (CISS Protocols)

C to carry out some another operation Y, while still acting as a client relative to the agent A. So the agent B is a client in relation to the agent A and a server in relation to the agent C, at the same time.

The second possibility would be to use the same common area for all inter-agent communications. This approach allows all agents to communicate via a common bus (common storage area), as opposed to a complex set of individual interconnections, which would itself increase the complexity of inter-agent communications and it would also inhibit the flexibility of the system. Since all requests are placed on a common bus, there should be a *driver module* to read, distribute and delete entries on the bus. Each agent must have the capability to send to the driver, to receive from the driver, and to recognize commands and parameters relevant to itself. This allows very easy protocol building and expansion of agent functions.

In this version, it would be important to define only the constraints on, and the standards to which protocols should be written, *not* rigidly define the protocols themselves. This allows flexible expansion of the protocols to cope with possible future agents, or implementations or architecture radically different from those commonly found at present.

All requests for security services will be primarily sent to the SSA. This agent receives a request and then carries it out to completion before being ready to accept and execute another request. Which other agents and security mechanisms the SSA must manage in order to fulfill a request depends on the nature of the request. On receiving a request the SSA will often contact the $SMIBA$ to find out what needs to be done in order to fulfill the request. Exactly what instructions are given to the SSA by the $SMIBA$ will depend on the protocols used to deal with the request. These in turn are evolved from the security policy and are then embodied in the capability (instruction) lists in the $SMIB$.

Although the exact data passed between agents in each of these protocols may be slightly different, the system is designed in a modular form, for both ease of interface and simplicity of software implementation. Each protocol is performed as a leading, header message, followed by a sequence of data messages. The formats of all protocols is therefore identical, with a defined *header message* containing control information pertinent to each specific protocol. This message is followed by a (free format) *data area*, following the Unix/DOS idea of an *IOCTL communication format*, comprising a series of *ASCIIZ* strings containing the parameters and details of the data to be proceessed by the required security mechanisms. This is, of course, one possible approach, i.e. to define the common structure of *API* calls and parameters.

The structure of the leading header message for all protocols may contain the following data:

```
{  Session.ID,
   Protocol.ID,
   Orginator.Agent,
   Recipient.Agent,
   Request.ID,
   Request.Reference,
   Date.Time.Group,
   f(TS),
   Security.Profile,
   Security.Level,
   Priority,
   Ack.Req.Flag,
   IOCTL.Length,
}
{  ASCIIZ IOCTL data  }
```

The fields are used as follows:

Session.ID – The serial number assigned to the request within the particular session, used within a multitasking environment, where identical request may refer to different calling applications.

Protocol.ID – The identification number of the protocol, as defined in the matrix in Figure 7.9.

Originator.Agent – The agent originating the request or data.

Recipient.Agent – The agent for whom the request or data is designated.

Request.ID – The serial number assigned to the request, used both for sequencing purposes in multi-function protocols, and for audit purposes.

Request.Reference – The serial number of the corresponding previous request to which this request is the reply.

Date.Time.Group – The date, time, or group stamp uniquely defining when the request was passed. This is vital for audit purposes.

f(TS) – A function of the time stamp. This is used in multi-function protocols, to chain the time stamps together. This allows verification of the true sequence of the protocols, and prevents replay attacks against the system.

Security.Profile – A set of security capabilities of the originator of the request (i.e. whether the request is within the purview of the security policy or not). This profile is usually established at the user registration time, and it contains all necessary security attributes and parameters for handling of the request.

Security.Level – A designator of the security level of the request, used both for audit purposes and for validating the calling entity privileges in connection with the request.

Priority – A designator quantifying the urgency of a request. In a multitasking environment, should two or more requests arrive simultaneously for the same service or mechanism, arbitration is carried out on the basis of the relative priority of the requests. Note that in the system as implemented, the *CISS* kernel is *not re-entrant*, so one request cannot interrupt another, even if it is of higher priority. It must wait for the protocol to terminate before taking control of the protocol itself.

ACK.Req.Flag – A flag indicating whether the calling agent requires acknowledgement of receipt of the calling protocol. This is in addition to the possible requirement that the called agent initiate a return protocol to the original caller.

IOCTL Length – The length of the following free-format *IOCTL* communication data field. This allows the recipient agent to be sure that it has received all parameters associated with the request, and that some have not been lost or truncated due to system error or sabotage.

The following table illustrates the typical field usage by the 44 *CISS* protocols defined in Figure 7.9:

Session.ID	* may be used by any protocol *
Protocol.ID	* always used by all protocols *
Originator.Agent	* always used by all protocols *
Recipient.Agent	* always used by all protocols *
Request.ID	* always used by all protocols *
Request.Reference	* may be used by some protocols *
Date.Time.Group	* always used by all protocols *
f(TS)	* may be used by any protocol *
Security.Profile	* always used by all protocols *
Security.Level	* used by protocols 01, 04, 05, 06, 07, 08, 09, 10, 11, 12, 15, 20, 26, 35, 42, 48
Priority	* used by protocols 08, 10, 30, 32, 39, 40, 42 *
Ack.Req.Flag	* may be used by any protocol *
IOCTL.Length	* always used by all protocols *
ASCIIZ IOCTL data	* may be used by any protocol *

The following examples illustrate typical data exchanges between selected agents of the *CISS:*

Protocol 01 : UA $\longrightarrow$ SSA

The *User Agent (UA)* is passing a request for a particular file to be accessed to the *Security Service Agent (SSA)*. The *ASCIIZ* strings contain the full system specification of the file.

Session.ID	9C (e.g.)
Protocol.ID	01 (unsigned byte)
Originator.Agent	01 (User Agent)
Recipient.Agent	03 (Security Services Agent)
Request.ID	3129 (e.g.) (file access)
Request.Reference	- - -
Date.Time.Group	12119007353412Z (e.g.) (longint)
f(TS)	- - -
Security.Flag	*TRUE*
Security.Level	002
Priority	03
Ack.Req.Flag	*FALSE*
IOCTL.Length	33 (unsigned integer)
ASCIIZ IOCTL data	c:\database\network\myfile.dat, 00h

Protocol 06 : SSA $\longrightarrow$ UA

The *Security Service Agent (SSA)* is passing a request for the user entity to authenticate himself to the *User Agent (UA)*, by passing the *ASCIIZ* strings containing the request information. This request is the response to the previous request, since (the security policy states that) the specific user may not access the requested file without additional authentication.

Session.ID	9C (e.g.)
Protocol.ID	06 (unsigned byte)
Originator.Agent	03 (Security Services Agent)
Recipient.Agent	01 (User Agent)
Request.ID	3165 (e.g.) (user authentication)
Request.Reference	3129 (e.g.) (file access)
Date.Time.Group	24029012040225Z (e.g.) (longint)
f(TS)	- - -
Security.Flag	*FALSE*
Security.Level	- - -
Priority	05
Ack.Req.Flag	*FALSE*
IOCTL.Length	27 (unsigned integer)
ASCIIZ IOCTL data	\$USER_NAME:\$USER_PASSWORD:, 00h

Protocol 39 : MA $\longrightarrow$ RA

The *Monitoring Agent (MA)* is passing a request for fault protection/error recovery to the *Recovery Agent (RA)* because an error has occurred during the current communications session. The *ASCIIZ* strings contain the request information.

Session.ID	3A (e.g.)
Protocol.ID	39 (unsigned byte)
Originator.Agent	09 (Monitoring Agent)
Recipient.Agent	10 (Recovery Agent)
Request.ID	8911 (e.g.) (comm. session recovery)
Request.Reference	- - -
Date.Time.Group	11039018451525Z (e.g.) (longint)
f(TS)	- - -
Security.Flag	*TRUE*
Security.Level	002
Priority	01
Ack.Req.Flag	*TRUE*
IOCTL.Length	27 (unsigned integer)
ASCIIZ IOCTL data	&&&& ERROR [47] &&&& ERROR [53], 00h

7.3.5 Guidelines for External Interfaces (API)

Although the *CISS* should be implemented as an application entity, it offers a full *OSI*-wide flexibility due to the appropriate *application programming interface (API)*. Such an interface must be designed to provide access to the *CISS* from various operational environments and by various users and applications. An advantage of this concept is the potential flexibility using the possibility of the *CISS* functions being called by other than operations in the Application Layer.

For the *OSI* environment, the *CISS API*, which could take the form of a software interrupt with appropriate parameters, for example, should be accessible from any of the *OSI* layers, not just the Application Layer. It is quite permissible for the Transport Layer, for example, to request data encryption services from the *CISS*. This conforms with the security recommendations of the *OSI*, which state that while the majority of security functions can be carried out at the Application Layer, there are a few which may need to be implemented in other layers.

When the *CISS* is invoked by some application, the appropriate *API* within the *OPEN Agent* is invoked. This module then acts as an interpreter between the application and the *CISS* activities. It is clear that the provision of such modules (*APIs*) increases the complexity of the *CISS* itself, since it must be able to interface with various applications and operational environments. This provision of an application translation front-end to a security system adds another sub-layer for the network passage to pass through. However, the extra path (sub-layer) can be seen as an insulator isolating the applications from the operations of the *CISS* and allowing the provision of transparent security services.

The *OPEN Agent* of the *CISS* will accept through the *API* the security request of the application. The request message will be broken down into its constituent parts, i.e. addressing data, other control data and content data. These parts of the security request are then passed on to the *SSA* via the *OPENA*. The parts which need to be kept in a plain form (e.g. routing data) are separated by the *OPEN Agent* from the sensitive data portion of the application output. The *API* module should be so designed as to be able to handle the request in this manner. Typically, the *API* modules for various applications and operational environments will differ, so each application needs its own interface module to the *CISS*, all within the *OPEN Agent*.

Should application requests conform to an *OSI* (or other operational environment) standard, they may be directly accepted by the *OPEN Agent*. This Agent translates the standard form of *OSI* request parameters lists into the format required by the *CISS*. This Agent should be suitable for all applications which conform to standard *OSI* requests. In this case it should not be necessary for each application to have its own *API* module. Because many applications may run at the same time in a multitasking environment, all standardized applications can share the same *API*. When standards become widespread, one *API* per standard operational environment will be satisfactory.

Standard *API* modules may be parts of the *OPEN Agent,* which is in turn part of the *CISS.* Creation of such modules allows the *CISS* to provide services to various applications, representing a truly comprehensive security system.

In Section 8.2 the design of the *API* modules for some standard operational environments (*OSI, ODP, TCP/IP, SNA, DECNET*) will be described. They will all be based on the design principles discussed in this section.

7.3.6 Security Management

Security management includes those aspects of secure operations which are outside normal instances of operations, but which are needed to support and control the security aspects of those operations. It is a very important aspect of network security, so that standardization of the activities of security management are very important to the *ISO.* An introductory discussion on *OSI* security management was given in Section 2.3.

Security management involves:

- The control and distribution (in real-time) of security-related information for use in the provision of security services.

- The logging of security-relevant events. These events include the detection of apparent violations of security, but may also include detection of normal security events, such as successful logins. The aim of the logging is to produce an *Audit Trail* that can be analysed to detect any security violations.

- The management (generation and dissemination) of various parameters needed for security mechanisms (like cryptographic keys).

- Security monitoring and recovery in case of security violations.

The *ISO Security Architecture* categorizes security management activities into four categories:

System Security Management: Concerned with event handling such as audit trail and system recovery.

Security Service Management: Concerned with the selection and invocation of security mechanisms to provide security services.

Security Mechanisms Management: Concerned with the management of cryptographic keys and the establishment of cryptographic parameters.

Security of OSI Management: Interactions between security management systems are necessary for the exchange of security information. These interactions are carried out through security management protocols. The functions of this management are to ensure that management information and protocols are adequately protected.

Many of the security management aspects have already been included in the concept of the *CISS*, described in Sections 7.2.1, 7.2.2, and 7.2.4. First, *SMIB* has been designed to keep and provide all data relevant for various aspects of security management. Next, there are several security agents, whose partial functions are concerned with management: *Monitoring Agent, Recovery Agent, Security Administrator Agent,* and *Inter-domain Communications Agent.* Finally, security protocols have been designed with operational and management aspects in mind.

For the purpose of operational coordination and synchronization, practical implementation of the *CISS* would need several "coordinating" modules for all the described agents. (They may be called "dispatchers"). They could be some kind of relatively simple module dispatchers for coordination of "working" agents.

Specific system security management functions would be covered by the appropriate agents: event handling by the *SSA*, security audit by the *MA*, security recovery by the *RA*.

The best approach in analysing and designing security management functions within the *CISS* would be to include all necessary security management aspects, functions, requirements and specifications together with operational aspects. In such a way, the resulting security system will be efficient, operational and consistent with all standardized specifications.

7.3.7 Generic Description of Usage of Security Services

Some examples of the use of security services by security profiles (sequencing data) have already been given in Section 7.3.1. The examples in that section were concerned with alternative security services and mechanisms. In this section a complete *CISS* is indicated. In fact, an example of a very simple "flow" between the application and the agents of the *CISS* will help to clarify the concepts.

Consider the diagram in Figure 7.10. This figure is related to Figure 7.5, but the specific sequences and steps are emphasized. A typical sequence of component interactions may be as follows:

The Request: The application (e.g. a secure *FTAM* or *MHS* module) calls the same security service from the *CISS* (in this example, for instance *user authentication* and *data confidentiality*), via its built-in *API* and *OPENA* (step [#1]). The application will have set up the control data for the *CISS* request, along with the information data upon which the *CISS* will act. The request for the service will be passed over the *API* (by means of a system interrupt, for example), to the *OPENA*.

Validation: The *OPENA* will note the source and location of the origin of the request

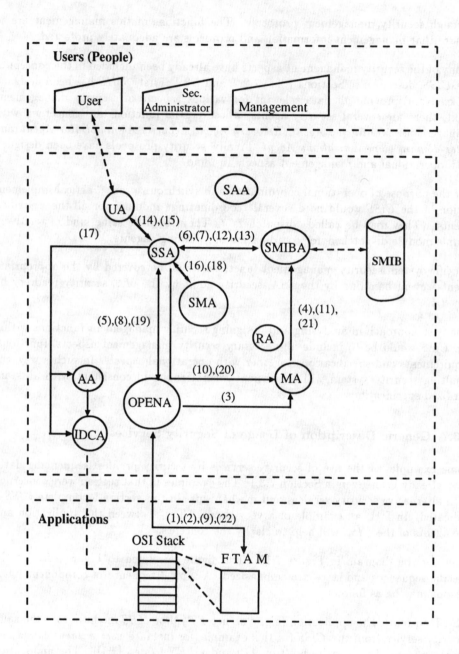

Figure 7.10. Usage of CISS for Secure Applications (Example)

and it will attempt to validate the request. Validation is performed at this stage only from the point of view of checking that the request is *recognized* by the *CISS* (via a look-up table) or syntax analysis, *not* to check that the request is permitted. (This will be performed later by the *SSA* and *SMIBA*.)

If the data structure in the request is not correctly built (in accordance with the structure described in Section 7.3.4), the *OPENA* will detect the error, initiate a request for a rebuild or corrections of the data and pass this back to the calling application (step [#2]).

At the same time, *OPENA* will pass the necessary information about the invalid request to the *MA*, which will record it in the security log (step [#3], protocol *(27)*). The *MA* will pass this information to the *SMIB* for effective writing into the *SMIB* (step [#4], protocol *(37)*).

Authorization: If the request and its data are valid and acceptable, the *OPENA* places them onto the internal *CISS* data bus. The control information (the part of the request) is routed to the *SSA* (step [#5], protocol *(24)*). The *SSA* examines the control data, and interrogates the *SMIB* via the *SMIBA* (steps [#6] and [#7], protocols *(09)* and *(20)*), as to whether the request is *(a)* valid and *(b)* legal (authorized).

If the request is *invalid,* the *SSA* will return the appropriate error code to the *OPENA* (step [#8], protocol *(10)*), which will inform the calling application process accordingly (step [#9]). The *MA* will also be informed about the illegal request (step [#10], protocol *(13)*) for logging in the *SMIB* via the *SMIBA* (step [#11], protocol *(37)*).

Action: If the request is *valid* and *authorized,* then the *SSA* will interrogate the *SMIB* via the *SMIBA* (steps [#12] and [#13], protocols *(09)* and *(20)*), as to the correct sequence of operations to be performed to execute the requested security service in line with security policy. If the *SMIBA* has informed the *SSA* that, for example, an additional password is required from the user (for the user authentication security service), then the *SSA* will request this from the *UA* (steps [#14] and [#15], protocols *(06)* and *(01)*).

The *SSA* will select and sequence the appropriate security mechanisms through interactions with the *SMA* (step [#16], protocol *(08)*) to fulfil the request. The request will be executed by passing control data as necessary. Selected security mechanisms for user authentication and data confidentiality will act upon the request information data on the *CISS* bus, which is to be processed, plus on the original data from the file that was requested for secure transfer by the *FTAM* application. Since the *FTAM* application has a remote destination location, user authentication and data confidentiality security services must be established across the communication path. For that purpose *SSA* calls either *AA* or *IDCA* in order to establish secure association (in the same or in a different security domain) (step [#17], protocol *(12)*).

Upon completion of the request, (i.e. the initiator of the *FTAM* request has been authenticated and all data during file transfer have been encrypted), signalled by the

SMA in turn to the *SSA* (step [#18], protocol *(15)*), the *SSA* will indicate task status to the *OPENA* (step [#19], protocol *(10)*), and it will also inform the *MA* of the security services performed (step [#20], protocol *(13)*), for whom it was provided, and the task status (return code). *MA* will log in the *SMIB* via the *SMIBA* (step [#21], protocol *(37)*) the appropriate information about the completion of this request.

Report: Finally, The *OPENA* will then retrieve the processed information data from the *CISS* bus, and return the processed data across the *API* to the correct calling location, along with the task status (return code) (step [#22]).

This sequence of actions is structured in the following table:

Step	Prot.	Agents	Action Description
(1)	API	FTAM $\longrightarrow$ OPENA	*(request for security services)*
(2)	API	OPENA $\longrightarrow$ FTAM	*(formal error in the request)*
(3)	27	OPENA $\longrightarrow$ MA	*(info: invalid request)*
(4)	37	MA $\longrightarrow$ SMIBA	*(recording into SMIB)*
(5)	24	OPENA $\longrightarrow$ SSA	*(valid request)*
(6)	09	SSA $\longrightarrow$ SMIBA	*(authorization and validity)*
(7)	20	SMIBA $\longrightarrow$ SSA	*(reply to the authorization and validity test)*
(8)	10	SSA $\longrightarrow$ OPENA	*(unauthorized or invalid request)*
(9)	API	OPENA $\longrightarrow$ FTAM	*(unauthorized or invalid request)*
(10)	13	SSA $\longrightarrow$ MA	*(unauthorized or invalid request)*
(11)	37	MA $\longrightarrow$ SMIBA	*(recording of unauthorized or invalid request)*
(12)	09	SSA $\longrightarrow$ SMIBA	*(request for sequencing data)*
(13)	20	SMIBA $\longrightarrow$ SSA	*(reply with sequencing data)*
(14)	06	SSA $\longrightarrow$ UA	*(request for additional parameters)*
(15)	01	UA $\longrightarrow$ SSA	*(reply with additional parameters)*
(16)	08	SSA $\longrightarrow$ SMA	*(selection of security mechanisms)*
(17)	12	SSA $\longrightarrow$ IDCA	*(establishment of a secure association)*
(18)	15	SMA $\longrightarrow$ SSA	*(completion of the action)*
(19)	10	SSA $\longrightarrow$ OPENA	*(completion of the action)*
(20)	13	SSA $\longrightarrow$ MA	*(completion of the action)*
(21)	37	MA $\longrightarrow$ SMIBA	*(logging of successful completion)*
(22)	API	OPENA $\longrightarrow$ FTAM	*(successful completion)*

8

IMPLEMENTATION ASPECTS
OF THE CISS

8.1 INTRODUCTION

This chapter is devoted to some practical implementations and operational aspects of the *CISS*. The purpose of this chapter is twofold: first, to elaborate further the concept of the *CISS*, as described in the previous chapter, and second, to describe some existing prototype implementations.

The practical implementations of the *CISS* cover three aspects: *(a)* consideration of the ideas of *API*, described theoretically in the previous chapter, but this time designed for some practical, popular operational environments: *OSI, MS-DOS, UNIX, TCP/IP, SNA, DECNET*, etc., *(b)* prototype implementations of some segments of the *CISS* system in order to show its applicability and feasibility, and *(c)* indications of the possibilities of use of the *CISS* in global (*EDI*) environments.

With coverage of these three aspects, the concept of the *CISS* will be more clear, and some indications of possible practical approaches to its implementation may be useful for this type of development in the area of computer security.

In Section 8.2 some partial implementations of the *CISS* will be described. In Section 8.3 some of its *APIs* to various popular operational environments, and in Section 8.4 possible uses of the *CISS* in a global operational environments will be indicated. The conclusions in this chapter indicate that the described practical implementations and considerations *(a)* prove the feasibility and the correctness of the *CISS* concept, and *(b)* give some practical guidance to possible implementations of the *CISS*.

8.2 SOME PROTOTYPE IMPLEMENTATIONS

8.2.1 Approach to Prototype Implementations

This section has two purposes: to describe some practical prototype implementations of the *CISS* and to demonstrate the feasibility of creating such a global system by modular design and implementation.

A system was considered which attempted to overcome the problem of duplicated services in individual applications and duplicated mechanisms in implementation of those services. This goal was achieved in several prototype implementations, using a modular approach:

a. all implemented security modules have been designed as self-contained, autonomous modules, which may be used as stand-alone programs or as parts of some larger system.

b. all intermodular communications were implemented as external calls, organized directly between modules, via a common area in memory or by inter-module communication areas on external storage devices.

c. all modules are independent of the underlying operational environment, i.e. they are all designed to interface to various application environments through specific *APIs*.

d. functional relations of modules belonging to the "higher" layers of the *CISS* structure on modules which are on some of the "lower levels" (see Figure 7.1) are not dependent on any specific "lower level" module.

In principle, in order to use the *CISS*, all software application packages should comply to *standardized security specifications* and *application interfaces*. For example, application layer entities within the *ISO/OSI* seven-layer model should conform only to the *ISO* reference model and functional specifications of the *CISS API* for the *OSI* environment.

However, this is far from the case in practice today. Had all existing software adhered strictly to *OSI* specifications, it may have been possible (albeit very tedious) to implement an *I/O redirection system*, which could cope with the widely differing interface, data and control requirements of all the various applications. Since the majority of software applications are written as an amorphous entity, with no obvious security interface standards, the concept of the *I/O* redirection system should be discarded as impractical. Even within the context of a local area network of personal computers, running *MS-DOS* for example, the amount of operating system interrupt handling to account for all secure *DOS* file *I/O* alone, proves to be an extremely difficult task.

The concept of providing a security system which is independent of, but available to, specific applications and various operational environments, implicitly or on request, is therefore only possible if the applications themselves are modified to utilize a standardized *application program interface (API)*, as described in Section 7.3.5. The requests for security services, control and data information and any other data must flow in a rigidly defined manner across the interface, which will enable analysis of the data flow protocols for formal demonstration of the strength of the security system. One version of this interface to the *CISS* system is described in Section 8.3.1.

8.2.2 Prototype Implementation of the CISS in a PC-LAN Environment

8.2.2.1 *Implementation of the CISS in a Single PC*

As described in Section 7.3, the *CISS* is a very powerful and therefore, in a full implementation, a very complicated system. But within the scope of this research, some initial prototype versions have been created which will be described here.

System Operations. This part is concerned with describing how the *CISS* works and not how the system was implemented. In practice, when such a global, modular system is designed, it will be implemented through a set of *drivers*, responsible for intermodular communications and individual modules. In this case the drivers will be simply *CISS drivers*, leading the user (or application) through the hierarchical tree of consecutive selections in order to reach the specific operational module. Individual operational modules are *CISS* agents and other modules on the lower layers of the *CISS* structure, as depicted in Figure 7.1. The implementation version of the *CISS* described in this subsection is rather limited in its functions, so it contains only one *CISS* driver and some operational modules, as described below.

When the system is initiated, the driver will be activated first and it will offer to the user two options:

    1. *User Interface*

    2. *System Administrator Interface*

If the user chooses *Option 1*, *CISS driver* will activate *UA*, and that agent will behave in the following sequence of steps:

Step 1: Prompt the user for his name.

Step 2: Prompt the user for his password.

Step 3: The *UA* will give the user three chances to enter the correct name and password. If he fails to do so, then the *UA* will notify the *MA* about this event, the *MA* will write a record in the System Log (via the *SMIBA*) and the *CISS* will terminate.

Otherwise the execution control will move to *Step 4*.

Step 4: UA will prompt the user for further action. At this stage the *CISS* is ready to read the user's command line. If the command is to logout, then the *UA* will terminate through the same sequence as in *Step 3*. Otherwise, it will move to the next step.

Step 5: UA will analyse formally the user's command. If the structure of the user's command line is invalid, then *UA* will display the appropriate message and return back to *Step 4*. Otherwise, it will move to the next step.

Step 6: UA will contact the *SSA* for the requested security services. The *SSA* will try to execute the requested service (by calling appropriate security mechanism(s) through the *SMA*). If it fails to do so for any reason, it will display the appropriate message and move to *Step 4*. Otherwise it will display the result and then move to *Step 4*.

If the user chooses *Option 2, CISS driver* will activate *SAA*, and that agent will display the following menu to the security administrator:

    1. *Add data in the SMIB*

    2. *Delete data from the SMIB*

    3. *Search for some data in the SMIB*

    4. *Display data from the SMIB*

If the security administrator chooses the first option in *Step 1*, then the *SAA* will display the following options:

    1. *Add a new user*

    2. *Add a new security service*

    3. *Add a new security object*

Depending on the administrator's choice, the *CISS* will display the proper data panel for the administrator to enter his data. If the data already exists in the *SMIB*, the administrator will be notified about that and data will not be added. Otherwise the *SMIBA* will add the data in the *SMIB*.

If the security administrator chooses *Option 2*, then the *SAA* will display to the administrator the following options:

    1. *Delete an existing user*

    2. *Delete some existing security service*

    3. *Delete some existing object*

Depending on the administrator's choice the *SAA* will prompt the administrator to enter the user name, or the service name, or the object name. If the data does not exist in the system, the administrator will be notified. Otherwise the data will be deleted from the *SMIB*.

If the administrator chooses *Option 3* in the main menu, then the *SAA* will display the following options:

    1. Search for user

    2. Search for service

    3. Search for token

Depending on the administrator's choice, the *SAA* will prompt the administrator for the user name, service name, or for the object name. If the data is found it will be displayed for the administrator, otherwise an error message will be displayed.

If the administrator chooses *Option 4*, then the *SAA* will display an index to the contents of the *SMIB* segments.

The User Agent Look-up Table. The current version of the *CISS* prototype implementation contains two types of data sets (segments) in the *SMIB*. The first type of segment is an internal look-up table, used by the *User Agent* to validate the structure of a user's command lines. The second type are segments of the integrated *SMIB*, which keep all the necessary security information about the whole system, its resources and users.

The user agent look-up table is scanned by the User Agent each time the User Agent wants to validate the structure of the user command line. The look-up table is constructed from an array of data structures. Each structure may be called *COM*. The structure *COM* in the current version of the implementation contains the following attributes:

1. *char command [15]:* This field holds *the command name* (e.g encrypt, decrypt, etc.). The command name is unique for each data structure and therefore is used as a search key by the User Agent.

2. *int arg:* This field is an integer and holds *the number of arguments* that any user should pass for this command.

3. *int type [4]:* This field is an array of four integers which represents *the type of each argument* the user should pass. The elements of this array may have the values 0, 2, or 8. The value 2 represents the type *integer,* the value 8 represents the type *real number,* and the value 0 represents the type *string.*

4. *int rights [4]:* This field is an array of integers which represents *the access rights* any user should have towards the corresponding arguments, if these arguments are security objects (e.g files) and not just ordinary numbers (e.g encryption key size). The values in this array would range from the number 0 (which corresponds to 000 in binary) to the number 7 (which corresponds to the number 111 in binary). This range of three bit numbers represents three types of access rights. The leftmost bit represents *read* access right, the middle bit represents *write* access right, and the rightmost bit represents *execute* right. Of course, these bits (access rights) may be extended with additional or combined access rights.

The Security Management Information Base Segments. The Security Management Information Base contains three types of segments (data structures): user security information, data sequencing information for security services, and security object tokens. In this particular implementation, the first type of data structure is called *REC*, the second type is called *SV*, and finally the third type is called *TOKEN*.

The first data structure *REC* contains four fields: *1. User-id, 2. Password, 3. User Group,* and *4. User Capabilities.* Fields one, two, and three are arrays of characters. The content of the array *user-id* is unique for each structure and therefore it is used as a search key by the *SMIB* agent. The fourth field, *user capabilities,* is implemented as an array of strings. The elements of this array are the names of the security services this user is allowed to execute by the security policy of the system.

The second data structure *SV* contains 2 fields: *1. char service [12]:* this field contains the service name and it is unique for each structure and *2. struct MECHANISM mechanism[ ]:* this field is an array of structures, each structure represents one of the relevant mechanisms and the arguments that should be passed to this mechanism. The data structure contains two fields: *2.a. int mech:* this is a positive integer which is used by the *SSA* as an identification number to the relevant mechanism agent; *2.b. int arguments[4]:* this is an array of integers, the elements of which can be positive or negative integers. The values in this array are used to identify the arguments for the security mechanism agent identified in the previous field.

The third type of data structure is *TOKEN*, which contains four fields: *1. char object [12]:* this field represents the name of the security object and it is unique for each structure of this type; *2. char owner [12]:* this field represent the name of the object's owner; *3. char group [12]:* this field represents the name of the owner's group; *4. int rights:* this is a 9-bit number that represents the access control rights of the object for the owner, owner's group, and other users. The access control rights for each group are of three types: *read, write, execute.* The leftmost triple in this number represents the owner's rights, the middle triple represents the owner's group rights, and the rightmost triple represents the other users' rights. In this scheme value '1' means that the corresponding right is granted, while bit value '0' means it is not.

Each *SMIB* segment is constructed from two files, a *data file*, and an *index file*. The index file contains three different indexes for each group of data structures (e.g. *REC,*

SV, TOKEN), while the data file contains the actual data. The index for each group is represented as an array of structures of type *EL*. An *EL* structure contains two fields: the first field is an array of 12 characters which contains the search key for one of the data structures in the *SMIB*, while the second file contains the address of this data structure in the data file. For example *structure EL [john, 134]* states that the location of user's *"john"* data structure is at address *134* in the data file. The advantage of the *SMIB* implementation is that the *SMIB* agent can access the data randomly in the data file instead of accessing this data in a sequential manner, which is a time consuming process for large data bases. This approach in implementing the *SMIB* was not used for the "look-up" data base, because that data base has a limited size and a sequential approach is adequate.

8.2.2.2 Prototype Implementation of the CISS on a LAN

Using the ideas developed in connection with the concepts, agents and protocols of a *Comprehensive Integrated Security System,* a practical system has been implemented using a *Novell Ethernet LAN* comprising three *IBM* personal computers, configured as one *SMC* and two user nodes ([SHEP90]) and also using a *TCP/IP LAN* with three PC stations on it ([MUFT92A]).

The API for the PC System. It has been stated in the conceptual model (in Chapter 7, Section 7.2) that the specific design of the *Application Program Interface (API)* is largely dependent on the host operating system. A popular operating system for *PCs* is *MS-DOS* and the *API* was designed for that system. It can be easily adjusted to other *PC* operating systems.

The *CISS* prototype implementation was written as an Application-layer *memory-resident (TSR)* software module. In one version ([SHEP90]), it is installed from a hardware ROM which takes control of the computer during the power-on self-test *(POST)*, and in another through a non-interruptable start-up procedure ([MUFT92A]). By this means, its activation cannot be prevented.

The *CISS* is capable of intercepting interrupt vectors controlling requests to operating system functions. In addition, the *CISS* monitors its own interrupt, which is used for passing security oriented requests to the *CISS* kernel. This distinction is necessary because the *CISS* can be invoked in one of three ways:

- The *user* can press a *hot-key* to activate the *CISS* directly. In this mode, the user can request a number of services directly, such as authentication at the start of a secure session on the terminal, or direct encryption of a file he wishes to transfer to floppy disk and send through the post.

- The *foreground application* can request security service of the *CISS* via a software interrupt reserved for that purpose. This approach may be used, for example, in part of a secure *E-mail* package which requires the services of encryption mechanisms under the control of the *CISS*.

- The *CISS* monitors all system requests for operating system services which may affect the security of the system and, if necessary, activates itself automatically. These cases include such services as file *I/O*, port control and program execution privileges.

It is important to note that the first two modes are *voluntary*, that is, the security services are available purely on a request by request basis, with no requirement to actually make use of the services offered. The third mode is *compulsory* and cannot be circumvented by the system.

For example, in the *File Encryption and Transfer (FET)* demonstration system (to be described briefly at the end of this subsection), all files have additional attributes specifying their security level as logical system *objects*. All file *I/O* requests are monitored by the *CISS*. Should an application, such as a text editor, attempt to open a file, the *CISS* intercepts the *DOS* request and determines whether the user has sufficient privileges for the operation. It does this at a local station by establishing contact with the *SMC* via the LAN, where the *Security Management Information Database (SMIB)* is held.

The *CISS* consults the *SMIB* which holds the rights and privileges of all the system *subjects.* As in the Bell and La Padula model, if the capability of the *subject* is equal or superior to the classification of an *object,* then the operation is permitted. If not, the operation is denied. The above scenario assumes that the user has *voluntarily* accessed the *CISS* at the start of the terminal session, and identified and authenticated himself to the system. If he has not done this, then on the first occurrence of identification/authentication being required, the *CISS* will suspend execution of the foreground application, and open a window requiring the user to identify/authenticate himself. Connection is then made with the *SMC* and *SMIB* as before, and an authentication process proceeds. If the user is accepted, the *CISS* closes the window and resumes execution of the foreground task.

Details of CISS API. The *CISS API* is implemented as a series of *interrupt handlers* to monitor software interrupt activities. These are:

- *INT $E0* which is an unallocated interrupt, and is used to pass voluntary requests from application processes to the *CISS* kernel for security services. The parameters associated with the request are built into a formalized data structure, and the service request code is placed in the *AH* register. Software interrupt $E0 is then called, and the *CISS*, monitoring the interrupt, intercepts the request and acts accordingly.

- *INT $09* which is the keyboard hardware interrupt is monitored for the *hot key* combination. If the user has pressed the hot-key to invoke the *CISS* voluntarily, a window is opened to receive user data.

- *INT $21* which is the *MS-DOS* function dispatcher. The *CISS* monitors the *AH* register on entry for operating system service requests of interest, and acts accordingly upon them. Requests which are not of any interest are simply passed on to the operating system. The monitoring of this interrupt is the compulsory component of the *CISS* activity.

Management of the SMIB Data. In the *PC*-based *LAN* system, the *SMIB* data is held at the *SMC* network server. The concept of the *CISS* requires the System Administrator to be physically present at this machine when amending or updating data in the *SMIB*. This is because of the digital signatures and creation of certificates, for which a *SA* secret key is needed. It would be quite simple to allow a higher level of system privilege at one of the user workstations, which would allow the System Administrator to log on with system privileges and amend the *SMIB* data remotely, but this was not done in this prototype version as an additional security precaution.

Secure Communications across the LAN. The *PC*-based *LAN* prototype implementation of the *CISS* may encrypt data for secure transmission over the *LAN* using any of the cryptographic algorithms. Currently a software (slow) version of some algorithms is used as a demonstration version. At the same time a hardware module is under development which will implement the fundamental arithmetic operations in hardware, and will serve as general-purpose "cryptographic (security) engine", and will considerably speed up the cryptographic (and other security) operations.

Other Security Measures. The prototype system also implements the following security features:

- *Timeout* after a predetermined period will clear the connection with the *SMC*, and place the *CISS* kernel at the *PC* user station in a dormant mode. This avoids the possibility of a user logging into a *PC*, and making a successful association with the *SMC*, and then inadvertently leaving the computer unattended, allowing an unauthorized person to carry out operations for which he is not privileged.

- An *audit file (security log)* of system activities is maintained at the *SMC* for system integrity auditing purposes.

All associations on a *LAN* are continually *supervised* by the *SMC*. A brief research program into the identification of users from their individual typing characteristics was carried out. Although an analysis of a short fragment is inconclusive, it is possible to make a continuous assessment of the style of typing, and hence possibly identify a change of user part way through a session. The preliminary results of this research will be reported in the future.

Limitations of the PC Demonstration System. The system, as currently implemented, suffers from the following shortcomings:

- The *CISS* software was written for procedural convenience and not functionally divided into agents as per the conceptual model from Chapter 7. This makes changing the function of a particular agent quite difficult. In a realistic system, presumably written and maintained by a large number of programmers, it is very important to modularize the software in this way to allow development and maintenance.

- Many of the weaknesses of protection of the *CISS* itself, which are anticipated at the conceptual level, may be circumvented in the implementation by placing critical parts of the *CISS* within a tamper-resistant hardware module. This would eliminate the requirement for many of the secure protocols linking the agents, as access to data in these protocols would not be possible.

- As stated, the encryption/decryption times, owing to software implementations, would need to be significantly improved, as encryption/decryption of a large file with the present system would be prohibitively slow.

- In a completely secure system it would be necessary to monitor and control other interrupts as well. For example the system time-out is dependent on the data read from the real-time system clock.

- To circumvent the time-out function, a user could keep resetting the clock every few minutes, to deceive the *CISS* into thinking that no time had passed. It would be necessary to monitor and control interrupt *$1A*, which controls the setting and reading of the real-time clock. The *CISS* should in that case make resetting the clock a privileged operation.

Many of the described limitations will be removed by the end of this research program. This text, however, reflects the status of the prototype products at the time of writing of this book.

File Encryption and Transfer (FET)

Within the framework of the ten-agent model described in Section 7.3, an implementation of some segments of the *CISS* for the *IBM-compatible PC* has been written using *Pascal* and *8086* assembler. A prototype of the *file encryption and transfer (FET)* protocol over the *LAN* has been coded, and tested between machines via serial port communications [SHEP90].

Another version of the same protocol has been created based on the Ethernet *LAN* and the *TCP/IP* software. This prototype implements a subset of the *X.509* protocol, based on transfer of files. Plain public keys (and not certificates) are recorded on the security server as individual files, they are accessed, transferred and used by protocol participants exactly according to the *X.509* specifications [MUFT92A].

8.2.3 Design of an X.32 DTE Prototype Workstation

8.2.3.1 Functional Specification

The *X.32* features described earlier in Section 3.2.3 may be incorporated in an *X.25* system for dial access to *PSDNs* and for the provision of security mechanisms for entity identification and authentication. Therefore the software design of the *X.32 DTE* prototype may be dictated by the design of the *X.25* system in terms of intertask communication, buffer structures, routing of events, etc.

In this section one possible *X.32* protocol implementation is described. The *X.25* system used for the prototype is based on the *MS-DOS* operating system with an *X.25* interface for accessing a packet switched or *X.25* network. Its operation is synchronous via dedicated leased lines. It comprises both hardware and software components.

The hardware consists of a *Zilog Z80 Serial Input/Output (SIO)* based communications board, which fits into one of the expansion slots in the *PC*. As a data communication interface, the *Z80 SIO* chip on the board provides two independent full-duplex channels. It performs serial-to-parallel and parallel-to-serial conversions and handles interrupt driven input/output via an *RS-232 C* interface.

The *SIO* supports both asynchronous and bit or byte oriented synchronous communication protocols such as *SDLC* (Synchronous Data Link Control) and *HDLC/X.25*. When transmitting an *HDLC* frame, zero insertion or bit-stuffing as well as *CRC (Cyclic Redundancy Check)* generation are automatically performed. Conversely, when receiving an *HDLC* frame, the *SIO* automatically deletes all zeroes (bit-stripping) inserted by the transmitter during character assembly and also checks the *CRC* to validate frame transmission.

Associated with each of the two channels are a number of control and status (*Read* and *Write*) registers. The *Write* registers must be programmed prior to operation. Modem control for each channel is provided by the *Request To Send (RST), Clear To Send (CTS), Data Terminal Ready (DTR)* and *Data Carrier Detect (DCD)* pins on the *SIO* chip. An external/status interrupt is used to monitor the signal transitions of the *CTS* and *DCD* pins.

The next component of the *X.25* is the software to drive the *X.25* protocol and the hardware. For this particular implementation the software was written in the C-programming language and is structured into specific modules, as follows:

- Pseudo-tasker or Executive;

- Application filters;

- X.25 Network, Link and Physical layer.

The *X.25* communication protocols for the three layers are defined in the *X.25* recommendation as a series of procedures to be carried out to establish, maintain and terminate communication between a host and a packet switched network. These procedures can be represented in the form of state diagrams where transitions from state-to-state is driven by events. These state-event transitions are then processed by software modules acting as finite state machines *(FSMs)*. Each of the *X.25* system software modules, with the exception of the pseudo-tasker, consists of a number of asynchronous task(s) and *Finite State Machines*.

At each level of the *X.25* system, with the exception of the pseudo-tasker, additional software has been incorporated to meet *X.32's* functional requirements. The *X.32* prototype was designed to meet the following prime objectives:

- The provision of dial-up access to/from a packet switched network.

- The provision of identification and authentication mechanisms.

- The provision of *X.32* optional user facilities.

- Compatibility with the software design of the *X.25* system used.

- Modularity so as to allow for easy integration within the *X.25 system*.

The integration of the *X.32* functionalities into the *X.25* system is illustrated in Figure 8.1.

8.2.3.2 Network Layer Security Procedures

The main concern at the Network Layer was how to provide the two levels of security and handle the exchanges of Registration packets based on *X.32's* identification protocol described in Section 3.2.3.

The initial design issue was deciding which logical channel to use for Network layer identification. The logical channel number field of Registration packets was always set to zero according to the definition of the format of Registration packets in *CCITT's* *X.25* recommendation. Therefore the most logical choice would be to carry out Network layer identification on the virtual channel zero. Virtual channel zero is currently used by the *X.25* system for handling incoming restart and diagnostic packets from the network. The additional handling of Registration packets can thus be catered for. After successful identification and allocation of a service type by the network, the *DTE* can then establish logical connections on a number of virtual channels. All connections on such channels will be offered the same service type.

8.2.3.3 The Network Security Finite State Machine (FSM)

The logical solution to handling the state-event transitions associated with *X.32's* authentication procedures is to have a path Network Security FSM which is then

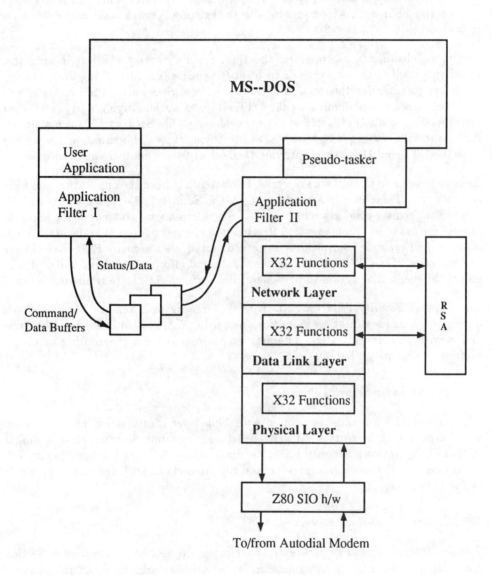

Figure 8.1. Integration of X.32 Functionalities into SCOM25

integrated within the existing Network layer design structure. Thus the structure of the Security FSM and its interactions with the existing network tasks and FSMs have to be specified.

During an identification procedure, the DTE can be either a *challenged party* (i.e. identifying itself to the network) or an *identifying party* (i.e. identifying the network). Therefore to cater for this dual situation, the Network Security FSM has two sets of states: a set corresponding to the DTE's role as an identifying party, and a set corresponding to the DTE's role as a challenged party. The Security FSM can maintain both a current Challenged state as well as Identifying state. This situation arises when both the DTE and DCE are identifying themselves to one another simultaneously.

Incoming events to the Network Security FSM originate from the application and from the network. These events are processed by the Security FSM based on its current state. The Security FSM assembles any security information to be sent to the network, in response to the incoming event, in Registration Request packets. On the other hand, if any invalid event or identification error is detected, then security FSM may initiate disconnection of the PSTN switched access path and inform the application, or it may ignore the event. The action to be taken is defined in $X.32$'s state transition tables.

The Network Security FSM interacts with the network task and the Network FSMs during the $X.32$ identification procedures using the $X.25$ system defined *I/O* streams and service primitives. These interactions are required for the routing of events to/from the Security FSM.

8.2.3.4 Link Layer Security Procedures

The state-event transitions associated with Link layer identification procedures are handled by a Link Security FSM. The structure of the link Security FSM is similar to that of the Network Security FSM, the main difference being the handling of *XID frames* instead of *Registration packets,* and the interactions with the tasks and FSMs at the Link layer.

8.2.3.5 Secure Dial-Back Procedure

The sequence of events in a secure dial-back procedure has been described in Section 3.2.3. It provides protection against replay security attacks by using the physical location of the *DTE* to establish its authenticity. The secure dialback procedure is initiated at the end of a Link layer or Network layer identification. The secure dial-back events are handled by the Link Security or Network Security FSM, depending on whether a Link layer or Network layer identification is in effect.

8.2.3.6 Application of the RSA System

The *RSA* system for the $X.32$ prototype can be implemented either in hardware or software. Hardware-based *RSA* systems have the advantage of speed over software implementations. The hardware option requires that an *RSA* chip be incorporated onto the *X.25* board, or the use of a separate RSA hardware board. Currently, stand-alone *RSA* hardware devices are not readily available. What is available is a number of *RSA*-based products which incorporate *RSA* hardware. Therefore for the *X.32* prototype, a software *RSA* module was implemented.

Both the Link and Network Security FSMs interact with the software *RSA* module during security grade two authentication. If the *X.32 DTE* is the challenged party, then the Security FSM has to pass the random number received from the *DCE* to the *RSA* system for signing (i.e. decryption). Conversely if the *DTE* is the identifying party, the security FSM has to pass the received signature from the *DCE* to the *RSA* system for encryption.

Key management is an important issue in the use of any cryptosystem. In the case of *X.32*, the means of conveying public keys has not yet been specified. For this *X.32 DTE* prototype the public keys for the *DCEs* are stored in a security file. Thus when the *DTE* receives a signed random number from a *DCE* (authenticating itself to the *DTE*), the Security FSM searches the security file for the *DCE's* public key using the identity element of the *DCE* as the index. The public key is then used by the *RSA* system for recovering the random number from the *DCE* signature. On the other hand, the secret key of the *DTE* used for signing is stored in the *X.32* system itself.

8.3 INTERACTIONS OF CISS WITH VARIOUS OPERATIONAL ENVIRONMENTS

In Section 7.3.5 some guidelines for the external Application Programming Interface *(API)* of the *CISS* to various operational environments were briefly described. The design of that interface depends, primarily, on the operational environment, and its usage depends on the particular application. The principles outlined in Section 7.3.5 will be applied in this section with more details, since each subsection will be concerned with one particular operational environment.

Conceptually, the *CISS* in some real life environment may be considered to be located "between" the applications using it and the operational environment. For instance, consider some regular File Transfer application over the *LAN* or the *X.25 WAN*. After the user has initiated the application (to send a file to a remote location, say) the application prepares all necessary parameters for the environment and transfers the execution of the protocol to the network control software.

If the *CISS* is available, during the initiation stage the user selects not only the *FTP* parameters, but also some additional security parameters. When the file is prepared for the transfer, before it is actually sent, the *CISS* gets into the action, transforms the outgoing file according to the required security specifications, and then initiates network control software for the actual transfer.

The same sequence may be sketched when receiving a file from a remote location. If the transfer was initiated with certain security options, those services will be performed (by the *CISS*) upon receipt of the file and before delivering it to the original File Transfer application.

This short example illustrates the logical "location" of the *CISS* with respect to the available applications and the underlying operational environment. Therefore, in order to perform all its functions, the *CISS* must have two types of interface: *(a)* *APIs* to various applications and *(b)* operational environment interfaces. This section is devoted to interfaces to various popular operational environments. These *APIs* must be created within those applications, since that is the only way to invoke the *CISS*, other than mandatory invocations, which should be implemented again through the operational environment interfaces (interrupts, etc.).

The operational environments for which the *CISS APIs* are described in this section represent the environments most often used. Designing *APIs* for the selected environments means at the same time a broad applicability of the *CISS*. The first subsection gives the design of the *API* for *OSI* and *ODP* systems as interactions of the *CISS* with some *OSI* layer entities. In the second subsection the *CISS API* is designed for *MS-DOS* and the *UNIX* operating systems, i.e. for the *CISS* implemented on a single user station. The third section is devoted to the application of the *CISS* on *LANs* through its interface to the *TCP/IP* protocol. Finally, in the last section, use of the *CISS* in private networks is treated for *SNA* and *DECNET,* as the most popular private networks.

Two approaches are possible to define the security service *APIs* for the various applications in the operational environments. One approach is to define the security within the scope of each specific application. This corresponds to the case where each application includes a security framework in its standards. The other approach defines a *common application programming interface* for security services which should be used by all applications, like *FTAM* (File Transfer, Access, and Management), *VT* (Virtual Terminal), *X.400* (Electronic Mail), etc.

Comparison and analysis of these two approaches indicates that the latter seems to have more merit for several reasons. The main one is that the security services implemented in each specific application seem to be limited to two or three common basic security services developed from the current *OSI* Security Architecture. Typical examples of specific security services are the authentication service, data integrity service, and data confidentiality service in existing *OSI* applications. Therefore, the fact that these similar requirements for security pertain to different specific application service elements encourages the need for a common application programming interface, specific to all security aspects in some environment. This idea is also supported by protocol designers who do not want to perform duplicate works; they expect to find a common security element that provides a full set of specific security services. Moreover, *ISO* and *CCITT* have accumulated important knowhow involving the extraction of common service elements from the early stages of specific application service elements. The extraction of *ACSE* (Association Control Service Element), *RTSE* (Reliable Transfer Service Element), and *ROSE* (Remote Operation Service Element) from *MHS* (message handling systems) are good examples.

Most of the ideas in this section are based on some available papers from the literature or on some original research materials. The original papers did not deal with design of *API* for the global security system, but merely with the implementation of some security services in some particular operational environment. Therefore, in this section, the original ideas were modified accordingly, to describe relevant details of the *CISS API* design and usage.

8.3.1 CISS API for OSI and ODP Systems

Since the *ODP* systems include data processing components, a combination of *API* interfaces at the application layer of the *OSI* stack with *APIs* in the host machines or user stations may provide a global *API* in the *ODP* system. Therefore, *APIs* in the data processing components of the *ODP* systems will not be treated in detail here. More important, some applications of the *CISS* in global *ODP* systems will be described in Section 8.4.

In *ISO/OSI* Security Framework [ISO88], interactions with security services may be performed through each of the *OSI* layers. This may be taken more as the principal (framework) suggestion. Recent research results, published in the literature, indicate that security for the *OSI* stack should be applied primarily at two layers:

    a. end-to-end communication security services should be implemented at the transport layer ([VOYD83], [UK90]), and

    b. application-oriented security services should be applied at the application layer [NAKA89].

Therefore in this section the concept of the two versions of the *API* for *OSI* systems will be described: an interface for *End-to-End Security Protocol (EESP)* on the transport layer and *Application Security Service Element (ASSE)* on the application layer.

8.3.1.1 CISS OSI API on the Transport Layer

The interface to the *CISS* on the transport layer may be the *End-to-End Security Protocol (EESP)* for provision of *ISO/ISO* security services, recently suggested by the UK delegation to the ISO/JTC 1/SC 21 [UK90]. The primary purpose of the *EESP* protocol is the the provision of *OSI* security services at the transport layer (for end-to-end protection). This protocol may be extended with ideas from [VOYD83], describing various possibilities for obtaining the working key by the transport entities. In that way the complete *CISS API* at the transport layer may be designed as a combination of ideas from [VOYD83] for obtaining the working key by the transport entities, plus application of the *EESP* for provision of end-to-end security services.

Obtaining the Working Key from CISS by the Transport Entity

In the class 4 protocol, a connection is established using a three-way handshake. Upon the receipt of a *T-CONNECT.request* from its user, a transport entity sends a *Connect Request (CR) TPDU* to the target transport entity. The *class* field of the *CR* indicates that a class 4 connection is desired. The receiving transport entity notifies the target transport user that a request to initiate a connection has arrived via the *T-CONNECT.indication* primitive.

If the target user wants to establish the connection, it notifies the transport entity via the *T-ACCEPT.request* primitive. This causes that entity to send a *Connect Confirm (CC) TPDU*. When the other end receives it, it notifies its user that a connection request has been accepted via the *T-ACCEPT.indication* primitive, and sends an *AK TPDU* to the sender of the *CC*. When the *AK* is received, the connection is established.

In [VOYD83] four possibilities are described how this mechanism can be enhanced in order to get a working key for a secure connection. Each of these possibilities assumes the existence of the special transport entity, called *Key Distribution Centre (KDC)*, and the four variants are concerned with various implementations of the *KDC*. All of them assume that the *KDC* maintains *(TE-ID, master key)* pairs for each transport entity, and generates and distributes session keys upon request.

The original concept of the *KDC* from [VOYD83] may be extended with use of the *CISS* for the same purpose. In that case only a single *TP* interface must be designed in order to use *CISS Key Generation* security service.

Let T_i denote the transport entity that received the *T-CONNECT.request* from its transport user. Let T_d denote the destination transport entity. Let $TE-ID_i$ and $TE-ID_d$ denote their respective transport entity identifiers. Let M_i and M_d denote their respective master keys which they share with the *CISS*. Let W denote the working key for the connection. Finally, let $E_K(X)$ denote the value of X encrypted under the key K.

Upon the receipt of a connect request, T_i obtains a working key for the connection from the *CISS*. Since the particular T_i is a *CISS* user, the *CISS* maintains in the *SMIB* the identity and a common key for that entity. The common (secret) key may be replaced by a pair of public keys, which may be exchanged between the *CISS* and the transport entity through the *X.509* protocol.

Two new *TPDU* types must be used for this connection: the *Key Request (KR) TPDU* and the *Key Deliver (KD) TPDU*. These two new *TPDUs* and the corresponding protocol between *TE* and the *CISS* constitute the transport layer *API* to the *CISS*.

This *API* is used in the following way: to request a working key, T_i sends a *KR PDU* to the *CISS*. It receives that key from the *CISS* in a *KD PDU*. The *KR PDU* contains the *TE-ID* of the target transport entity and a 64-bit *unique identifier*, that is used by T_i to verify the time integrity of the *KR/KD* exchange:

$$\text{KR PDU} : [\ TE - ID_d, \ u - id \ ]$$

Upon receipt of the *KR PDU*, by the *OPENA* of the *CISS*, that agent requires from the *SSA: (a)* generation of a working key W for the session, *(b)* generation of two temporary keys, denoted by B and C, *(c)* provision of connection time integrity by a time stamp, and content integrity by a *MAC*. The *SSA* interacts with the *SMA* which effectively generates a working key, the two temporary keys, a time stamp, and calculates the *MAC*. All of this data is returned to the *OPENA*, which passes the entire *KD PDU* back to the transport entity. Reconstruction of that message, in order to obtain the working key, depends on its structure and content. The details are described in [VOYD83].

When the session working key has been obtained and exchanged, other *OSI* security services on the transport layer may be provided according to the specification of the *End-to-End Security Protocol (EESP)*. In order to achieve high assurance implementation of such a protocol it is desirable that the *End-to-End Security Protocol (EESP):*

- be independent of "non-security" *Protocol Control Information* in either the network and transport layer;

- operate on units of data passing between the network and transport layer, i.e. on *NSDUs.*

The second item above indicates that the *EESP* must be functionally located "at the bottom" of the transport layer.

The *EESP* protocol is designed to provide the following *OSI* security services: *(1)* peer entity authentication, *(2)* data confidentiality, *(3)* data integrity without recovery, *(4)* data origin authentication, and *(5)* access control. The *EESP* protocol also supports *traffic flow confidentiality.*

The *EESP* operates by encapsulation of *NSDUs* (network service data units).

Security control information needed by the *EESP* resides in a *Security Management Information Base (SMIB)* located at host systems of each communicating entity. The information may either be pre-distributed to the *SMIB* by procedures outside of the *EESP* or may optionally be exchanged at connection establishment for a connection orientated network service. This version, therefore, implements completely a distributed *CISS* system, without special *SMCs.*

There are two variants of the *EESP* protocol which are:

- **EESP-CL:** provides at its upper boundary (towards the transport layer) a secure connectionless network service and assumes at its lower boundary (towards the network layer) a connectionless network service.

- **EESP-CN:** provides at its upper boundary a secure connection orientated network service and assumes at its lower boundary a connection orientated network service.

The *EESP* protocol contains the concept of a *secure association,* which may exist outside of a specific connection. For that reason, when the *CISS* is used by this protocol for security services, the *AA* must allow for:

- a secure association to endure beyond a lifetime of connection;

- a secure association to be pre-arranged or set up with the connection.

For *EESP-CL* the secure associations between *EESP* entities are set up by the *CISS Association Agent,* external to the *EESP-CL.*

For *EESP-CN* the security associations are set up by the *CISS Association Agent* when the connection is established. Cryptographic keys associated with the secure association may be transferred during the connection set up, or may have been already established by previous security associations or by *CISS* procedures, external to the *EESP.*

When the secure association exists outside of a connection, the *AA* must hold in the *SMIB Secure Association* segment the association parameters, like association reference number, identities of the parties involved, security keys, *QOS* parameters, etc.

Two options for connection integrity are provided in order to avoid duplication of message sequence numbers when class 4 transport is in use. The options are termed:

- *SDU* integrity (for use with transport class 4);

- sequence and *SDU* integrity (for use with transport class 0, 1, 2, or 3).

If sequence errors are detected by the *EESP,* this causes a *RESET* of the association upwards and downwards.

From the original material [UK90], it should be noted that the *EESP* is not responsible for protecting against the loss of last messages before closing an association. This is assumed to be the responsibility of the session layer.

Traffic flow confidentiality is provided by *CISS* based on the use of the *integrity padding* and *confidentiality padding* fields within a message and by the generation of additional traffic.

Network layer access control is not defined in detail in the *EESP* protocol ([UK90]). The *EESP* protocol can support the transfer of parameters associated with access control within the *LABEL* field. The processing of such information is defined to be a local matter, i.e. the function of the *CISS*, and not of the *EESP*.

The *API* between the *CISS* and the *EESP* consists basically of two primitives, namely *EESP-UNITDATA Request* and *EESP-UNITDATA Indication*. In fact, in the original material [UK90] *EESP* is responsible in both, *establishing* a secure association and *providing* security services to that association. Use of the *CISS* separates these two functions, so that the *CISS* is in charge of security services, and the *EESP* is in charge of management of secure associations. With this arrangement *(a) EESP* is used by the transport entity for management of secure associations, *(b)* the *CISS* is used by the *EESP* for provision of security services, and *(c) API* is an interface between the *EESP* and *CISS*.

Of the security services provided by the *CISS* to the *EESP-CL*, some are always provided, while others are requested as part of the *EESP UNITDATA Request.*

1. *EESP-CL* requires that the *CISS* provides integrity of the *EESP Userdata* (connectionless integrity), if requested, via the *integrity requested* parameter.

2. *EESP-CL* requires that the *CISS* provides confidentiality (connectionless confidentiality) of the *EESP Userdata,* if requested, via the *confidentiality requested* parameter.

3. If requested via the *security label requested* parameter, *EESP-CL* will accept and validate a security label and deliver it to the *CISS* with *EESP Userdata.*

4. *EESP-CL* indicates to the *CISS,* via the *integrity indicated* parameter, whether connectionless data integrity is needed for this unit.

5. *EESP-CL* indicates to the *CISS,* via the *confidentiality indicated* parameter, whether confidentiality is needed for this unit.

6. *EESP-CL* may also require data origin authentication. This security service is supplied by the *CISS* via appropriate key management techniques.

7. *EESP-CL* supplies to the *CISS* as the indication (*security label indicated* parameter) a representation of a security label which has been carried with integrity.

8. *EESP-CL* also may requre from the *CISS* the access control security service. The key generation security service of the *CISS* (external to *EESP*), may choose, for access control reasons, not to make a key available for communication between two *EESP* entities. This decision by the *CISS* implies that the access control service must be applied at the upper interface of *EESP* towards the transport layer. *EESP* will not allow communication if an appropriate key

has not been established. In addition, if a security label is provided for the data, then *EESP* will require information from the *CISS* to make an access control check against label on both transmit and receive.

8.3.1.2 CISS OSI API on the Application Layer

The interface between the *CISS* and the application layer should be a new type of common *ASE* in the application layer. Since it is a service element for security, it may be called an *Application Security Service Element (ASSE)*. This element, as a common interface to the *CISS*, should provide different security services for various *OSI* applications.

To define the details of the *ASSE* service and protocol, a model of *ASSE* is necessary. Figure 8.2 shows the proposed *ASSE* model, located at the application layer, between the *OSI* application (application layer user) and the *ACSE*. This model is based on ideas from [NAKA89], but in the original paper, which is concerned primarily with communications security, the corresponding element is called *Secure Comunications Service Element (SCSE)*. It is designed to provide only (some) *ISO/OSI* security services. The *ASSE* described in this subsection, as an interface to the *CISS*, provides in fact the possibility to use all security services available with the *CISS*. For the same reasons, the original prefix *"SC"* for the *SCSE*, meaning *"secure communications"*, is replaced by the prefix *SS*, meaning *"security services"*.

The *SMIB* is used to store the information related to the protection context (user security profiles in the *Extended Security* segment), such as the encryption algorithm identity, mode of operation, encryption key, initialization vector, and so on. This information is necessary for the *CISS* to provide various security services and it is registered initially or negotiated dynamically with the *CISS*. That process is therefore completely outside the use of the standard *OSI* applications in the *ASSE* environment.

With the introduction of the *ASSE*, an *OSI* application, instead of going directly into the *ACSE*, it now communicates first with the *ASSE*. That element routes the request directly to the *ACSE*, if security is not needed, otherwise it interfaces the application to the *CISS*.

The application layer interface to *CISS*, i.e. *ASSE*, consists of a number of service primitives and protocols. A list of service primitives and corresponding protocol elements for the *ASSE* is described below:

A. *SS-OPEN Service.* This service provides a confirmation type of service to establish the secure connection, by a negotiation of the security services, between *ASSE* users. The secure connection is defined as a secure communication association and a secure data processing environment between the two end-systems.

This service belongs to the interface of the *ASSE* and the application, and it may contain the request parameters for any of the security services which are described

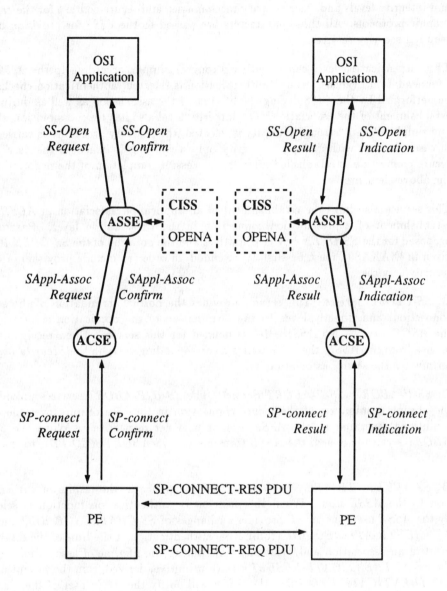

Figure 8.2. Extention of the Standard ACSE with the ASSE

in Table 4.1. Those parameters may be: categories of security services, authentication and integrity levels and their security mechanisms, and secure context for the cryptographic protocols. All those parameters are passed to the *CISS* for provision of the required security services.

The authentication level can be either strong or simple, according to the *X.509* recommendation. When "strong" authentication is selected, authentication checks will be performed by the *CISS* during the lifetime of the association as well as during the establishment of the association. The integrity level also has two possibilities: strong and simple. When "strong" integrity is selected, the recovery procedure is carried out in case of error; with "simple" integrity only a warning is issued to the user. The secure connection is established after the successful completion of the negotiation on the above elements.

This service also links the establishment of an application association in *ACSE* with establishment of a presentation connection in the Presentation layer. Parameters proposed for the *SS-OPEN* service primitives and the notation of the *SS-OPEN PDUs*, given in [NAKA89], must be slightly extended, in order to include provision of other security services.

B. *SS-CLOSE Service.* This service provides the normal termination of the secure connection, and directly leads to the termination of the application association in the *ASCE* service. No *ASSE PDU* is defined for this service. Upon receipt of this service from the *ASSE*, the *CISS* writes a corresponding entry in the *Security Log* and terminates the secure association.

C. *SS-U-ABORT, SS-P-ABORT Service.* The *SS-U/P-ABORT* services provide for the abrupt termination of the secure connection in the case of unrecoverable error conditions generated by the *ASSE* user or provider respectively. When the *SS-U-ABORT* service is issued, the *ASSE* transfers the *SS-ABORT-REQ PDU* to the peer entity.

D. *SS-AUTHENTICATE Service.* This service indicates the results of authentication to the *ASSE* user. When the peer entity authentication function is selected by the *ASSE* user, the *ASSE* provides exchanges of *SS-CHALLENGE REQ* and *SS-AUTHENTICATE REQ PDUs* for mutual authentication at the time of the establishment of an association and/or at any time during the lifetime of association. Using the *SS-AUTHENTICATE RESULT* service primitive, derived from the receipt of *SS-AUTHENTICATE REQ PDU*, the *ASSE* will notify the *ASSE* user of the result of the authentication procedure performed by the *CISS*.

E. *SS-TRANSFER Service.* After the establishment of the secure connection at the *SS-OPEN* service, the *SS-TRANSFER* service is available within the secure connection to provide the user with data integrity and/or data confidentiality services. When providing the selective field data integrity/data confidentiality services, the parameters of *Integrity Part Indication* and *Confidentiality Part Indication* are passed to the *CISS* to indicate the parts requiring the application of the corresponding services.

8.3.2 CISS API for MS-DOS and UNIX (API on a Single Station)

The operational environments considered in this subsection are popular operating systems on a single user station, i.e. *MS-DOS* and *UNIX.* These operational environments are widely used for many applications and microcomputer *LANs.* The same ideas may be applied to another popular *PC* operating system, *OS/2.*

8.3.2.1 CISS under MS-DOS

Each application executed on a *PC* will use *DOS* to access the secondary storage of the *PC.* Further, all keyboard and screen *I/O* use calls to the operating system. Most *I/O* calls on the *PC* are implemented using the software interrupt *21 X.* This interrupt has many subfunction routines, each carrying out a separate *I/O* function. Which routine is executed depends on register values when the interrupt is triggered.

The *interrupt handler* is an integral part of the operating system. A call to interrupt *21 X* (or any other interrupt) causes the system to look up the interrupt vector table. This table contains the addresses of the routines to be carried out when an interrupt is triggered. Control passes to the instructions at that address and so the desired *I/O* is carried out.

For example, if the user has selected data confidentiality security service, this service will be provided by the *CISS* by application of some symmetric encryption mechanism.

In this case the *CISS* will act as follows: the request and later user data will be passed to the *CISS* via the *OPEN Agent.* The control will be passed to that Agent when the application produces an output. This Agent will contact *SSA,* which will in turn contact *SMA* to carry out the desired security operations on the output. Assume that the *OPEN Agent,* which receives the control first, is implemented as a subroutine to be found at memory location *1000 X,* and assume that each agent knows memory addresses of all other agents it calls.

The *CISS* must first get the address of the output interrupt routine, whose interrupt number is, say, *9X.* The *CISS* finds out the vector of interrupt routine *9 X.* It then resets the vector value to *1000 X.* At the end of the agent code, the *CISS* chains the control back to the original output routine's address. Suitable commands on modern *C* compilers, such as Turbo C and Microsoft C, are *get-vector ( )* and *set-vector ( ).*

Some significant problems about this solution arise:

1. Application programs, when loaded into primary memory, tend to take over all available *RAM.* This speeds up their execution by reducing the number of disk accesses by the application.

2. Some output from the application may be directed to places other than the

local addresses; when using networks some outputs may be directed to the network access point, i.e. some output will be to a local sink and some to a remote sink.

3. The *CISS* will cause considerable overhead, because *DOS* interrupts are typically invoked very often by application programs and in this concept each one must be checked if relevant for the *CISS* action.

The problem of exclusive use of memory can be dealt with using *Terminate-and-Stay-Resident (TSR)* type of programs. Such programs run in *RAM* and are not unloaded to disk when the next application is loaded. Instead they reserve as much *RAM* as they require for a working set and remain resident in primary memory. So they have an address to which the interrupt vector can be redirected. If the system is short of memory, a stub of the *TSR* program can be left in memory, allowing it to be loaded when invoked. One method for invoking the *TSR* is to run it as a line in the batch file used to load the application. A later line can then be used to unload the *TSR*.

In order to overcome the problem of message destination for the case of the network (remote) addresses, the *CISS* must be able to comprehend the headers used by the application. This is quite a problem, threatening the viability of the interrupt-driven *CISS* concept. A method should be found in order to place only the detours on the network output. Perhaps knowing the network logical port address will allow the *CISS* to write directly into the output buffer of that port.

No solution to the overhead problem is obvious. Each call to the interrupt routine must be checked by some *TSR* component of the *CISS* to see if it is a relevant interrupt. Further, security-related processing will also occur for each network output, slowing the system considerably.

The following conclusions may be suggested concerning the interrupt driven *CISS API* to the *MS-DOS*. Modifying the *DOS* interrupt table provides a method of processing the output from an application in a manner transparent to the application itself. Implementation of such a scheme should be quite straightforward, but the scheme involves significant overheads, and the *CISS* will need to be able to interpret the control data on the application output.

A preferable solution would be a method for diverting all values written to the relevant logical port address. It must be noted that if the *CISS* can divert interrupt vectors, then so can an attacker. Therefore, another conclusion is that *DOS* itself is not a fully secure operating system.

8.3.2.2 CISS under UNIX

The *UNIX* operating system is organized in three basic components: kernel, shell (*UNIX* command interpreter), and file subsystem. The *kernel* is a residential part of the operating system. The *shell* is an interface which provides (user or process) communications with the operating system. This component interprets and executes the keyboard commands or commands from the shell's programming files.

The *CISS* consists of several modules and they may be linked under *UNIX* through the appropriate *UNIX* shell commands. In particular, the command **sh** is used to activate the interface to the operating system, and the **shl** command may be used to activate simultaneously several parallel processes under *UNIX* control. The active processes initiate each other by use of individual **shl** subcommands. Since shell subcommands may be combined in various executable command sequences, such sequences may be prepared in advance, for the most frequent user requests, or they may be created dynamically, for specific user requests.

Network aspects of *CISS* operations, when a *UNIX* station is connected to a network, may be implemented as a *CISS API* to the *LAN* operating system or to the *OSI* stack. Implementation and use of the *CISS* on *UNIX* stations in global *OSI* systems have been described in Section 8.3.1 and use of *CISS* in *LANs* (under *TCP/IP*) will be described in the next section.

8.3.3 CISS API for the TCP/IP Protocol (LANs)

In this subsection use of the *CISS* to provide security services in local area networks is described. For that purpose the *Transmission Control Protocol/Internet Protocol (TCP/IP)* is selected and the *CISS API* for that operating environment is created. *TCP* is a popular *LAN* protocol, located at the fourth (transport) layer and most of the *LAN* applications interact directly to that protocol. Therefore *LAN API* can be located between an application and the *TCP*. Following that principle *CISS API* may be based on use of *TCP* entry points (called *sockets*).

CISS API may be implemented in a local network environment with *socket compatibility interface (SCI)* and *transport level interface (TLI)* library packages available with the *TCP/IP*. These packages provide an interface to the lower level network services. Their principal purpose is to enable applications at higher layer protocols to be implemented without knowledge of the underlying network protocol suite.

These two *TCP/IP* types of interfaces do not provide any network security services; therefore, a security system for *LAN* resources and users must be designed as an "add-on" system.

Since in each *LAN* data processing components are primarily user stations, the primary three *CISS* agents which will be involved in security operations are:

1. User Agent (UA);

2. Association Agent (AA);

3. Security Services Agent (SSA).

The *UA* is an agent responsible for interactions between a network user and *AA* or *SSA*. When a user wants to communicate with a remote entity, the user will initiate his/her request by calling the *UA*. The *UA* would in turn ask the user to provide the following information for a secure association: *(a)* the host address of the remote entity; *(b)* the identity of the remote entity; *(c)* action to be taken (*send, receive, mail, rlogin*, etc.); and *(d)* the desired security services. The identity of the remote entity may designate a user, a program or a file name. The action to be taken may be in the form of the application call or just some primitive network operation (*send* or *receive*). The desired security services may be many of the services available in the network.

The *AA* is in charge of establishing (secure) associations between any two cooperating application processes, users or programs. This agent uses security services provided by the *SSA*. The *AA* handles all security aspects in the association and after processing requests by the *SSA*, it sends back the resultant response to the *UA*.

The Security Services Agent (*SSA*), in cooperation with the *SMA* and *SMIBA*, performs various security-related functions.

The *CISS* interface to the three relevant agents is just a *command interpreter* to be associated with the user. It must be capable of processing and interpreting the security commands and parameters passed directly from the user. In [RAMA89] the following security commands and parameters (and their meanings) are suggested:

/Local-Authen: the sender is willing to authenticate himself/herself to the remote user.

/Remote-Authen: the sender wants to check authenticity of the remote user.

/Encrypt: the sender wants his/her outgoing data to be sent in encrypted form.

/Local-Authen-Encrypt: the sender wants to authenticate himself/herself as well as to transmit data in encrypted form.

/Remote-Authen-Encrypt: the sender wants to send his/her data in encrypted form as well as to transmit data in encrypted form.

/Local-Remote-Authen-Encrypt: the sender wants to authenticate himself/herself as well as to check the authenticity of the remote user and also wants to transmit the data in encrypted form.

/Integrity: the sender wants the data received by the receiver at the other end to be exactly the same as those transmitted by the sender.

/0: Null or empty set. It indicates that no security service was requested.

As soon as the *API* module receives the complete set of parameters from the upper layers (user or application), it should start checking for the logical presence of the security service request parameters. If the security parameter(s) is (are) not present, then the *TCP/IP* connection establishment phase is initiated; otherwise, if the security service request is present, then the control is passed to the *CISS* for further processing.

The *CISS* handles all security service functions. The details of providing the security service functions and mechanisms should be transparent to the user. Some users may explicitly request certain security services, while to some other users some services will be mandatory and therefore will be applied automatically.

The same security commands may be used for programming modules (applications) running on the *LAN*. In that case the same *API* may be used with input coming from the application module and the output (security request) will be directed from the *API* to the *OPEN* Agent instead of the *UA*.

One example of the prototype *CISS* implementation with direct user interactions, similar to commands suggested above, has been described in Section 8.2.2. For the system described in that section *TCP/IP* was not used, since the primary concern was the development of the *CISS* itself, but network aspects described in that section may be modified to the *TCP/IP* protocol, as described in this section.

8.3.4 Interactions with Other Environments (SNA and DECNET)

The use of the *CISS* in *SNA* and *DECNET* proprietary network architectures is now described. Those are the two most widely used network architectures and the *CISS* interfaces for them will make the *CISS* widely available in the network environment. The same principle as with the other proprietary network operating systems (i.e. *TCP/IP*) may be used here: *CISS API* will be established by using various entry points available with the *SNA* and the *DECNET* components. Both of these two network operating systems are in fact global networking environements. This means that they include many different types of network components, so that the *CISS* will interface with those environments through several of their components, depending on specific actions or resources to be protected.

8.3.4.1 CISS API for the IBM System Network Architecture (SNA)

The *System Network Architecture (SNA)* is the network architecture for *IBM* systems. The various protocol layers in the *SNA* are comparable to the *ISO/OSI* Reference Model. The highest layer in the *SNA* is the *Function Management Data Services (FMDS)* layer. It has the functionality of the *ISO* layer 6, but also some of the functions of layer 7. It provides a collection of services to the end user, including presentation services – (transfer) syntax selection and, if necessary, the associated data transformations – and some additional network management services. There are not application entities as such, however, and they are assumed to be provided by end-user processes.

In a *SNA* network, all communications between end-users (application processes) are through entities known as *logical units (LUs)*. Unlike *OSI* systems, end-users do not have a network identifier, instead it is the *LUs* that have a network address. *LUs* are also refereed to, therefore, as *network addressable units (NAUs)*. Communication between *LUs* is accomplished by exchanging messages known as *request/response units (RUs)*. Then, as in *OSI* systems, headers containing protocol control information are added as *RUs* pass down through the lower layers. This includes control information relating to the transmission control (session/transport), path control (network) and data link control layers.

As in *OSI*, no communication can take place (between *LUs* in the case of *SNA*) until a session connection has been establish between them. Within *SNA*, a session connection and a transport connection are one and the same. Thus, the data flow control and transmission control layers collectively provide a similar set of services as the *ISO* session layer and the part of the transport layer. Session connection is established and maintained by the *session control* component of the transmission control layer. The data flow control layer is then responsible for the subsequent data exchange, including interaction management, synchronization and exception reporting.

Unlike the *ISO* transport layer, the transmission control layer can not only transfer a message in response to a request from the data flow control layer (that is, an *RU*), but also from an end-user directly, or indeed from within its own layer. All messages to be transferred across the (path control) network carry protocol control information generated by the *connection point manager* component of the transmission control layer. This is then used:

1. to determine the intended destination of the message – that is, within the layer or a layer above;

2. to apply flow control and other control functions on the message units (*RUs*) exchanged between two LUs.

The *path control* and *data link control layer* collectively provide a similar set of services to the *ISO* network and data link layers. A typical *SNA* network comprises a mesh topology with a group of one or more physical links connecting each node in the network to an adjacent node. The flow of data units across each physical link is under the control of the data link control layer protocol. In *SNA*, this is *SDLC*, which is almost identical to the *ISO HDLC* protocol.

The provision of a group of links between adjacent nodes is done to achieve enhanced *reliability:* on receipt of a data unit for transmission, the *transmission group control* sublayer initiates the transmission of the data unit on the first available physical link to the intended destination node, rather than on a fixed link. Clearly, however, although this improves reliability, because of the use of a separate error control procedure on each link, data units may arrive at their destination out of sequence. To allow for this, the transmission group control protocol employs a *sequence numbering scheme* to ensure that the order of data units may be re-established by the receiving (destination) node. Also, when only a single physical link is available, improved performance is obtained by the protocol *blocking* a number of smaller data units into a single information frame prior to transmission. It may be concluded from this that the transmission group control sublayer simply enhances the performance of the data link control layer, and hence collectively these are equivalent to the *ISO* data link layer.

Finally, the *virtual route control* sublayer provides the transmission control layer with the means of establishing a logical connection – analogously to a virtual circuit/logical channel in a packet-switched network – with a peer transmission control layer. This may then be used to carry message units (*LUs*) relating to different sessions. The virtual route control protocol then applies flow control on the message units exchanged across this logical link and also fragmentation (and reassembly) of long messages. In *OSI*, the latter is, of course, a function of the transport layer, and hence the two layers are shown to overlap.

Obviously, the *SNA* is a complex network architecture and it includes not only data communication functions and components, but also data processing components. In those aspects where communication protocols in the *SNA* are similar (equivalent) to the *OSI* layers, similar *CISS API* may be used. In this case they may be on the top *SNA* layer, *FMDS* layer, which would be equivalent to the described *OSI ASSE*, and on the fourth transmission layer, equivalent to the *EESP*.

However, the most important *IBM* operating system component for communication functions is the *Virtual Telecommunications Access Method (VTAM)*. Parallel with *ASSE* and the *EESP*, *VTAM* standard security features and exits may also be used to interface the *CISS* with the *SNA* operating environment.

VTAM Security Features. *VTAM* is a subsystem that provides basic modules for constructing a data processing program, to perform and control transmission of data between logical units. *VTAM* executes in the host computer and operates with *IBM 37X5* communication controllers, which contain a resident program for communications, called *Network Control Program (NCP)*.

VTAM directly provides two security services: *data integrity* on communication lines, and *application (process) identification*. In addition, *VTAM* provides multiple exit points in the session establishment processing path at which *CISS API*, if provided, may be invoked. This *API* may be used to implement all other security services provided by the *CISS*.

Process Identification. Before an application program and a logical unit can communicate with each other, a connection, referred as a *session* or an *association* [VOYD83], must be established between them. Session establishment is a process by which *VTAM* establishes an association between internal control blocks, that represent a logical unit and an application program. During that process various security tests and communication security mechanisms may be applied, in order to establish a secure, reliable and authorized session.

When a user (logical unit) wants to establish a session with a particular application program, it sends a logon message to *VTAM* specifying, among other parameters, the *application program's name* (process identification). *VTAM* has facilities for verification of an application *LOGON* requests. *VTAM* determines where the application resides, whether it is available to accept the requested session and, at the user's option, whether the requester is permitted to establish the session.

Access Control. The systems programmer defines a valid logon message for each application program. The format of the standard logon message may be expanded by some additional (optional) parameters. If a user-written *CISS API* for the authorization security service is supplied, these parameters may be used by *CISS* to restrict *access* to an application program, or they may be used by the *LOGON exit routine.* A user identity or his/her password may be used by the *CISS* to verify user identity, his/her authentication and authorization. If available, *CISS API* should be invoked before *VTAM* processes a session establishment request. Therefore, *CISS* may prevent any security violations before a session is established.

The *Virtual Telecommunications Access Method (VTAM)* may, in cooperation with the *CISS,* provide some additional security functions for data protection in the communication system:

   a. it is possible to control *access* of terminals or users to interactive services or applications, or

   b. the Encrypt/Decrypt function of *VTAM*, which may be used in conjunction with hardware in user stations, may be combined with *CISS* cryptographic facilities to form a complete set of cryptographic mechanisms for *IBM* systems.

Data Integrity. Various error detection and recovery procedures of *VTAM* are in fact implementations of *data integrity* communication security services. They can verify the correctness of data, equipment, channels or operations. They may be combined with *CISS MAC* security mechanisms to ensure better data integrity guarantees.

Other security features of the *CISS,* which may be used by various components of *IBM* systems, may be invoked through the appropriate *API,* based on exits existing in those components. The details of those exits, mainly in the mainframe systems, may be found in the literature [MUFT92A].

8.3.4.2 CISS API for the DEC Digital Network Architecture (DNA)

Digital Network Architecture (DNA) is the network protocol architecture of *DEC.* The various protocol layers in *DNA* are also comparable with the *ISO Reference Model.*

The lowest three layers in a *DNA* collectively provide a similar service to an *ISO* connectionless (datagram) network. The data link layer in the *DNA* is known as the *Digital Data Communications Message Protocol (DDCMP)*. It is responsible for the management and transfer of data messages across the data link connecting adjacent network nodes. It is not a *HDLC*, but it is a character (byte)-oriented protocol. The control characters used are the *ASCII* control characters, but the content of data messages may be either *ASCII* characters or simply strings of 8-bit bytes.

To allow for this, therefore, each data message has a *count field* in its header that indicates the numbers of characters/bytes in the message. Also, the *error check field* is a *16-bit CRC*. *DDCMP* is based on a continuous *RQ* protocol and supports full-duplex data transfers. It also utilizes piggyback acknowledgements.

The *DECNET transport* layer is equivalent to the *ISO* connectionless network layer. It thus provides a basic datagram service. The *DNA* transport protocol, however, in addition to performing routing, also performs flow control and some other network management services.

The *network services* layer performs connection management and data transfer services. Connection management is concerned with the establishment (and clearing) of a full-duplex logical channel (equivalent to a combined *ISO* transport/session connection) between two peer network service layers. Once established, this can be used for both the exchange of messages between two user processes and for the transfer of protocol control and other messages.

The *session control* sublayer, which is considered part of the network services layer, performs two functions. The first is analogous to the *ISO* session connection management and the second to the address resolution part of the *ISO* directory services. In the *DNA*, as in *OSI*, user programs (processes) utilize symbolic names when initiating a (session) connection with another user program, and it is the session control sublayer that performs the necessary mapping between the symbolic names used by the user processes and their corresponding physical network addresses. Thus, on receipt of a connection request from a user process, the session control sublayer, after determining the required network address, passes a connect command to the network services layer. The latter then generates a connect (initiate) message and transfers this to the required correspondent network services layer. On receipt of this, the latter passes a connect command to the (peer) session control sublayer which, assuming the required user process is available, returns an accept command to the (peer) network service layer. Alternatively, if the called user process is not currently active, the session control sublayer first initiates its protocol before returning the accept command. The network services protocol then generates and returns a connect confirm message to the initiating layer which, in turn, informs the session control sublayer of the result of the connection attempt. Then, assuming this was successful, user messages may be exchanged across this connection without any further intervention from the session control sublayers. Finally, after all messages have been exchanged, the session sublayer is used to release the connection.

Being equivalent to the *OSI* Reference model, *DECNET* architecture may be linked to the *CISS,* and various security services may be provided in that environment, with the same principles as with standard *CISS APIs* for the *OSI* stack: the *ASSE* on the application layer and the *EESP* on the transport layer. Since *DEC* systems easily operate in *LANs,* the *CISS API* for the *TCP/IP* protocol may also be used for the *DECNET* environment.

8.4 POSSIBILITIES FOR USAGE OF CISS IN GLOBAL EDI SYSTEMS

Global *EDI* are considered in this context as network systems with additional functions (and therefore security requirements) as compared with (regular) simple *MHS* systems. In particular, *EDI* objects are documents, rather then messages; therefore, they not only have a content, but also certain special delivery implications. Those documents may be contracts, tenders, proposals, software modules, etc. and they, in principle, need higher level of protection than simple messages.

In addition, in almost all security requirements for standard *MHS* systems, it is always assumed that two mutually trusted users are communicating in the untrustful environment. This may be stated as the fact that the sources of threats are always "outside" of the regular associations. In the *EDI* systems this is not always the case. The sender sometimes is not willing to deliver the letter (software module, a contract, etc.) unless he is absolutely certain that he will receive a confirmation (payment acknowledgement, etc.). Standard digital seal and digital signatures mechanisms and ordinary third parties assistances are not efficient in this case because of the mutual suspicion.

These kinds of requirements may be generally resolved by special protocols for cooperation of mutually suspicious users. These protocols need a third party, but not a regular arbitrator, but the party executing specially designed protocols. Since the concept of *CISS* is based on cooperating *SMCs,* these *SMCs* may provide at the same time those special protocol components.

The purpose of this section is to indicate some additional security requirements in the *EDI* environments and to suggest use of a *CISS* as the solution for these requirements. With these examples a *CISS* is suggested as a global security system, suitable not only to fulfill regular, but also even certain special security requirements.

8.4.1 Certified (Registered) Electronic Mail

As an example of the use of a *CISS* in global systems, secure, certified (registered) electronic mail is described in this subsection. This is an extention of the standard *E-mail* exchange of letters between two regular users, with the following additional security requirements:

1. The third party (intruder) cannot read confidential letters.

2. The sender must be certain that only the intended receiver will receive (and understand) the letter.

3. The receiver must be convinced that the indicated sender has really sent the letter.

4. Both the sender and the receiver must be convinced that the content of the letter is original.

5. Both the sender and the receiver must be convinced that the letter will be delivered within a reasonable time without getting lost. If the letter does not arrive at all, the sender has to receive a notice about that.

6. Both the sender and the receiver must receive the confirmation of delivery.

7. In case of mutually suspicious users, the sender is not willing to deliver the letter unless it is absolutely certain that it will receive a receipt for it, confirming both the intended recipient and the contents of the letter.

This type of global system requires special security services and protocols, not only between the two users involved and against the third party, but also as mutually suspicious users. Standard authentication, confidentiality and integrity security services are not sufficient to provide the stated requirements. Therefore some protocol for cooperation of suspicious users is required.

The protocol may be based on sending a message called *"confirmation of delivery"*, equivalent to the counterpart in classical (physical) postal services. This message is included in the original letter as a separate item. The message contains the name and the address of the sender and the receiver, the date of sending, the secret symmetric key by which the letter has been encrypted and a random number. The message is signed by the sender and also encrypted by the receiver's public key.

The receiver has first to handle the *"confirmation of delivery"* message and after that he can receive (read) the letter. He decrypts the message by his secret key, checks the signature, fetches the secret symmetric key from the message, appends to the message the receiving date and time, signs the complete message, encrypts it by the original sender's public key and sends it back to the sender.

Based on those protocols it is possible to guarantee that:

1. Since the letter is encrypted with a secret session key, the mail system agents or any other intruders cannot read the letter.

2. The receiver can be convinced that the letter really came from the original sender, because the letter must be signed by the sender and it must guarantee the integrity of addresses of both parties.

3. Mail system agents cannot modify the confirmation of delivery message, because they do not possess the association secret key.

4. The sender can be convinced that the letter has been received by the receiver, if the confirmation message contains the same random number sent by the sender and if the integrity of both addresses is guaranteed.

However, with mutually suspicious users, this protocol cannot be used. It is obvious that if the receiver wants to cheat, he will not return any confirmation message to the sender. Therefore, the receiver has received (and read) the message and the sender has been left without the proof of delivery.

There are two possibilities to resolve this situation, both relying on certain special protocols for cooperation of mutually suspicious users. The first protocol is based on the concept of so-called *"beacons"* [RABI83], special network components which emit certain special signals to all participants in the protocol. Upon the receipt of these signals, the sender of the registered mail and its receiver may simultaneously recover earlier received special messages, which to the receiver provide a possibility to reconstruct the letter, and to the sender a possibility to generate an authenticated confirmation of the receipt.

Another equivalent protocol for this special service is again based on special network components, called *"antennas"* [MUFT90B]. The concept suggests the use of "trustful" network components, so that the equivalent goal may be achieved as with "beacons", but with much more efficient protocols.

8.4.2 The Notary Service

The main function of the notary service is to provide assurance of the following requirements:

a. When a person A has sent a document to a person B, B cannot later claim that he has never received the document in question or that the document has arrived with a different content.

b. When a person A has sent a document to a person B, A cannot later claim that he has never sent the document in question or that the document has been sent with a different content.

The notary service should be provided by a third trustworthy party. This party is called here an *arbitrator (V)*. The notary service system must verify, that

- the document has been really sent by A;

- the document will really reach B; and

- neither party can later modify the document content.

Additionally the following protocol functions may be offered by the notary:

1. The arbitrator should not be able to read the content of the document sent by user A.

2. The arbitrator must store the document or the signature of the document with the time-stamp.

3. Fraudulent activity of two parties, A and V or B and V, against the third party, B or A, could not be possible.

4. Fraudulent denial of service by the arbitrator could not be possible.

The notary service protocol transfers the original letter via a special notary server (Arbitrator) from the sender to the receiver. The protocol is based on storing by the arbitrator the signed document including the receiving date and additionally including the confirmation of delivery in the message. The retrieval key will be delivered both to the sender and to the receiver, so that they can request it later with the key.

The Arbitrator signs the received item (containing also the letter itself) and sends it to the receiver. The receiver checks the validity of the message and obtains from it the retrieval key, the original letter, and the *"confirmation of delivery"* item. He modifies the message in a similar way as in the case of the certified electronic mail, sends it back to the Arbitrator, and consequently to the original sender of the letter. There is a double confirmation of delivery in this protocol and the user may choose to store the *"confirmation of delivery"* message without degrading the security provided by the notary service.

It may be stated that the described protocol has the following properties:

1. The sender A cannot repudiate the sending of the document, because the record of sending is stored with time stamp in the arbitrator's file.

2. The sender A cannot later (and neither can V on behalf of the sender), modify the content of the document, because the signature of the document is also encrypted with B's public key. Otherwise, the receiver B can check that by decrypting the signature with his secret key and with the sender's public key.

3. Neither V nor A can later modify the time stamp of the document registration, because B has the signature of the delivered item dated and signed by V.

4. The arbitrator V can not read the document, because it does not know the secret session key, which was used to encrypt the document text. The arbitrator V cannot modify the document content with the help of the receiver B, because neither of them have A's secret key, which has been used to produce the signature. The receiver cannot later modify the document, because for that A's secret key is needed.

5. Since the confirmation of delivery will be sent from B to A, A can be convinced that the document has been really registered and that B has really received it. This confirmation practice is a double guarantee of message delivery to B.

6. Both parties A and B have the retrieval keys created and signed by the arbitrator and they can request from the arbitrator's file registration records to verify their conformity.

8.4.3 The Document Service

The final example of a secure global system is an overview of a prototype document service system containing the basic security mechanisms incorporated into the application functions. Heavy emphasis has been laid on different security mechanisms which may all be available through the usage of the *CISS*.

The Document Service, as described in this subsection, is a generic service which may be used in many different global *EDI* systems: libraries, public information systems, national or corporate document archives, etc. Such systems need special protection features, dealing with suspicious users, generation of unauthorized information, search of large volumes of documents, etc. The protected application, described here just as a prototype of some larger, global document system, consists of the following subsystems:

    a. User workstation;

    b. Document Server System;

    c. Security Directory Service;

    d. Protocol/Network System;

    e. RSA Key Generation and Delivery System.

The security aspects of this system are incorporated into different application functions in the application development phase. A user interactive interface to the document server runs in a user workstation. Command messages and user data in this prototype implementation are transferred through the transmission *LAN* using the *TCP/IP* transmission protocol.

The document service system functions are the following:

- Query to the document base directory, its delivery to the workstation, scrolling it on a display, and selection of specific requests.

- Requesting a named document from the server to the workstation.

- Sending a specific document for storing into the document base.

- Deleting a selected document in the document base.

- Sending an operator message to the document server display.

The key exchange protocol in this Security Document System has been developed as a stand-alone system according to the *CCITT Recommendation X.509.* The conventions followed for generating the *RSA* keys are taken from the literature and they produce cryptographically strong keys. Below are listed the directory server functions targeted in this implementation:

- Public key storage and delivery upon request;

- Complete notarization service;

- Common system time delivery.

8.5 SUMMARY AND CONCLUSIONS

As conclusions for this chapter, it may be emphasized that the described practical implementations and considerations of the *CISS* system: *(a)* prove the feasibility and the correctness of the *CISS* concept described in the previous chapter, and *(b)* give some practical guidance to possible implementations of the *CISS* system.

All these practical implementations had been implemented at the time of writing of this book. At the time of its publishing the prototypes will be further developed and synthesized, resulting at that time in the first version of the complete, global implementation of the *CISS* system.

Appendix

SMIB Segments (ASN.1 Notation)

In this Appendix the structure of *SMIB* segments in *ASN.1* notation is given. Standard (*X.500*) segments are object classes 1–14 (with additional attributes in italic), while additional *SMIB* segments needed for implementation of security in the *ODP* environment are object classes 15–20.

Standard (X.500) Object Classes with Additional Security Attributes

1. **Top:**

   top   Top ::= { objectClass 0 }

2. **Alias:**

   alias   Alias ::= { objectClass 1 }

3. **Country:**

   country OBJECT-CLASS
            SUBCLASS OF top
            MUST CONTAIN {
                countryName }
            MAY CONTAIN {
                description,
                searchGuide }
            ::= { objectClass 2 }

4. Locality:

```
locality  OBJECT-CLASS
        SUBCLASS  OF  { top | country | organization }
        MAY  CONTAIN  {
            description,
            localityName,
            stateOrProvinceName,
            searchGuide,
            seeAlso,
            streetAddress }
        ::=  { objectClass 3 }
```

5. Organization:

```
organization  OBJECT-CLASS
        SUBCLASS  OF  { top | country | locality }
        MUST  CONTAIN  {
            organizationName }
        MAY  CONTAIN  {
            organizationalAttributeSet }
        ::=  { objectClass 4 }
```

6. Organizational Unit:

```
organizationalUnit  OBJECT-CLASS
        SUBCLASS OF  { locality | organization }
        MUST  CONTAIN  {
            organizationalUnitName }
        MAY  CONTAIN  {
            organizationalAttributeSet }
        ::=  { objectClass 5 }
```

7. Group of Names:

```
groupOfNames  OBJECT-CLASS
        SUBCLASS OF  { locality | organization |
            organizationalUnit }
        MUST  CONTAIN  {
            Name,
            member }
        MAY  CONTAIN  {
            description,
            organizationName,
            organizationalUnitName,
            owner,
            seeAlso,
            businessCategory }
        ::=  { objectClass 9 }
```

8. Residential Person:

```
residentialPerson  OBJECT-CLASS
      SUBCLASS OF locality
      MUST  CONTAIN {
            localityName }
      MAY  CONTAIN {
            UserPassword,
            localAttributeSet,
            postalAttributeSet,
            preferredDeliveryMethod,
            telecommunicationAttributeSet,
            businessCategory }
      ::=  { objectClass 10 }
```

9. Application Process:

```
applicationProcess  OBJECT-CLASS
      SUBCLASS OF { organization | organizationalUnit }
      MUST  CONTAIN {
            Name }
      MAY  CONTAIN {
            UserPassword,
            description,
            localityName,
            organizationalUnitName,
            seeAlso }
      ::=  { objectClass 11 }
```

10. Person:

```
person  OBJECT-CLASS
      SUBCLASS OF { locality | organization |
            organizationalUnit }
      MUST  CONTAIN {
            Name,
            surname }
      MAY  CONTAIN {
            description,
            seeAlso,
            telephoneNumber,
            userPassword }
      ::=  { objectClass 6 }
```

11. Organizational Role:

```
organizationalRole  OBJECT-CLASS
        SUBCLASS OF { organization | organizationalUnit }
        MUST  CONTAIN {
        Name }
        MAY  CONTAIN {
        UserPassword,
        description,
        localAttributeSet,
        organizationalUnitName,
        postalAttributeSet,
        preferredDeliveryMethod,
        roleOccupant,
        seeAlso,
        telecommunicationAttributeSet }
        ::=  { objectClass 8 }
```

12. Organizational Person:

```
organizationalPerson  OBJECT-CLASS
        SUBCLASS OF { organization | organizationalUnit }
        MUST  CONTAIN {
        Name,
        surname }
        MAY  CONTAIN {
        UserPassword,
        localAttributeSet,
        organizationalUnitName,
        postalAttributeSet,
        telecommunicationAttributeSet
        title }
        ::=  { objectClass 7 }
```

13. Application Entity:

```
applicationEntity  OBJECT-CLASS
        SUBCLASS OF applicationProcess
        MUST  CONTAIN {
        Name,
        presentationAddress }
        MAY  CONTAIN {
        description,
        localityName,
        organizationName,
        organizationalUnitName,
        see Also,
        supportedApplicationContext }
        ::=  { objectClass 12 }
```

14. Device:

```
device  OBJECT-CLASS
        SUBCLASS OF { organization | organizationalUnit }
        MUST  CONTAIN {
            Name }
        MAY  CONTAIN {
            description,
            localityName,
            organizationName,
            organizationalUnitName,
            owner,
            seeAlso,
            serialNumber }
    ::=  { objectClass 14 }
```

Additional Security Object Classes and their Attributes

15. Extended Security:

```
extendedSecurity  OBJECT-CLASS
        SUBCLASS OF { person | applicationProcess |
            residentialPerson | organizationalPerson |
            organizationalRole }
        MUST  CONTAIN {
            Name }
        MAY  CONTAIN {
            Certificate,
            publicAuthenticationParameters,
            thresholdGroupOfNames,
            thresholdSize,
            thresholdValue,
            conferenceName,
            conferenceCommonBase,
            conferenceModulus }
    ::=  { objectClass 17 }
```

```
Certificate  ::=        SIGNED SEQUENCE {
        version  [0]                     Version DEFAULT v1988
        serialNumber                     CertificateSerialNumber,
        signature                        AlgorithmIdentifier,
        issuer                           Name,
        validity                         Validity,
        subject                          Name,
        subjectPublicKeyInfo
            SubjectPublicKeyInfo }


Version  ::=        INTEGER { v1988(0) }


CertificateSerialNumber  ::=  INTEGER


AlgorithmIdentifier  ::=
        SEQUENCE {
            algorithm OBJECT IDENTIFIER,
            parameters ANY DEFINED BY algorithm
                OPTIONAL }


Validity  ::=
        SEQUENCE {
            notBefore                    UTCTime,
            notAfter                     UTCTime }


SubjectPublicKeyInfo  ::=
        SEQUENCE {
            algorithm                    AlgorithmIdentifier,
            subjectKey                   BIT STRING }
```

16. Confidential Parameters:

```
confidentialParameters OBJECT-CLASS
        SUBCLASS OF { person | applicationProcess |
            residentialPerson | organizationalPerson |
            organizationalRole }
        MUST CONTAIN {
            Name,
            userPassword }
        MAY CONTAIN {
            secretSymmetricKey,
            secretAuthenticationParameters,
            CA-Modulus,
            publicCA-Key }
        ::= { objectClass 18 }
```

17. Secure Association:

```
secureAssociation  OBJECT-CLASS
        SUBCLASS OF { person | applicationProcess |
            residentialPerson | organizationalPerson |
            organizationalRole }
        MUST  CONTAIN {
            associationIdentity,
            InitiatorIdentity,
            peer-entityIdentity }
        MAY  CONTAIN {
            sessionSymmetricKey,
            RNG-seed,
            initializationVector,
            subliminalChannelKey,
            conferenceKey,
            messageSequenceNumber,
            timeStamp }
        ::=  { objectClass 19 }
```

18. Attribute Set:

```
attributeSet  OBJECT-CLASS
        SUBCLASS OF { person | applicationProcess |
            residentialPerson | organizationalPerson |
            organizationalRole | applicationEntity | device }
        MUST  CONTAIN {
            Name,
            superiorCommonName,
            ATTRIBUTE-SET }
        MAY  CONTAIN {
            description,
            localityName,
            organizationName,
            seeAlso,
            supportedApplicationContext }
        ::=  { objectClass 20 }
```

19. Extended Access Control:

extendedAccessControl OBJECT-CLASS
    SUBCLASS OF { person | applicationProcess |
        residentialPerson | organizationalPerson |
        organizationalRole }
    MUST CONTAIN {
        subjectCommonName,
        attributeSetCommonName,
        AC-parameters }
    MAY CONTAIN {
        description,
        localityName,
        owner }
    ::= { objectClass 21 }

AC-parameters ATTRIBUTE-SET
    MUST CONTAIN {
        AC-right,
        AC-conditionModule }
    MAY CONTAIN {
        AC-parameters }
    ::= { attributeSet 4 }

20. Security Log:

securityLog OBJECT-CLASS
    SUBCLASS OF { person | applicationProcess |
        residentialPerson | organizationalPerson |
        organizationalRole }
    MUST CONTAIN {
        entryTypeIndicator,
        subjectCommonName,
        timeStamp }
    MAY CONTAIN {
        subjectPublicKeyInfo,
        certificate,
        messageContents,
        messageSeal,
        secureAssociationParameters }
    ::= { objectClass 22 }

REFERENCES
AND LITERATURE

1. Contributions to the COST-11 Ter "Security" Project

[COLO90]   Colon, R., *Secure Protocols And Applications In The OSI Environment*, University of Madrid, Madrid, Spain, 1990.

[EKBE85]   Ekberg, J., *Tietosuojan tulevaisuuden nakymia*, Sahko 58, 5, 1985.

[EKBE86A]   Ekberg, J., *New Solutions in User Identification and Authentication Mechanisms*, Technical Research Center of Finland, Helsinki, Finland, 1986.

[EKBE86B]   Ekberg, J., Karila, A., *A Layered Security Management Model*, Technical Research Center of Finland, Helsinki, Finland, 1986.

[HEIJ85]   Heijnsdijk, J.W.J., *Some Thoughts on Security and Privacy in Computer Networks*, Delft University of Technology, Delft, The Netherlands, 1985.

[HEIJ87]   Heijnsdijk, J.W.J., *Cryptographic Key Management in Computer Networks*, Delft University of Technology, Delft, The Netherlands, 1987.

[LAWM89A]   Law Min, F., Patel, A., *Security In OSI Applications*, Department of Computer Science, University College Dublin, Belfield, Dublin, Ireland, 1989.

[LAWM89B]   Law Min, F., Patel, A., *Security Functional Reference Model For Open Distributed Processing Environments*, Department of Computer Science, University College Dublin, Belfield, Dublin, Ireland, 1989.

[MARO86]   Maroulis, D., *Entity Authorization and Access Control Mechanisms*, The Greek Computer Society, Athens, Greece, 1986.

[MARO89]   Maroulis, D., *Security Architecture in the OSI Environment*, The Greak Computer Society, 1989.

[MUFT85]   Muftic, S., *Communication Protection for Computer Networks*, IRIS-ENERGOINVEST, Sarajevo, Yugoslavia .

[MUFT88A]   Muftic, S., *Survey of Network Security Services And Mechanisms*, University of Sarajevo, Yugoslavia, 1988.

[MUFT88B]   Muftic, S., *N–Level Approach For Raiting of Security Mechanisms*, University of Sarajevo, Yugoslavia, 1988.

[PATE86A]   Patel, A., Law Min, F., *Study of Security Measures within the OSI Framework*, University College Dublin, Dublin, Ireland.

[PATE86B]   Patel, A., Law Min, F., *Entity Authentication*, University College Dublin, Dublin, Ireland.

[PATE86C]   Patel, A., Law Min, F., *Entity Authentication*, University College Dublin, Dublin, Ireland.

[PATE89A]   Patel, A., Law Min, F., *Management Implications in the Provision of X.32 Services*, University College Dublin, Dublin, Ireland, 1989.

[PATE89B]   Patel, A., *General Introduction to Computer Security*, Department of Computer Science, University College Dublin, Dublin, Ireland, 1989.

[PATE89C]   Patel, A., Law Min, F., *Management Implications In The Provision Of X.32 Services*, Department of Computer Science, University College Dublin, Belfield, Dublin, Ireland, 1989.

[PRIE85A]   Prieto, A.R., *Security Solutions in Data Transmission Networks*, Universidad de Madrid, Madrid, Spain, 1985.

[PRIE85B]   Prieto, A.R., *Cryptography and Data Protection for Computer Networks in ISO Context*, Universidad de Madrid, Madrid, Spain, 1985.

[PRIE86]   Prieto, A.R., Garcia Tomas, J., *Encryption-Decryption Quality Rating*, Universidad de Madrid, Madrid, Spain, 1986.

[PULK88]   Pulkkinen, U., Sanders, P., *Document Handling System With Security Management Centers (SMC)*, Plymouth University, England, 1988.

[PULK89A]   Pulkkinen, U., *Some Comments in COST 11 Ter Papers*, Technical Research Centre of Finland, Graphic Arts Laboratory, Helsinki, Finland, 1989.

[PULK89B]   Pulkkinen, U., *Extended OSI Security Architecture*, Technical Research Centre of Finland, Graphic Arts Laboratory, Helsinki, Finland, 1989.

[PULK90A]   Pulkkinen, U., *Protected Application Description*, Technical Research Centre of Finland, Graphic Arts Laboratory, Helsinki, Finland, 1990.

[PULK90B]   Pulkkinen, U., *Application Security Protocols*, Technical Research Centre of Finland, Graphic Arts Laboratory, Helsinki, Finland, 1990.

[SAND88A]   Sanders, P.W., *Extended Security Architecture*, Polytechnic South West, Plymouth, England, 1988.

[SAND88B]   Sanders, P.W., *Security Architecture Discussion Paper*, COST-11 Ter, Polytechnic South West, Plymouth, England, 1988.

[SAND90]   Sanders, P.W., *An Optimization Technique For Large Scale Security Networks*, Polytechnic South West, Plymouth, England, 1990.

[SHEP90]   Shepherd, S., *Implementation Aspects Of Security On a PC Station*, Polytechnic South West, Plymouth, England, 1990.

[VARA86]   Varadharajan, V., Sanders, P.W., *Mechanisms for Protection of Data Confidentiality*, Plymouth Polytechnic, Plymouth, UK, 1986

[VARA87]   Varadharajan, V., Sanders, P.W., *Some Communication Security Measures and Techniques for Protecting Data Confidentiality and Integrity in Networks*, Plymouth Polytechnic, Plymouth, UK, 1987

[VARA88]   Varadharajan, V., *A Formal Methodology For Secure System Design*, EEC COST-11 Ter Security Project, 1988.

[ZAMP90]   Zamparo, R., *Strong Authentication in FTAM*, Swedish Telecom, COST-225 Project, Sweden, 1990.

2. General References

[ACHE86]   Achemlal, M., et al. *Dynamic Signature Verification*, Proceedings of the IFIP/SEC '86 Conf., Monte Carlo, 1986.

[AKL 83]   Akl, S.G., *Digital Signatures: A Tutorial Survey*, Computer, Feb 1983.

[AYOU83]   Ayoub, F.N., *Some Aspects of the Design of Secure Encryption Algorithms*, Hatfield Polytechnic, M.Sc. Thesis, March 1983.

[BABI77]   Babic, G., Liu, M.T., Pardo, R., *A Performance Study of A Distributed Loop Computer Network (DLCN)*, Proc. 1977 Computer Networks Symposium, Gaithersburgh, USA, Dec 1977.

[BART84]   Barton, B.F., Barton, M.S., *User-Friendly Password Methods for Computer Mediated Information Systems*, Computers & Security, 3(4), Nov 1984.

[BAUE83]   Bauer, R.K., Berson, T.A., Feiertag, R.J., *A Key Distribution Protocol Using Event Markers*, ACM Transactions on Comp. Systems, Vol. 1, No. 3, Aug 1983.

[BEKE82]   Beker, H., Piper, F., *Cipher Systems*, Northwood Books, London, 1982.

[BELL73]   Bell, D.E., LaPadula, I.J., *Secure Computer System: Unified exposition and Multics interpretation*, MITRE Corporation, MTR-2997, 1976.

[BENN84]   Bennett, C.H., Brassard, G., *Quantum Cryptography: Public Key Distribution and Coin Tossing*, Proc. of the Int'l Conf. on Computers, Systems and Signal Processing, India, 1984.

[BERG85]   Berger, R., Peralta, R., Tedrick, T., *A Provable Secure Oblivious Transfer Protocol*, Proc of the EUROCRYPT '84, Springer-Verlag, 1985.

[BLAC89]   Black, U., *Data Network: Concepts, Theory and Practice*, Prentice-Hall, Inc., 1989.

[BLUM81]   Blum, M., *Three Applications of the Oblivious Transfer: Part I : Coin Flipping by Telephone; Part II : How to Exchange the Secrets; Part III : How to send Certified Electronic Mail*, Dept EECS, Univ. of California, USA, 1981.

[BLUM83]   Blum, M., *How to Exchange (Secret) Keys*, ACM Trans. Comp. Systems, Vol. 1, No. 2, May 1983.

[BLUM85]   Blum, M., *All-or-Nothing Certified Mail*, Workshop on Mathematical Aspects of Cryptography, Edicot House, MIT, 1985.

[BOLO87]   Bolognesi, T., Brinksma, E., *Introduction to the ISO Specification Language LOTOS*, Computer Networks & ISDN Systems, Vol. 14, 1987.

[BOND84]   Bond, D.J., *Practical Primality Testing*, Int'l Conf. on Secure Communication Systems, IEEE, London, 1984.

[BOYD86]   Boyd, C., *Digital Multisignatures*, Proc. I.M.A. Conference on Coding and Cryptography, Cirencester, Gt. Britain, Dec 1986.

[BRAN76]   Branstad, D.K., Gaits, J., Katzke, S., *Report on the Workshop on Cryptography in Support of Computer Security*, NBS, USA, IR 77-291, 1976.

[BRAN87]   Branstad, D.K., *Considerations for Security in the OSI Architecture*, IEEE Network Magazine, Vol. 1, No. 2, April 1987.

[BRAS87]   Brassard, G., *Cryptology in Academia : A Ten Year Retrospective*, IEEE Compcon Conference, San Francisco, USA, Feb 1987.

[BUDK87]   Budkowski, S., Dembinski, P., *An Introduction to Estelle: A Specification Language for Distributed Systems*, Computer Networks & ISDN Systems, Vol. 14, 1987.

[BUSS80]   Bussolati, U., Martella, G., *On Designing Security Management System for Distributed Data Bases*, Proc of the COMPSAC 80 Conference, USA, 1980.

[BUSS81A] Bussolati, U., Martella, G., *Access Control and Management in Multilevel Database Models*, Trends in Information Processing Systems : Lecture Notes in Comp. Science, Vol. 123, Springer, 1981.

[BUSS81B] Bussolati, U., Martella, G., *Managing Data Privacy in Data Base Management Systems*, Proceedings of the Informatique Latine Conference, 1981.

[CAPE88]   Capel, A.C., Lafarriere, C., and Toth, K.C., *Protecting the Security of X.25 Communications*, Data Comm., pp. 123-139, Nov 1988.

[CCIT86]   CCITT / ISO Directory Convergence Document No. 3 *The Directory - Authentication Framework*, Melbourne, April 1986.

[CHAM75]   Chamberlin, D.D., Gray, J.N. and Traiger, I.L., *Views, Authorization and Locking in Relational Data Base Systems*, Proc. AFIPS NCC, USA, Vol. 44, 1975.

[CHAU81]   Chaum, D., *Untraceable Electronic Mail, Return Addresses, and Digital Pseudonyms*, Communications of the ACM, Vol. 24, No. 2, Feb 1981.

[CHAU85]   Chaum, D., *Security without Identification : Transaction Systems to Make a Big Brother Obsolete*, Communications of the ACM, Vol. 10, 1985.

[CHAU87]   Chaum, D., *Demonstrating that A Public Predicate Can Be Satisfied Without Revealing Any Information About How,* Proc of the CRYPTO'86, Springer-Verlag, 1987.

[CHOR86]   Chorley, B.J., Price, W.L., *An Intelligent Token for Secure Transactions,* Proceedings of IFIP / SEC '86, Monte Carlo, 1986.

[CHRI87]   Christoffersson, P., *Message Encryption and Authentication,* Tele-K, Swedish Telecom, Stockholm, Sweden, 1987.

[CHRI88]   Christoffersson, P., *Message Authentication and Encryption Combined,* Computers & Security, 7(1), 1988.

[CLAR87]   Clark, D.D., Wilson, D.R., *A Comparison of Commercial and Military Security Policies,* Proc. 1987 IEEE Symp. on Security and Privacy, CS Press, Los Alamitos, USA, 1987.

[CNUD90]   Cnudde, H. *CRYPTEL: The Practical protection of an existing Electronic Mail System,* Computer Security and Information Integrity in our changing world, Finland, May 1990.

[COHE85]   Cohen, J.D., Fisher, M., *A Robust and Verifiable Cryptographically Secure Election Scheme,* Proc of the 26th IEEE Symp on Foundations of Computer Science, 1987.

[COMM86]   Commission of the European Communities, *Beyond OSI – Future Basic Research into Distributed Systems,* Brussels, 1986.

[COMM89]   Commercial Computer Security Committee, *UK Commercial Evaluation Criteria,* DTI, London, UK, 1989

[CONW72]   Conway, R.W., Maxwell, W.L., Morgan, H.L., *On the Implementation of Security Measures in Information Systems,* Communications of ACM, Vol. 15, No. 4, April 1972.

[COPP86]   Coppersmith, D., *Cheating at Mental Poker,* Proc. of CRYPTO'85, Springer-Verlag, 1986.

[CREP87]   Crepeau, C., *A Zero-Knowledge Poker Protocol That Achieves Confidentiality of Player's Strategy,* Proc. of CRYPTO'86, Springer-Verlag, 1987.

[DATE83]   Date, C.J., *An Introduction to Database Systems,* Addison-Wesley, Reading, Massachusetts, 1983.

[DAVI80]   Davis, D.W., Price, W.L., *The Application of Digital Signatures Based on Public Key Cryptosystems,* NPL Report DNACS 39/80, England, Dec. 1980.

[DAVI83]   Davis, D.W., *Applying the RSA Digital Signature to Electronic Mail,* Computer, Feb 1983.

[DAVI84]   Davies, D.W., Price, W.L., *Security for Computer Networks,* Wiley, New York, 1984.

[DEC 84]   *Guide to VAX/VMS System Security,* Digital Equipment Corporation, Massachusetts, Sep 1984.

[DeMI83]   DeMillo, R., Merritt, M., *Protocols for Data Security*, Computer, Feb 1983, pp. 39-50.

[DEMO77]   Demo, B., *On the Data Base Integrity Concept*, Proc. INFORMATICA 77 Computer Conf., Bled, Yugoslavia, Oct. 1977.

[DENN76]   Denning, D.E, *A Lattice Model of Secure Information Flow*, Communications of the ACM, 19(5), May 1976, 236-243.

[DENN79]   Denning, D., Denning, P.J., *Data Security*, ACM Computing Surveys, 11(3), Sept. 1979, 225-249.

[DENN81]   Denning, D., Sacco, G.M., *Timestamps in Key Distribution Protocol*, Communications of the ACM, 24(8), August 1981.

[DENN82]   Denning, D.E., *Cryptography and Data Security*, Addison-Wesley, Reading, 1982.

[DENN83]   Denning, D.E., *Protecting Public Keys and Signature Keys*, Computer, Feb. 1983.

[DENN87A]   Denning, D.E., *Views for Multilevel Database Security*, IEEE Transactions on Software Engineering, Vol. SE-13, No. 2, Feb. 1987.

[DENN87B]   Denning, D.E., *An Intrusion-Detection Model*, IEEE Transactions on Software Engineering, Vol. SE-13, No. 2, Feb. 1987.

[DIFF76]   Diffie, W., Hellman, M.E., *A Critique of the Proposed Data Encryption Standard (DES)*, Communication of the ACM, Vol. 19, No. 3, 1976.

[DIFF81]   Diffie, W., *Cryptographic Technology: Fifteen Years Forecast*, BNR Inc., Mountain View, USA, 1981.

[DoD 83]   Department of Defense, *Trusted Computer System Evaluation Criteria*, Aug. 1983.

[ECMA86]   European Computer Manufacturers Association, *Framework for Distributed Office Applications*, ECMA TC32-TG5, Dec. 1986.

[ECMA88]   European Computer Manufacturers Association, *Security Framework (TR46)*, ECMA, June 1988.

[ELOF83]   Eloff, J., *Selection Process for Security Packages*, Computers & Security 2, 256-260, 1983.

[EVEN85]   Even, Sh., Goldreich, O. and Lampel, A., *A Randomized Protocol for Signing Contracts*, Comm. ACM, 28(6), June 1985.

[FEIG86]   Feigenbaum, J., *Encrypting Problem Instances*, CRYPTO '85, 477-488, 1986.

[FIAT87]   Fiat, A. and Shamir, A., *How to Prove Yourself: Practical Solutions to Identification and Signature Problems*, Proc. CRYPTO'86 Conf., Springer-LNCS 263, 1987.

[FIPS77]   FIPS Publication 46, *Data Encryption Standard (DES)*, U.S. Department of Commerce, National Bureau of Standards, 1977.

[FIPS80]   FIPS Publication 83, *Guideline on User Authentication Techniques for Computer Network Access Control*, U.S. Department of Commerce, National Bureau of Standards, 1980.

[FREE88]   Freer, J., *Computer Communications and Networks*, Pitman Publishing, 1988.

[FUMY90]   Fumy, W., *Asymmetric Authentication Schemes for Smart Cards - Dream or Reality?*, Proc. Conf. "Computer Security and Information Integrity in Our Changing World", FUB, Rome, Nov. 1990.

[GLAS87]   Glasgow, J.I.,   MacEwen G.H.   *The Development and Proof of a Formal Specification for a Multilevel Secure System*, ACM Transactions on Computer Systems, Vol. 5, No. 2, May 1987.

[GOGU82]   Goguen, J.A., Messeguer, J., *Security Policies and Security Models*, Proc. 1982 IEEE Symp. on Security and Privacy, New York, USA, April 1982.

[GOGU84]   Goguen, J.A., Messeguer, J., *Unwinding and Inference Control*, Proc. 1984 IEEE Symp. on Security and Privacy, New York, USA, 1984.

[GOLD82]   Goldwasser, S., Micali, S., *Probabilistic Encryption and How to Play Poker Keeping Secret all Partial Information*, Proc of the 14th ACM Symposium on Theory of Computing, 1982.

[GOLD83]   Goldwasser, S., Micali, S., Yao, A.C., *Strong Signature Schemes*, Proc of the 15th ACM Symposium on Theory of Computing, 1983.

[GOLD84]   Goldreich, O., Goldwasser, S., Micali, S., *How to Construct Random Functions*, Proc of the 25th IEEE Symp. on Foundations of Computer Science, 1984.

[GOLD85]   Goldreich, O., Goldwasser, S., Micali, S., *On The Cryptographic Applications of Random Functions*, Proc. of the CRYPTO'84, Springer-Verlag, 1985.

[GOLD86]   Goldreich, O., Micali, S., Widgerson, A., *Proofs That Yield Nothing But Their Validity and A Methodology of Cryptographic Protocol Design*, Proc of the 27th IEEE Symp on Foundations of Computer Science, 1986.

[GOLD87]   Goldreich, O., *Towards A Theory of Software Protection*, Proc. CRYPTO'86, Springer-Verlag, 1987.

[GRAH72]   Graham, G.S. and Denning, P.J., *Protection–Principles and Practice*, Proc. SJCC, USA, 1972.

[HARD83]   Hardy, G.H., Wright, E.M., *An Introduction to The Theory of Numbers*, Oxford University Press, 1983.

[HARR76]   Harrison, M.A., Ruzzo, W.L., Ullman, J.D., *Protection in Operating Systems*, Communications of the ACM, 19(8), August 1976.

[HART76]   Hartson, R., Hsiao, D.K., *Context Oriented Protection and Consistent Control*, The Computer and Information Ssystems Dept. TR, The Ohio State University, 1976.

[HELL76]   Hellman, M.E., et al. *Results of an Initial Attempt to Cryptanalyse The NBS Data Encryption Standard*, Stamford University, USA, 1976.

[HELL80]   Hellman, M.E.,   A Cryptanalytic Time-Memory Trade Off,   IEEE Transactions on Information Theory, Vol. IT-26, No. 4, 1980.

[HENS88]   Henshall, T., Shaw, S. OSI Explained: End-to-End Computer Communication Standards, Ellis Horwood, England, 1988.

[HERZ86]   Herzberg, A.,   Pinter, S.S.,   Public Protection of Software,   Proc of CRYPTO'85, Springer-Verlag, 1986.

[HSIA79]   Hsiao, D.K., Kerr,D.S., Madnick, S.E., Computer Security, Academic Press, New York, 1979.

[HUMP86]   Humphreys, E.,   Network Security and the OSI Reference Model, BRITISH TELECOM, Ipswich, UK

[IBM]   International Business Machines Corporation,   Advanced Communications Functions for VTAM (ACF/VTAM) - Installation, SC 27-0464-0

[INGE82]   Ingemarsson, I., et al.   A Conference Key Distribution System,   IEEE Trans. on Information Theory, Vol. IT-28, No. 5, Sept. 1982.

[ISO 86A]   International Standard Organization,   Use of Encipherment Techniques in Communication Architectures, ISO/TC 97/SC 20/WG 3, N 66, Sept. 1986.

[ISO 86B]   International Standard Organization,   Data Integrity Mechanism using a Cryptographic Check-Function employing an N-bit algorithm with Truncation, ISO/TC 97/SC 20/WG 1, N 73, Oct. 1986.

[ISO 87A]   International Standards Organization,   Discussion Paper on Trusted Functionality, ISO / TC 97 / SC 21 / N 2026, June 1987.

[ISO 87B]   International Standards Organization,   Peer Entity Authentication Mechanisms using an N–bit Secret Key Mechanisms, ISO / TC 97 / SC 20 / WG 1, July 1987.

[ISO 88]   International Standards Organization, Information Processing Systems – OSI RM. Part 2: Security Architecture, ISO/TC 97 7498-2, 1988.

[ISO 91]   International Standards Organization, (1) CD Access Control Framework SC21 N6168; (2) WD Integrity Framework SC21 N6163; (3) WD Confidentiality Framework SC21 N6164; (4) WD Non-repudiation Framework; (5) WD Framework Overview SC21 N6166; (6) CD Audit Framework SC21 N6169; (7) WD Guide to OS Security SC21 N6167;   July 1991.

[ITSEC90]   Commission of the European Communities,   Information Technologies Security Evaluation Criteria (ITSEC),   CEC, Brussels, 1990.

[JUEN87]   Jueneman, R.R.,   Electronic Document Authentication,   IEEE Network Magazine, Vol. 1, No. 2, April 1987.

[JUEN89]   Jueneman, R.R., Integrity Controls for Military and Commercial Applications, II, Workshop for Data Integrity, NIST, Gaithersburgh, USA, Jan 1989

[KNUT81]   Knuth, D.E.,   The Art of Computer Programming: Vol. 2: Seminumerical Algorithms, Addison-Wesley, 1981.

[KONF78]   Konfelder, L., *A Method for Certification*, LCS MIT, USA, May 1978.

[KONH81]   Konheimer, A.G., *Cryptography: A Primer*, John Wiley, 1981.

[KOWA84]   Kowack, G., Healey, D., *Can the Holes Be Plugged?*, Computerworld 18, 39B, Sept. 1984, 27-28.

[LAMP81]   Lamport, L., *Password Authentication with Insecure Communications*, Communications of the ACM, Vol. 24, No. 11, Nov. 1981.

[LAND81]   Landwehr, C.E., *Formal Models for Computer Security*, Computing Surveys, 13(3), Sept. 1981.

[LEXA76]   Lexar Corporation, *An Evaluation of Data Encryption Standard*, Los Angeles, USA, 1976.

[LIND76]   Linden, T.A., *Operating System Structures to Support Security and Reliable Software*, Computing Surveys, 8, 4.

[LIPT81]   Lipton, R., *How to Cheat at Mental Poker*, Proc. of the AMS Short Course on Cryptology, 1981.

[LIST75]   Lister, A.M., *Fundamentals of Operating Systems*, Macmillan Press, 1975, 113-123.

[LUBY86]   Luby, M., Rackoff, C., *Pseudo-Random Permutations and Cryptographic Composition*, Proc of the 18th ACM Symposium on Theory of Computing, 1986.

[McCU87]   McCullough, D., *Specifications for Multi-Level Security and a Hook-up Property*, Proc. 1987 IEEE Symp. on Security and Privacy, IEEE CS Press, Los Alamitos, USA, 1987.

[McLE85]   McLean, J., *A Comment on the "Basic Security Theorem" of Bell and LaPadula*, Information Processing Letter, 20, North-Holland, 1985.

[McLE87]   McLean, J., *Reasoning about Security Models*, Proc. 1987 IEEE Symp. on Security and Privacy, IEEE CS Press, Los Alamitos, USA, 1987.

[McLE90]   McLean, J., *Security Models and Information Flow*, Proc. 1990 IEEE Symp. on Security and Privacy, IEEE CS Press, Los Alamitos, USA, 1990.

[MEIJ82]   Meijer, A., Peeters, P., *Computer Network Architectures*, Pitman Publishing, 1982.

[MERK78]   Merkle, R.C., Hellman, M.E., *Hiding Information and Receipts in Trap-Door Knapsacks*, IEEE Trans. Inf. Theory, Sept 1978.

[MEYE78]   Meyer, C.H., *Ciphertext/Plaintext and Ciphertext/Key Dependence vs. Number of Rounds for the DES*, AFIPS Conf. Proceedings, Vol. 47, 1978.

[MEYE82]   Meyer, C.H., Matias, S.M., *Cryptography*, John Wiley and Sons, 1982.

[MILE82]   Miler, G.L., *Riemann's Hypothesis and Tests for Primality*, Proc. of the 7th ACM Symposium on the Theory of Computing, 1982.

[MILL84]   Millen, J.K., Cerniglia, C.M. *Computer Security Models*, MITRE, MTR-9543, Bedford, USA, Sept. 1984

[MITC89]   Mitchell, C., Walker, M., Rush, D., *CCITT/ISO Standards for Secure Message Handling*, IEEE Journal on Selected Areas in Communications, pp. 517-523, May 1989.

[MORR79]   Morris, R., Thompson, K., *Password Security: A Case History*, Communications of the ACM, Vol. 22, No. 11, Nov. 1979, 594–597.

[MUFT77]   Muftic, S., Kantardzic, M., *Some Problems of Information Generation During Data Retrieval from Files*, Proceedings of ETAN Conf., Banja Luka, Yugoslavia, 1977.

[MUFT78]   Muftic, S., *On Functionally Distributed Computing Systems*, Proc. IEEE Distributed Systems Conf., Gaithersburg, MD, USA, 1978.

[MUFT83]   Muftic, S., Underhill, L.H., *Security Aspects of Computer Networks*, Proc. of the CEC EUTECO'83 Conference, Varese, Italy, Oct 1983.

[MUFT86]   Muftic, S., *Secure Exchange of Sensitive Data in Computer Networks*, Proceedings of IFIP/SEC'86, Monte Carlo, Dec 1986.

[MUFT88C]   Muftic, S., *An Integrated Network Security Mechanism*, Proc. of the CEC EUTECO'88 Conference, Vienna, April 1988.

[MUFT88D]   Muftic, S., *Security Mechanisms for Computer Networks*, Ellis Horwood, Ltd., Chichester, England, Dec 1988.

[MUFT90A]   Muftic, S., *Security in IBM Systems*, Computer Technology Research Corp., New York, USA, 1990

[MUFT90B]   Muftic, S., *Transaction Protection by "Antennas"*, Computers & Security Journal, 1992

[MUFT92A]   Muftic., S., *CISS: Implementation of Network Security on Generalized Security Servers*, Proc. 3rd RARE JENC, Innsbruck, May 1992

[MUFT92B]   Muftic., S., *Security Requirements for Open Distributed Systems*, Proc. 7th COMPASS Conference, IEEE, Gaithersburg, MD, USA, June 1992

[MUFT92C]   Muftic., S., *CISS: Generalized Security Libraries*, Computers & Security Journal, 1992

[MUFT92D]   Muftic., S., *Implementation of A Generalized Security System for EDI Applications*, Proc. 7th European Conference on Information Systems, Audit and Control, Brussels, Nov. 1992

[NAKA89]   Nakao, K., *Proposal on a Secure Communications Service Element (SCSE) in the OSI Application Layer*, IEEE Transaction on Communications, Selected Areas in Communications, Vol. 7, No. 4, May 1989.

[NBS 76]   National Bureau of Standards, *Report of the 1976 Workshop on Estimation of Significant Advances in Computer technology*, NBS, USA, 1976.

[NBS 83]   National Bureau of Standards, *Proceedings of the Sixth Seminar on the DOD Computer Security Initiative*, NBS, USA, 1983.

[NEED78]   Needham, R.M., Schroeder, M.D.,   *Using Encryption for Authentication in Large Networks*, Communications of the ACM, Vol. 21, No. 12, Dec. 1978, 993-999.

[PAPA83]   Papadimitrou, C.H., Thanos, C.,   *Concurrency Control in Distributed Databases: State of the Art*, Proc. of EUTECO'83, Varese, Italy 1983.

[PETE84]   Peterson, J.L., Silberschatz, A.,   *Operating System Concepts*, Addison-Wesley, 1984, 387-419.

[PFIT87]   Pfitzmann, A., Waidner, M.,   *Networks Without User Observability*, Computers & Security, Vol. 6, 1987.

[RABI76]   Rabin, M.O.,   *Probabilistic Algorithms*, Proc. of the Symposium on New Directions and Recent Results in Algorithms and Complexity, Academic Press (Ed. J.F. Traub), 1976.

[RABI81]   Rabin, M.O.,   *How to Exchange Secrets by Oblivious Transfer*, Technical Memo TR-81, Harvard University, 1981.

[RABI83]   Rabin, M.O.,   *Transaction Protection by Beacons,* Journal of Computer and System Sciences, 27, 256-267, 1983.

[RAMA89]   Ramaswamy, R.,   *Security Architecture for Data Transfer through TCP/IP Protocols,* Computers & Security Journal, Elsevier, 8 (1989),

[RIVE78]   Rivest, R.L. Shamir A. and Adleman, L.,   *A Method for Obtaining Digital Signatures and Public Key Cryptosystems*, Comm. ACM, 21(2), Feb. 1978.

[RUSH83]   Rushby, J., Randell, B.   *A Distributed Secure System*, IEEE Computer, July 1983.

[RUSH86]   Rushby, J. *Introduction to "Dependable Computing" for Communications,* Comm. ACM, 29(11), Nov. 1986.

[RUTL86]   Rutledge, L.S., Hoffman, L.J.,   *A Survey of Issues in Computer Network Security,* Computers & Security, Vol. 5, No. 4, Dec 1986.

[SALT74]   Saltzer, J.H.,   *Protection and the Control of Information Sharing in Multics*, Communications of the ACM, Vol. 17, No. 7, July 1974.

[SAND88]   Sandhu, R.S.,   *The Schematic Protection Model: Its Definition and Analysis for Acyclic Attenuating Schemes,* Journal of the ACM, 35(2), 1988.

[SHAM85]   Shamir, A.,   *Identity Based Cryptosystems and Signature Schemes*, Proc of CRYPTO'84, Springer-Verlag, 1985.

[SHAM79A]   Shamir, A.,   *How to Share A Secret*, Communications of the ACM, Vol. 24, 1979.

[SHAM79B]   Shamir, A., Rivest, R.L., Adleman, L.,   *Mental Poker*, MIT / LCS / TR-125, 1979.

[SHAN49]   Shannon, C.E.,   *Communication Theory of Secrecy Systems*, Bell Systems Technical Journal, Vol. 28, 1949.

[SIDH86]   Sidhu, D.P.,   *Authentication Protocols for Computer Networks: I*, Computer Networks and ISDN Systems, Vol. 11,   April, 1986.

[SIMM79]   Simmons, G.J.,   *Symmetric and Asymmetric Encryption*,   Computing Surveys, Vol. 11, No. 4, 1979.

[SIMM84]   Simmons, G.J.,   *A Prisoner's Problem and The Subliminal Channel*,   Proc of CRYPTO'83, Plenum Press, 1984.

[SIMM86]   Simmons, G.J.,   *A Secure Subliminal Channel(?)*,   Proc of CRYPTO'85, Springer-Verlag, 1986.

[SOLO77]   Solovay, R., Strassen, V.,   *A Fast Monte-Carlo Test for Primality*,   SIAM Journal of Computing, Vol. 6, 1977.

[SUMM84]   Summers, R.C.,   *An Overview of Computer Security*,   IBM Systems Journal, 23, 4, 1984, 309-325.

[SUTH86]   Sutherland, D.,   *A Model of Information*,   Proc. 9th National Computer Security Conference, Gaithersburgh, USA, Sept. 1986.

[TANE81]   Tanenbaum, A.S.,   *Computer Networks*,   Prentice Hall, USA, 1981.

[TATS88]   Tatsuaki, O.   *A Digital Multisignature Scheme Using Bijective Public–Key Cryptosystems*,   ACM Transactions on Computer Systems, Vol. 6, No. 8, Nov. 1988.

[UK90]   ISO/JTC1/SC6 (UK),   *Proposed Draft for an End–to–End System Security Protocol*,   Project JTC1.06.3506, UK, 1990.

[VARA89]   Varadharajan, V.,   *Verification of Network Security Protocols*,   Computer & Security, Vol. 8, Dec 1989.

[VAZI84]   Vazirani, V.V., Vazirani, V.V.,   *Efficient and Secure Pseudo Random Number Generation*,   Proc. of the 25th IEEE Symp. on Foundations of Computer Science, 1984.

[VOYD83]   Voydock, V.L., Kent, S.T.,   *Security Mechanisms in High-level Network Protocols*,   Computing Surveys, Vol. 15, No. 2, June 1983.

[WARE67]   Ware, W.,   *Security and Privacy in Computer Systems*,   Proceedings of the SJCC, USA, 1967.

[YAO 82]   Yao, A.C.,   *Protocols for Secure Computations*,   Proc of the 23rd IEEE Symposium on Foundations of Computer Science, 1982, pp. 160-164.

[YAO 86]   Yao, A.C.,   *How to Generate and Exchange Secrets*,   Proc of the 27th IEEE Symp. on Foundations of Computer Science, 1986.

[ZSI 89]   ZSI, Zentralstelle für Sicherheit in der Informationstechnik,   *IT Security Criteria - Criteria for the Evaluation of Trustworthiness of Information Technology (IT) Systems*,   Bundesregierung, Bundesanzeiger Verlagsgesellschaft mbH, Bonn 1989, ISBN 3-88784-200-6

INDEX

16–bit checksum, 57

A

access condition, 192
access control, 31, 34, 41, 45, 47, 56,
    59, 67, 73, 87, 151, 152, 183
access control information base, 35
access control management, 50, 53
access control models, 101
access control service, 152
access policy, 109
access rights, 192
access subjects, 73
action, 213
acyclic attenuating schemes, 102
add, 71
address identifier, 57
anonymous communications, 83, 87,
    153, 189
Application Common Service Element
    (ACSE), 9
application entity, 3, 5
application layer, 3
application layer model, 6, 8
application layer service, 6
application process, 3, 5, 119
application programming interface (API),
    172, 204, 209, 216, 217, 222,
    229, 230, 231, 236, 239, 243, 246
application service element, 6, 231,
    236
ASN.1 notation, 192
assessment of security, 90, 147
asset, 21
association-accepted operation, 134, 138
association-active state, 134, 138, 140,
    142
Association Agent, 89, 180, 200, 241

Association Control Service Element
    (ACSE), 8, 230
association-modified operation, 134,
    138, 139
association-negotiated operation, 134,
    137, 138
association-rejected operation, 134, 138,
    139
association-requested operation, 137,
    138, 139
association-terminated operation, 136,
    139
associations, 121, 126, 132
associations security model, 93
asymmetric algorithms, 34
audit trail, *see* security audit trail
auditing, 87, 119, 146
authentication, 35, 76, 151, 238, 242
authentication exchange, 36, 41, 152
authentication management, 50, 53
authentication models, 101, 115
authentication protocols models, 102,
    116
authenticity, 123, 129, 130, 131, 132,
    136, 137, 140
authorization, 108, 123, 129, 130, 131,
    132, 136, 140, 213, 214
authorization security policy, 72
authorship, 68
availability, 123

B

basic security theorem, 105
Bell-LaPadula model, 102
bilateral contract signing, 84
Bind macro, 71, 72
biometrics, 36
boundedness, 116, 117